WILFRED OWEN

Wilfred Owen in 1916

WILFRED OWEN

JON STALLWORTHY

OXFORD UNIVERSITY PRESS

AND

CHATTO AND WINDUS

London 1974

Published jointly by Oxford University Press and
Chatto and Windus

Distributed by

Oxford University Press, Ely House, London W.1

GLASGOW NEW YORK TORONTO MELBOURNE WELLINGTON
CAPE TOWN IBADAN NAIROBI DAR ES SALAAM LUSAKA ADDIS ABABA
DELHI BOMBAY CALCUTTA MADRAS KARACHI LAHORE DACCA
KUALA LUMPUR SINGAPORE HONG KONG TOKYO

ISBN 0 19 211719 X

Filmset and printed by BAS Printers Limited, Wallop, Hampshire

*To the
memory of
Harold Owen*

FOREWORD

This book is dedicated to the memory of the man it was Wilfred Owen's good fortune to have as a brother, and mine to have as a friend. Harold Owen's *Journey from Obscurity* and the fine edition of the poet's *Collected Letters*, on which he collaborated with John Bell, provide the biographer of Wilfred Owen with his principal asset and his principal problem. How to fit the old cloth into the new garment? Too many fragments of direct quotation, with their varying tones and obtrusive stitching of quotation marks, could only make an uneven patchwork. I have preferred, with Harold Owen's approval, to base sections of my narrative – particularly some early sections – on indirect quotation, interspersing these with an occasional piece of some length from the *Journey* or the *Collected Letters*. My sources are detailed in the Notes, which have been placed at the end of the book where they will be available to the scholar and offer no distraction to the general reader.

Although this biography draws heavily on those others, and although it contains a good deal that they do not, it is in no sense a substitute for them. I see it, rather, as complementary; a portrait of the man as artist to balance Harold Owen's portrait of the artist as elder brother, and Wilfred's own careful self-portrait – in his letters (four fifths of them to his mother) – of the artist as son. I see the *Collected Letters*, *Journey from Obscurity*, and this biography as together forming the foundation for an edition of the *Complete Poems of Wilfred Owen*, on which I am now engaged.

Biographies as a rule embody the perceptions and researches of many people other than their authors, and this is no exception to that rule. Unlike many of its kind, however, it could never have been written at all but for two acts of generosity. My greatest debt of gratitude is to Harold Owen, and my greatest regret that he did not live to see the book completed. Had he done so, it would have been a better one, but there would have been no book at all had he not entrusted his brother's books and papers to me, and himself given me so many hours of his time when we both knew that his hours were numbered.

We have no testimony but Harold Owen's to much of his brother's childhood and to many incidents in his later life, and the evidence of the single witness will always be questioned. I believe him to have been an unusually faithful witness, even when writing of events that took place decades before, but it must be remembered that his view of his brother was necessarily the ugly duckling's of the swan.

Despite Harold Owen's generosity, this book could not have been undertaken – or at least undertaken on this scale – but for the generosity of the Warden and Fellows of All Souls College, Oxford. A year spent as a Visiting Fellow under their most hospitable roof enabled me to assemble my material and my thoughts and write for some months undistracted by anything more intrusive than a blackbird on my window sill and a fountain beneath it. One of Wilfred Owen's greatest regrets was that he never got to Oxford, and I like to think that he would have shared my satisfaction that his *Life* should owe so much to an Oxford College dedicated to the memory of King Henry V and those who perished in the French Wars.

I am happy to be able to record my gratitude also to Mr. George Derbyshire for sharing so generously his unrivalled knowledge of the history of the Manchester Regiment; to Miss Dorothy Gunston and Mr. Leslie Gunston for their vital recollections of their cousin; and to Mr. Dominic Hibberd for assistance in dating and deciphering the manuscripts. I am grateful, too, to many others who helped me in my researches: Mr. J. E. Allison, the Rev. J. Biddlestone, Professor Louis Bonnerot, Miss Blanche Bulman, Mrs. Elizabeth Cameron, the Librarian and staff of the Codrington Library, Miss Marie Dauthieu, Mrs. Edith Dymott, Dame Helen Gardner, Mr. Eric Garton, Mr. John Harris, Sir Rupert and Lady Hart-Davis, Mrs. M. Hirth of the Library of the University of Texas at Austin, Mr. K. D. Holt, Mr. and Mrs. Ikin, Miss Dorothy Iles, Professor Gwyn Jones, Sir Geoffrey Keynes, Miss Dorothy Kitchingman, Mr. Evan Lane, Mr. Murray McClymont, Mr. A. K. Newboult, Miss M. Newboult, Mr. Foy Nissen, Mr. D. Norman, Mr. Alec Paton, Miss M. and Miss K. Paton, Mrs. Arthur Philips, Mr. C. H. Wallace Pugh, Miss Mary Ragge, the Registrar of the University of Reading, Mrs. Ian Reid, Mr. J. H. Rowsell, Mr. Jeffrey Sains, Mr. William St. Clair, Mr. Eric Smallpage, Mrs. Angus Stewart, Dr. P. H. Tooley, Mr. H. Walpole of the Oswestry Public Library, Mr. David Yates, Miss Elizabeth Varet, and Sister Valerio.

I am also indebted to the following: Mrs. C. T. A. Beevor, for permission to reprint Jessie Pope's poem, 'The Call'; Sir Rupert Hart-Davis, for permission to print Siegfried Sassoon's unpublished poem, 'Vision', and prose; Mr. G. T. Sassoon, for permission to reprint 'They' from Siegfried Sassoon's *Collected Poems* and an extract from *Siegfried's Journey*; A. P. Watt

& Son for permission to print 'Two Fusiliers' by Robert Graves from his *Poems 1914–1927*; and Macmillan and G. P. Putnam's Sons, New York, for permission to print an extract from Captain Cyril Falls's *History of the Great War: Military Operations: France and Belgium 1917*, copyright © 1959 by Cyril Falls.

Acknowledgements are due to the Director and Trustees of the Imperial War Museum for the photographs reproduced on pp. 151, 164, 165, and 179; to the Director and Trustees of the British Museum for the photographs reproduced on pp. 84, 120, 138, 212, 213, 217, 219, 220, 221, 224, 225, 226, 238, 240, 241, 243, 244, 250, 251, 254, and 255; to the Librarian of the Academic Center, the University of Texas at Austin, for the photographs reproduced on pp. 122 and 175; and to Mr. Steve Hartley for the photograph reproduced on p. 68.

Few authors are so fortunate in their friends and publishers, and *Wilfred Owen* owes much to the ministrations of Mr. John Bell, Miss Catharine Carver, Mr. D. J. Enright, Miss Susan le Roux, Mr. Ian Parsons, Mrs. Norah Smallwood, and to Carol Buckroyd, who helped at every stage and prepared the index.

Finally, I want to thank Mrs. Harold Owen for her continuing encouragement, and my wife for accepting Wilfred Owen as a ghostly addition to the family so long.

October 1973   The Mill House
                                                               Wolvercote

CONTENTS

Note on Abbreviations and Texts   xii

List of Illustrations   xiii

1 Oswestry   1

2 Birkenhead   13

3 Shrewsbury   37

4 Dunsden and After   63

5 France 1913–15   94

6 Training   126

7 The Somme   149

8 Craiglockhart   189

9 Scarborough and Ripon   235

10 France 1918   269

Afterwords   287

Notes   289

Appendixes   304

Select Bibliography   324

Index   325

A NOTE ON ABBREVIATIONS
AND THE TEXTS OF OWEN'S POEMS

In my footnotes and endnotes the following abbreviations appear:

EB   *The Poems of Wilfred Owen*, edited with a Memoir by Edmund Blunden, 1931.

LG   Leslie Gunston.

CDL   Cecil Day Lewis

CL   *Wilfred Owen: Collected Letters*, edited by Harold Owen and John Bell, 1967.

BM   British Museum.

CP   *The Collected Poems of Wilfred Owen*, edited with an Introduction and Notes by C. Day Lewis, 1963.

HO   Harold Owen.

JFO   Harold Owen, *Journey from Obscurity*, 1963, 1964, 1965.

SO   Susan Owen.

WO   Wilfred Owen.

SS   Siegfried Sassoon.

Wilfred Owen lived to see only five of his poems in print. So, in an attempt to bring the reader more fully into his life and work, I reproduce (somewhat reduced) the manuscripts of poems quoted in full, except in cases where either there is a typescript or the manuscript is indistinct or much corrected. A page-reference is given to every poem appearing in *The Collected Poems*; unpublished poems and fragments are listed in Appendix B on pp. 305–7.

LIST OF ILLUSTRATIONS

Wilfred Owen, 1916 · · · · · *frontispiece*

Chapter 1. Oswestry · · · · · *page*
'Boy' Tom Owen's Certificate of Discharge · · · 6
Plas Wilmot · · · · · 8
Family group at Plas Wilmot, 1895 · · · 9
Wilfred, aged three, and his parents · · · 11
Auctioneer's catalogue for the sale of Plas Wilmot · · 12

Chapter 2. Birkenhead
Wilfred in his mother's uniform · · · · 15
Wilfred with his father's yacht · · · · 15
Susan Owen · · · · · 16
The Birkenhead Institute · · · · 22
The Owens on Scarborough beach, 1905 · · · 31

Chapter 3. Shrewsbury
The Uffington ferry · · · · · 43
The canal at Uffington · · · · 47
William and Mary Owen's Golden Wedding group, 1909 · 50
Mahim · · · · · 51

Chapter 4. Dunsden and After
The Rev. Herbert Wigan · · · · 64
Dunsden Vicarage · · · · · 65
Dunsden Church · · · · · 68
Wilfred Owen aged nineteen · · · · 77
Midshipman Harold Owen and family · · · 87

Chapter 5. France 1913–15
The Villa Lorenzo, about 1914 · · · · 103
Wilfred Owen with Laurent Tailhade, September 1914 · 108
Le Châlet, Mérignac · · · · · 114

page

Family group at Mérignac, 1915   115

Chapter 6. Training

Harold Monro and customer in the Poetry Bookshop   128
The Officers of the 5th (reserve) Manchester Regiment, 1916   137
Officer Cadet Owen, 1916   145

Chapter 7. The Somme

German dead near Guillemont, September 1916   151
'You will proceed to ABBEVILLE'   160
Manchester Regiment working party, January 1917   164
Soldiers in a trench, February 1917   165
Distant view of St. Quentin, April 1917   179

Chapter 8. Craiglockhart

Cover of *The Hydra*   200
Siegfried Sassoon, 1916   207
Robert Graves, September 1917   223
Wilfred Owen with Arthur Newboult, July 1917   232
Robert Ross   237

Chapter 9. Scarborough and Ripon

Borage Lane, Ripon   259
Charles Scott Moncrieff, May 1918   264

Chapter 10. France 1918

The Sambre and Oise Canal, November 1918   284

1

OSWESTRY

THE TIMES, Saturday, March 18, 1893, reported the launching of the second-class cruiser *Astræ*; from Berlin, the rejection by the Reichstag's Army Bills Committee 'of the second reading of the whole of the Government measures'; and from St. Petersburg, that 'The Tsar, accompanied by the Tsarina and the members of his family, will leave . . . for Livadia, in the Crimea, where a stay of several weeks duration will be made.' Cold, changeable weather was forecast for most districts, while the TO-DAY column announced: 'Performance of *Becket*, by command of the Queen, at Windsor Castle, by Mr. Irving, Miss Ellen Terry, and Lyceum Company.' Unannounced and unrecorded in the august pages of *The Times*, an event noticed only in *The Oswestry and Border Counties Advertizer*, under the heading BIRTHS: 'OWEN – March 18, at Plas Wilmot, Oswestry, the wife of Tom Owen of a son.'

Wilfred Edward Salter Owen, born in an upper room of that creeper-covered house, inherited two of his names from a man born almost a century before.[1] Edward Salter came from Chester to Oswestry sometime before November 1820 when he married Mary C. Cross Simpson shortly after her twenty-first birthday. They had five children: Mary, Edward who died at eighteen months, Harriet, Edwin, and Francis. Edward Salter must have been a man of some means, for he decided to build a house of comfortable proportions on several acres of good land to the south of the town.

In a black leather notebook fastened with a metal clasp,[2] he wrote:

Oswestry July 18th 1829

Copy of – Memorandum of agreement made between Edwd Salter of Chester & James Payne of Oswestry – the said James Payne undertakes to throw up the Clay temper and make into Bricks complete, also to make the Kiln and Burn forty thousand Bricks in Edw Salter's Croft at Croes Wyllan[3] before the 1st Day of October next E Salter paying unto the sd. J Payne the sum of nine shillings per thousand allow one Pound for making & levelling the ground – the s^d E Salter not to be liable to any further charges

Signed James Payne

Other memoranda of agreement follow – with brick-layer, carpenter, and carrier – and the day-by-day building expenses, scrupulously set out, testify to Edward Salter's business acumen. Sadly, however, he died at the early age of thirty-two, before Plas Wilmot was completed, but his widow lived there until her death twelve years later.[4] In 1848 three of their four surviving children married, leaving Mary, the eldest, alone but for her servants in the large redbrick house.

Two years after this, there arrived in Oswestry an energetic young man called Edward Shaw. He had been born at Shobden, near Leominster, in 1821 and now set up as an ironmonger at number 16 Bailey-street.[5] His business affairs prospered so that when, in 1857, he made his proposal of marriage to Mary Salter and was accepted, it must have seemed a highly suitable match. Both were thirty-six. He had a respectable business and she a respectable property, and at first life went well for the Shaws of Plas Wilmot. They had four children, Emma, Mary (known as May), Susan, and Edward, who were educated at home by a series of governesses of whom the favourite was the daughter of a local doctor, Nellie Roderick. Edward Shaw's business went from strength to strength and he began to play an increasingly prominent part in the affairs of the Town Council. He was elected a councillor in 1863 and filled the office of Mayor of Oswestry with marked success in 1869. He was a Justice of the Peace, a Governor of the Oswestry Grammar School, and a founder member of the Oswestry District Agricultural and Horticultural Societies. The long list of his civic appointments set out in his obituary ends on a resonant Victorian note:

Mr Shaw was a strong Churchman, and in all movements affecting the welfare of the Church, he took a deep interest. He was a faithful communicant at Holy Trinity Church, and shortly after coming to the town he was appointed superintendent of the Sunday School, which post he held for some years. In politics he was a Conservative, and, at one time, he was chairman of Mr. Stanley Leighton's election committee. He was also a knight-harbinger of the St. Oswald Habitation of the Primrose League.[5]

In 1884 his daughter Mary married Dr. Richard Loughrey, L.R.C.P., M.R.C.S., and moved with him to the East End of London where they devoted themselves to the relief of suffering in the dockland tenements and, after lives of great hardship, died early and within weeks of one another.[7] Emma Shaw in 1886 married a businessman, John Gunston, and like her sister took the road to London, albeit to a more comfortable suburb south of the Thames.

In these years business was as brisk as ever in the premises of Edward Shaw, 'general ironmonger & nail manufacturer & agricultural implement maker, locksmith, bellhanger & tin plate worker', but the situation at Plas Wilmot was less happy. While Susan Shaw delighted her parents with her painting, her needlework, her accomplished playing of harp and piano, and the general behaviour expected of a dutiful daughter, her brother Edward was beginning to give cause for concern. Councillor Shaw's only son was a formidable sportsman. An international footballer, he has an aura of aggressive energy as he stares from the sepia photograph of the Welsh team about to play Scotland at Glasgow on 29 March 1884.* The face is broad, the eyes narrow, there is a truculent tilt to the chin, and a sense of animal vitality barely contained by the folded arms and crossed legs. His prowess on the playing field led him into rougher company than he would have found in his parents' drawing room. A spirited boy became a wild young man; but had he been otherwise, the sister who had to put him to bed when he came home drunk might never have become the mother of Wilfred Owen.

The Owen family tree has its tap-root in Wales. Wilfred inherited from his father the legend that they were descended from Baron

---

* Wales, with E. G. Shaw at centre-forward, lost to Scotland 4–1. He also played for Wales against Ireland in 1882 and 1884, Wales winning both matches, 7–1 and 6–0 respectively.

Lewis Owen who, during the reign of Henry VIII, was Sheriff of Merionethshire.[8] The truth of this tradition, passed down through generations of yeoman stock, can never be established. All that is known is that the line crossed the border into England sometime before Queen Victoria's accession to the throne. It emerges, appropriately, in Welsh Row (the road leading to Wales), Nantwich, where on 2 December 1837 a son was born to John Owen, a thirty-seven-year-old shoemaker, and his wife Hannah, who was ten years his junior.[9] The boy was christened William and before he was thirteen was apprenticed to his father in the little Cheshire salt-town whose brine-pits had been used by the Romans. On 24 January 1859 he was married to Mary Millard in the magnificent rose stone parish church of St. Mary[10] and brought her back, over the river Weaver, to Number 1 Nixson's Row where father and son together plied their needles. In that small cottage, the first of a line of eight leading off Welsh Row, were born their three daughters, May, Emily, and Anne, and in 1862 a son, Tom, whose birth-certificate shows that his father had by then changed his occupation to that of tailor. In 1862 the Nantwich cotton mill closed down during the cotton famine, and it would seem that William Owen too was gradually forced out of business. His old father died in 1870 and ten months later his mother followed him to the churchyard. In due course William and his family moved to Shrewsbury where, forfeiting his independence, he worked for Maddox the drapers until his retirement.

There was little enough money for the children's schooling, but Tom was eager to learn and such was his thirst for reading that he was able to turn to advantage his years at a Dame-school owned by an old woman who made savage use of the rod. At the age of fifteen he applied, successfully, for a post as junior clerk with the Great Western Railway and was posted to Oswestry. An energetic and cheerful young man, he enjoyed playing cricket and football and it was at the local cricket club, sometime in the late 1870s, that he first met Edward Shaw.

It is easy to imagine the relief at Plas Wilmot when Edward first introduced his new friend to his family. Tom Owen may have been only a railway clerk, living in furnished rooms on wages of a few shillings a week, but he was courteous, clearly hard working, and at once high spirited and high principled. Moreover, he had a pleasant singing voice and was better acquainted with the words of hymnal and psalter than with the songs of the locker-room. Under the circumstances it was hardly surprising that Tom Owen and Susan Shaw should fall in love. His prospects with the GWR, however, were not such that he could hope to keep the beautiful daughter of the former mayor of Oswestry in the manner to which she was accustomed, so he resolved to seek his fortune elsewhere. Still only eighteen, he succeeded in obtaining a post with the Great Indian Peninsular Railway, on the understanding that he must himself finance his passage out. Having no money but considerable determination, he took the train to Liverpool and hunted the docks until he found a ship's captain prepared to let him work his passage. On the morning of 23 September 1880 he signed on as an Ordinary Seaman on the *Benalder*, 1,330 tons, Captain Buchanan. After an adventurous voyage of four weeks he reached India, took his discharge certificate from the ship, and by Christmas was ensconced on an office stool in Bombay.

His certificate, however, he kept and was to treasure all his life. His son Harold remembers it as

one of his most prized possessions. During the dullness of his later life it became emblematic of early adventure, and a signal mark to him of real manhood . . . he had at least once been a sailor before the mast. It became as well one of the earliest bonds between him and me. I so well remember as a very small boy when, one day finding ourselves alone together in the house, he, having with enormous solemnity first of all bound me to secrecy, showed me this certificate and told me the story of his voyage, exaggerating the terrible storms, near shipwreck, and the barefoot work about the decks and up aloft, painting all the time a gruesome picture of the dark fo'c'sle, the decomposing food, and the strangely dangerous sailors who were his companions. In my imagination it became a tingling mixture of nightmare terror and breath-holding enchantment.[11]

Tom Owen seems to have adapted himself to life in India as successfully as he had settled down in Oswestry. He joined the Great Indian Peninsular Railway Volunteer Rifles and a sailing club, and his work found favour in the eyes of his employers. 'Owen T. Clerk,

Dis. 1.

CERTIFICATE OF DISCHARGE

FOR SEAMEN DISCHARGED BEFORE THE SUPERINTENDENT OF A MERCANTILE MARINE OFFICE IN
THE UNITED KINGDOM, A BRITISH CONSUL, OR A SHIPPING OFFICER IN BRITISH POSSESSION ABROAD.

SANCTIONED BY
THE BOARD OF TRADE
JANUARY, 1869.

№ 164

Name of Ship.	Offic. Number.	Port of Registry.	Regist.ᵈ Tonnage.
Benalder	83011	Leith	1330

Horse Power of Engines (if any.)	Description of Voyage or Employment.
240	Foreign

Name of Seaman.	Age.	Place of Birth.	N.º of R.N.R. Commiss.ⁿ or Certif.	If Mate or Engineer, N.º of Certif. (if any.)	Capacity.
Tom Owen	18	Nantwich	—		Boy

Date of Engagement.	Place of Engagement.	Date of Discharge.	Place of Discharge.
23 Sept 81	Skool	Nov 81	Bombay

I certify that the above particulars are correct, and that the above named Seaman
was discharged accordingly; and that the character described on the other side hereof
is a true copy of the Report concerning the said Seaman.
Dated this ____ day of ____ 186_

AUTHENTICATED BY

W. Buchanan MASTER.

SIGNATURE OF SUPERT. CONSUL, OR SHIPPING OFFICER.

OFFICE
SEAL
OR
OFFICIAL
STAMP

Signature of Seaman

A SIGNATURE THESE WORDS IF THEY DO NOT APPLY

NOTE. Any Person who makes, assists in making or procures to be made any false Certificate or Report of the Service Qualifications, Conduct, or Character of
any Seaman, or who forges, assists in forging, or procures to be forged, or fraudulently alters, assists in fraudulently altering or procures to be
fraudulently altered, any such Certificate or Report, or who fraudulently makes use of any Certificate or Report or of any Copy of any Certificate or Report
which is forged or altered or does not belong to him, shall for each such offence be deemed guilty of a misdemeanor and may be fined or imprisoned.

Note. The Characters are to be inscribed only in the appropriate ornamented spaces below. All of these spaces
which are not filled in with particulars of Character must be marked over with a thick Cross in Ink by the
Superintendent, Consul, or other Shipping Officer, before the Certificate is given out of his possession.

Character for Ability
in whatever Capacity
engaged.

VERY GOOD · GOOD · DECLINES TO REPORT

Character for Conduct.

VERY GOOD · GOOD · DECLINES TO REPORT

**✳✳ CARE IS TO BE TAKEN THAT THE ABOVE CIRCLES
ARE CROSSED THROUGH OR FILLED IN.**

General Traffic Manager's Office G.I.P.R. Bori Bunder', as he appears in the *Times of India* Calendar and Bombay Directory for 1884, must have shared in the excitement of those expansionist years in the G.I.P.R. He would have watched the magnificent Italian-Gothic railway station, designed by F. W. Stevens and opened in 1888, rising at Bori Bunder to dominate the skyline in a manner befitting its proud name: the Victoria Terminus. For eleven years Tom and Susan wrote to each other two or three times a week, and clearly he had visions of her coming out to join him and their settling down in India. Then in 1891 he fell dangerously ill. After months in hospital he recovered and was recommended for leave in England. As he was hesitating over whether he should not, rather, take local sick-leave – fearing that if he left India he might not be accepted back – there came disturbing news from Oswestry. Susan wrote that her mother was dying, her brother Edward was drinking and gambling more wildly than ever, and her father was worried about his financial affairs. There could be no question of her joining Tom in Bombay, so he immediately decided to return to England.

He arrived to find that Mrs. Shaw had died and that Edward had disappeared. His sporting friend's excesses had reached epic proportions. Edward's homecomings in the small hours were frequently heralded by the firing of his shotgun in the stableyard. Having been put to bed by Susan or a servant, he would awake next morning to face parental prophecies of fire and brimstone. Alderman Shaw (as he had become in 1886), the Sunday School superintendent, was a rigid Calvinist by upbringing and conviction. The Old-Testament father and his black-sheep son made life so intolerable for each other that a crisis was inevitable. One night Edward failed to come home. He was at first assumed to be sleeping off a hangover under some more sympathetic roof, but a day or so later a friend brought his parents the news that he was leaving for America and intended never to return. He never did. In 1893 he was reported to be in Denver, Colorado, but that was the last they heard of him.

His wife's death, his son's disappearance, and the precarious state of his finances (a result of Edward's gambling and the cost of keeping up Plas Wilmot) left Alderman Shaw with only one wish: that his daughter should marry Tom Owen as soon as possible and that they

Plas Wilmot: Wilfred Owen was born in the upstairs room on the right

should set up house with him. Suppressing his dreams of a return to India, Tom rejoined the Oswestry Branch of the GWR on a clerk's salary of £75 a year, and on 8 December 1891 he and Susan were married in St. Oswald's Church. The bride was dressed in deep mourning for her mother.

Despite this ill omen, the next five years were a period of Indian Summer at Plas Wilmot. The young couple managed to introduce some sensible economies into a way of life that old Mr. Shaw could no longer afford. He had sold his business to his partner, Mr. Gardner, in 1892, and now spent much of his time breeding prize ducks, geese, and Brahma hens. He mellowed considerably in his seventies, but could not bring himself to introduce the major retrenchments that alone could have checked the erosion of his capital.

And so the lawns were cut, the orchard pruned, the lamps on the pony carriage polished when, on 18 March 1893, Wilfred Owen was

Family group at Plas Wilmot, 1895
Wilfred is on his mother's knee, next to Grandfather Shaw, Aunt Emma Gunston standing, left. In front, Gordon, Dorothy, and Vera Gunston. The parrot was called Jubilee

born in that upper room. With the coming of the summer, his baby carriage was put out on the croquet lawn under the shade of his mother's favourite trees, the mulberry, the walnut, and the weeping ash. Later, he learnt his way about the six bedrooms – one with a four-poster bedstead – and tottered downstairs to follow Mrs. Onion, the charwoman, around kitchen, back kitchen, wash house, and laundry; or, in the drawing room with the blue chintz chairs and sofa, listened to his mother playing the 'excellent pianoforte by *Lange*'.[12] Susan Owen wrote on a small twist of paper, subsequently committed to her jewel box: 'The hair of Sir Wilfred Edward Salter-Owen at the age of $11\frac{1}{2}$ months – in the year 1894'. The title and the hyphen are eloquent of her hopes for her son, and shed a revealing light on her view of the relative importance of her family and her husband's.

Susan, with her fair complexion and striking blue-black hair, had inherited her father's strength of will and his belief in a Divine Will. Throughout her life she was to enjoy the comforting assurance – that did not always comfort her more practical husband – that 'God will provide'. Tom, a short but sturdy man, had a brisk vitality that gave him a presence, an air of physical strength out of all proportion to his small stature. He was still suffering from sea-fever and this, coupled with hopes – altogether different from Susan's – for his son's future, led him to build Wilfred a model ship in one of the Plas Wilmot coach-houses. Touchingly if ironically christened the *S.S. Susan*, she was three feet from stem to stern,

most exquisitely wrought throughout with superb craftsmanship. The steering system was exact and could be set to steer a course; the steering wheel itself, carved in one piece from the lid of a cigar box, was masterly in execution; the lifeboats were gems in themselves, complete with minute – but removable – canvas covers, and could be correctly lowered to the water-line by working davits. It was properly equipped with regulation navigation lights, binnacle and real compass; so delicately carved was everything about it that even the skylights were glazed with real glass. Fitted into the ship were real boilers with furnaces fired by methylated spirit and cotton-wool for fuel, which drove the engine geared to the propeller shaft. The fog-horn fitted to the foremast funnel was operated from the bridge by lanyard. It was here that the small Wilfred, hand in hand with my mother and father, would watch with ecstasy the manoeuvres of the miniature ship as it steamed around and across their lake. One of his earliest and most treasured memories was of the day when the little ship caught fire in mid-lake, and of my father plunging into the water fully clothed and swimming out to submerge it.[13]

To Tom's disappointment, Wilfred's interest in the *S.S. Susan* was to prove less durable than his devotion to the hussar's tunic and tent made for him by his mother.

One evening in May 1895 the Owen's second child was born, a girl whom they christened Mary. She was small and frail and at first they despaired of her life, but she survived to delight her parents and her ageing grandfather with her gentle presence. In these years old Mr. Shaw found in his grandson some consolation for the loss of Edward. But in the winter of 1896 his health began to deteriorate, although nothing could keep him from his garden and the prize birds to which he was so attached until, on the morning of 15

January 1897, he was found to have suffered a stroke. A doctor was called but could do nothing, and at a quarter to seven that evening he died. His will revealed his financial position to be even worse than had been feared.[14] He left £132 to his eldest daughter Emma Gunston, and to her and her sisters a third share each of the proceeds from the sale of Plas Wilmot, its furniture, implements, and effects.

Wilfred, aged three, and his parents

And so that March the Owens watched their world disintegrate under the blows of the auctioneer's hammer, saving from the wreck only some of the silver, linen, pictures, and a few of the lighter pieces of furniture. Tom Owen applied for a transfer from the Oswestry district and was appointed to a slightly better post in Birkenhead.

Throughout the country brass bands were practising for Queen Victoria's Jubilee celebrations, as the Owens packed their cases and passed through the gates of Plas Wilmot.

> Some natural tears they dropped, but wiped them soon;
> The world was all before them, where to choose
> Their place of rest, and Providence their guide. . . .[15]

PLAS WILMOT,

Near OSWESTRY.

MESSRS.

WILLIAMS & NICHOLSON

Have received instructions from the Representatives of the
late EDWARD SHAW, Esq., to offer for

SALE BY AUCTION,

On the premises as above, (subject to Conditions
to be then read),

ON TUESDAY, THE 16th DAY OF MARCH, 1897,

THE WHOLE OF THE

HOUSEHOLD & FURNITURE,

Implements & Effects.

Sale of the OUT-DOOR EFFECTS to Commence
at 11 a.m., and the Household FURNITURE
at 12 o'clock Noon.

Goods on view the day prior to Sale.

Auctioneers' Offices—
Salop House, Oswestry.

W. Hope, Excelsior Printing Works, Bailey Street, Oswestry.

2

BIRKENHEAD

After leaving Plas Wilmot, Tom Owen could at first find no adequate 'place of rest' for his family at all. Susan was some months pregnant and, in April, despairing of finding a suitable house that he could afford, he applied for another transfer. This second application cannot have helped his professional prospects, but he was posted to Shrewsbury where, in a shabby little house in Canon Street, Harold Owen was born on 5 September 1897. The following spring Tom was reappointed to Birkenhead as Stationmaster of Woodside Station, on the understanding that he would in due course be promoted to Assistant Superintendent at Shrewsbury. Before this move, their third in less than a year, they had a holiday in Ireland and Harold's earliest memories were of their return by sea and their arrival at 14 Willmer Road, in the Tranmere district of Birkenhead:

My next moments of consciousness came to me as I was being unloaded from a dark and dripping cab on to a black wet pavement in a dank and evil-smelling street outside one of a long line of small, squalid, and near-slum dwellings. Our cab driver, who was terribly drunk, threw off our boxes and bags, somehow regained his seat and drove away, cursing and singing very loudly. When we had groped our way into the house, and my father had made a light, the floor and walls of the passage and the small room leading from it appeared to surge and lift as if covered with a simmering treacle. We had been welcomed to our new home by armies of black beetles. The disgusting crunching as our feet pressed down on these horrible insects, the loathsome smell of the air in the house, following as it did the nightmarish crossing from Ireland, with the wet cold blackness of my arrival in the slummy street, was more than my small body could withstand. I was immediately and very violently sick, and the last impression I had before consciousness once again drifted away from me, was of Wilfred's protective rush towards me, the feel of his arms around me, and the fearful sight of the racing heaving mass of beetles converging upon what I had thrown up.[1]

Later that year they moved again, to 7 Elm Grove, a semi-detached house in a quieter street. This had a small garden and, after the privy that had dominated their Willmer Road yard, the comparative luxury of an indoor lavatory. Wilfred was now learning his alphabet at his mother's knee and, in 1898, wrote her what was probably his first letter. It is surrounded by a border of kisses:

my dear mother
  i no that you have got there safely. We are making huts. I have got a lantern, and we are lighting them up to-night.
            With love from Wilfred I remain your loving son Wilfred[2]

These were dark years for the Owens. Tom had as little love for the railways as had Susan for the neighbourhood in which they now found themselves. With them on their repeated moves they took a mental picture – more vivid than any oil painting of Susan's – of Plas Wilmot, an ikon held up to the inward eye every time she set out the family silver, the cut-crystal pepper-pot and salt-cellar, on one of her damask tablecloths. This emblem of happier days was at once an inspiration and, to Tom particularly, a reproach. His salary was barely sufficient for the necessities of life, but Plas Wilmot standards had to be maintained. The children had to be well turned out and, lest their accents and manners should be corrupted by those of the stevedores' and dock-workers' children up and down the street, it was insisted that they keep themselves to themselves. The situation was somewhat improved when, in the winter of 1898/9, the Owens moved to their third and last house in Birkenhead, 51 Milton Road. This was again semi-detached, but in a slightly better-class locality. Tom at first considered it beyond their means, but allowed himself to be persuaded otherwise when he learnt that the old lady next door was the widow of a sea-captain with two sea-

Wilfred in his mother's uniform and with his father's yacht

captain sons who used to stay with her when their ships were docked in Birkenhead. In the event, this move made life a good deal more pleasant for him as well as for his wife and children. He was persuaded

to attend church and was soon to become a churchwarden and honorary secretary and treasurer of various charitable juvenile clubs and activities in connection with church affairs. All this in itself was unimportant to him, but it pleased my mother and did open to him a source of interest away from his work and helped a bit to satisfy a genuine wish to be of some social use.

Possession of a beautiful tenor voice made him welcome any excuse to sing, and by this time he had taught himself an almost endless range of songs which included nearly all the Gilbert and Sullivan works and many excerpts from serious opera. His passion for music was second only to, if not equal to, his love of the sea. Not unnaturally, he was in great demand for the many concerts taking place for various charities.[3]

After one such concert, he was asked by the Secretary of a Seamen's Mission if he would sing to an audience of sailors in some dockland hall in Liverpool. He agreed and was such a success that the Mission authorities asked him whether he would be prepared to help as a voluntary worker. He had none of his wife's evangelical fervour, but was happy to take on the task of distributing tracts about the docks for the contact it gave him with ships and sailors. And so on Sunday

Susan Owen

mornings – or occasionally, in summer, on a Sunday evening – he and Harold would set off for the Mission to collect their tracts, which they would stuff deep into their pockets, before boarding the launch that was to carry them out to the cliff-sided vessels in the stream. Tom could never persuade Susan to accompany them on these Sunday expeditions. Moreover, she strongly disapproved of Wilfred going and he, sensing the conflict between his parents, was happy to side with his mother. Her possessiveness where he was concerned was beginning to cause a rift between Wilfred and his father and divide the family in two: herself, Wilfred, and Mary on the one side;

Tom, Harold (and later, Colin) on the other. Tom loved Wilfred deeply, but his bitterness at the gulf growing between them caused him to be increasingly critical of his ways and ambitions.[4] Susan, for her part, had no great sympathy for her husband's nautical nostalgia, and an evening when a Scandinavian captain and his wife were invited to supper was not a success. By happy contrast, there was the occasion when Tom insisted on inviting home four Lascar seamen who had missed their ship. The opportunity to practise his Hindustani was too good to be lost, and Harold remembers that his mother

was duly instructed to prepare a special curry, the recipe for which he had brought home from Bombay. The evening when he did bring these Indians home created something of a stir in the road we lived in. For some reason, not one of them would walk abreast with my father but insisted on shuffling along behind him, in single file with their flimsy slippers clipping and slapping on the pavement as they moved along. Following closely behind them came the young street rabble, shouting and calling out rude insults. The Indians like my father remained stoical and impassive. Ceremonial was gone through before entering our home, slippers were carefully removed and the beautifully ornamented round silk caps retained on their heads. They were perfect guests, appreciative and complimentary and delightfully courteous. They enjoyed the food immensely and ate entirely with their fingers. Knowing from my father their national weakness for sweetmeats, my mother had placed four or five pounds of home-made treacle toffee on the table. The sight of this seemed to have a mesmeric effect on them in a most extraordinary way; at the expense of the other carefully prepared dishes, they could not stop eating it, and although they did this with restraint and dignity, they finished every bit.

Perhaps their nicest touch of all was the trouble they had taken previously to find out from my father how many children he had; all of the four Indians had prepared a separate little gift for each of us, carefully wrapped in Indian tissue paper and tied with tinsel thread. My mother was presented with glass trinkets and my father with a bundle of cheroots. All were tendered in the most graceful manner with low bows and spoken benedictions. Altogether the evening was a success, although my mother did not give the proceedings quite her full approval. We children were completely fascinated with these brown seamen, especially their dark skins and to us curious garb, and most of all by the eight bare feet so carefully arranged underneath the table. This was very much Wilfred's evening, as he was old enough now to be a small person in his own right in a different way from the rest of us who could still be lumped together as children.

He had begged my father to teach him a few polite phrases of Hindustani, and had taken special pains to become word perfect. He did not do this with any special desire to please my father or the Indian seamen, but more because this was, as it appeared to him in his serious small way, an opportunity for gaining knowledge and, best of all, a knowledge that if he was able to acquire at all he would be able to test out immediately. The characteristic of wishing to prove to himself the actuality of his knowledge presented itself very early in his life and was, I think, brought about by a perpetual doubt about his own ability for true scholarship. . . . The Indians were intrigued to be addressed with such serious intent by the small English boy in their own language, but when the visit was over Wilfred's interest in Hindustani died almost immediately.[5]

Tom Owen had a firm belief, befitting a one-time cricketer and footballer, in the value of physical exercise. In a further attempt to establish a common (and nautical) bond with his sons, particularly with Wilfred, he decided to teach them to swim. A splendid swimmer himself, he decreed that they should all be able to swim the breadth of the Livingstone Street Corporation Baths at six years old, and the length before they were eight. Wilfred accomplished this, to his father's pride and pleasure – if not his mother's, who did not approve of Tom throwing him in from the middle diving board – but Harold was almost drowned on one of these occasions.

The Stationmaster, of course, could only lead such expeditions on a Sunday. For the rest of the week the children were largely confined to the house and garden. Their mother, who was in poor health much of the time, was disinclined to take them out and still did not like them mixing with the neighbours' children in the street. For these reasons, and because of Wilfred's growing passion for books,[6] his parents decided to send him to the Birkenhead Institute. Tom Owen was perhaps influenced in his choice of school by the enamelled advertisement for the Institute on one of the walls of the station whose platform he patrolled daily.[7] Opened in January 1889 by no less a personage than the Duke of Westminster, the school had made a strong start under its vigorous headmaster, Mr. W. S. Connacher. Among the first notices to appear on its walls was a set of maxims that may have come from his worthy Scottish hand:

'Idleness is the first step to all unhappiness.'

'One thing mastered is better than a dozen half-done.'
'Acting a lie is worse than telling a lie.'
'A bully is invariably a coward with an empty head.'
'An honest boy makes a confession, a coward makes an EXCUSE.'
'When a bad boy is popular, the school is bad.'

Many of these precepts were no doubt reproduced over the years in the form of lines by boys who had failed to live up to them.

The Preparatory School was only a few minutes walk from Elm Grove, and on 11 June 1899 Wilfred set off for the first time in his grey school cap with its red vizor device.[8] That year there joined the school two masters whose teaching was later to be an important factor in his development: Mr. Harry Bennett, a strict disciplinarian who taught French and German, and Mr. Harry Plant Wood, a mathematician with a knowledge and love of the classics and English literature. For his first term or two, however, Wilfred was in the hands of a Miss Farrell,

a lady who took a great interest in small boys' knees and limbs and seemed to be always studying and comparing them as they protruded underneath the narrow desks. . . . She was much given to favourites. . . . This office entailed being a general sort of run-about, with many rewarding kisses for chores well done, and also the ritual of preparing her 11-o'clock break coffee. This was effected with the aid of a gas-ring and a bottle of Camp coffee and meant, of course, losing one's break and being confined with Miss [Farrell] in the classroom.[9]

If, as seems likely, his mother or Miss Farrell introduced Wilfred to the fairy tales of Hans Andersen and the Brothers Grimm, that could partially account for the dark Gothick streak in his imagination that began to appear at about this time. He would put the younger children into cupboards or darkened rooms and, dressing himself up as a ghost, terrify them with shrieks, solemn incantations, and banging doors.[10]

In July 1900, with the newspapers full of the Boer War then entering its final phase, Colin Owen was born and Susan Owen's health deteriorated further. The other children were left even more to their own devices and Wilfred, in his school holidays, was often put in charge. He would sometimes take them to play in a dingy park abutting on to an area of desolate waste-land. Harold and Mary used to find this place, with its scrofulous trees and bushes, drear and frightening.

Wilfred did little to dispel this atmosphere, and his natural instinct to dramatize the surroundings and make them a backcloth for the imaginative stories he was then absorbing with such avidity, led him to exaggerate the latent eeriness of the place.

The nearby waste-land ran up to a piece of dark and mangy wood, and sometimes if it suited the particular story that Wilfred was trying to bring to real life, he would persuade us to penetrate into these forbidding depths. Any entry into this wood was always full of misery and foreboding for me, especially if Wilfred insisted upon secreting us separately, which he sometimes did, without thought of harm: he was not very old himself. It was on one of these occasions, when I was hiding in this horrible wood, that a man slouched by. He was filthily bearded and clothed in rags. I remember that patches of the yellow skin of his dirty body showed through in many places. Suddenly catching sight of me, he whirled and sprang on me and lifted me up in a loathsome embrace, pushing his hairy face into mine. Such a shaft of burning fear tore through my small body that it must have actuated it to frenzy. I remember biting and screaming and kicking and tearing with all my four limbs in an ecstasy of desire to hurt. This must have been effective for he dropped me in a few seconds and himself fell to the ground doubled up. I expect one of my little flailing boots had caught him, with a perfection of splendid accident, full in the testicles.[11]

Harold – by no means always through his own fault – was the most accident-prone of the four children, and sometime after the encounter with the tramp he had another fortunate escape. Colin was in bed with scarlet fever, and his mother had isolated him and herself behind a sheet soaked in carbolic that no one else was permitted to pass. Wilfred had taken Harold and Mary out on a long walk into the country and, pretending he was driving a pair of horses, had made them reins out of a clothes line. One of these tightened on Harold's arm, stopping the circulation, and could not be released. In the ensuing panic a woman brought up a rough-looking man who cut Harold free with his pocket-knife and then turned on Wilfred, threatening to thrash him for bullying his brother. Fortunately, he was restrained by the woman while the three children made their escape. On their return home, the quarantine was broken and the arm put through the carbolic-soaked sheet for examination. It was then swabbed with hot water by Wilfred and later bandaged by Tom, who ended the day on a cheerful note by initiating a game of wounded soldiers.[12]

Wilfred was doing well at the Birkenhead Institute, moving up from the Preparatory School to the Junior, which was housed in the main Institute building on Whetstone Lane. Behind its grey stone façade, classrooms, with tall windows set too high for children to look out and be distracted from book or blackboard, opened off cavernous passages. In this world of brown tile and dark stain, its air heavy with chalk-dust and the smell of floor-polish, Wilfred began to make friends. The first and closest was Alec Paton. Their friendship was based on shared interests in the classroom. Both boys were clever and worked hard, and there developed between them an amicable rivalry as to which would be top of the form and which second.[13] Naturally enough, the other boys called them 'swots', which further strengthened their alliance. In Mr. Bennett's English classes they were introduced to Shakespeare, Scott's *Marmion*, and Dickens's *A Christmas Carol*. From the start, Wilfred was interested in words and evolved a game with Alec, whereby they read downwards the words at the right-hand end of the lines on a printed page to see what sense or nonsense might emerge.

Another similar game was the invention of names for people we met on our way home from school. One such was a young man with large dark eyes whom we nicknamed 'Nigoc' from the Latin 'niger oculus'. On one occasion we were enjoying our joke as he was passing and, assuming we were laughing at him, he stopped and boxed Wilfred's ears.[14]

Alec being unusually tall and Wilfred unusually short, they were sometimes called 'the long and the short of it'. At break, in the playground, they were generally to be found talking together,

seemingly unaware of the yelling and screaming of the rest of the boys around them. When, as sometimes happened, some tail-end of a horse would accidentally charge them they hardly seemed to notice, but would move quietly out of the way without any interruption.[15]

Alec became a frequent visitor at 51 Milton Road. There, he and Wilfred would fight battles with two armies of toy soldiers or, particularly on days when there were other children present, would

The Birkenhead Institute

play charades with elaborate dressing-up.[16] At Susan Owen's instigation – she was determined that Wilfred should not follow in his uncle Edward's unsteady footsteps – both boys joined the Young Abstainers' Union and sported its badge in their buttonholes. Lectures on the dire consequences of involvement with the Demon Drink were held in certain of the better-class homes in the Tranmere area, another factor commending the Union to Mrs. Owen. Both boys went to the Christ Church Sunday School where, in due course, to please his wife, Tom began conducting the older classes.

This phase did not last very long. My father was not good at mixing with other Church enthusiasts and disliked the whole atmosphere. He met with open disapproval from them through his habit of talking to his boys' classes about ships and sailors and foreign ports – instead of instilling the Gospel as he was supposed to do. As most of them were sons of sailors or stevedores, this was not unnatural, but he soon gave up the work. It was typical of him that he kept in touch with the boys themselves and visited them in their homes.[17]

Wilfred's Sunday School teacher was a Miss McHutcheon. Visiting her house with Alec one day for tea, he tripped as she opened the door and fell full-length at her feet. He blushed to the roots of his hair and was so embarrassed that he hardly spoke a word all afternoon.[18]

In April 1902 he went to stay with his Owen grandparents in Shrewsbury, and wrote back to his mother:

Grandpa has given me as much garden as what you see from the dining room window only where the bricks are and I have got about six potatos planted, I have made another path and on the right side of it is the Vegeatble Garden and on the left is the fruit and the one you saw is the flower. It has just been raining a little for the first time but now it has stopt. We are going to Market this afternoon and I might buy some seeds.[19]

Old William Owen was devoted to his garden, growing all his own vegetables and taking pride in the fact that every year his new potatoes were in advance of his neighbours'. Any grandchild that came to stay was allotted his or her plot, and the botanical interests that were to have such an important relationship to Wilfred's poems may well have sprung from the garden at Hawthorn Villa.

That summer Tom Owen took his family back to Ireland for a holiday.[20] They rented rooms in Tramore, near Waterford, in the white-washed cottage of a fisherman called Fleury. He and his wife were kindly hosts and the holiday began propitiously. The weather was fine and the mornings were spent on the beach, with Tom and Wilfred swimming, the smaller children playing in the dwindling surf at the sea's edge. One rougher day, when Tom had insisted that he and Wilfred must have their swim, though begged by Susan not to, Wilfred got into difficulties and had to be helped ashore by a fisherman. Exhilarated rather than alarmed by this, Tom waved aside all counsels of caution and plunged back into the tossing waves. His shivering children watched him and must have separated, for another fisherman found Colin wandering by himself. He took him to his mother in the Owens' bathing hut and helped her rub some warmth into the little boy's frozen limbs. Meanwhile, Tom had returned from battling with the billows to find three children where he had left four. Wilfred was promptly despatched, dragging Harold and Mary with him, to search the water's edge, while their desperate father enlisted the aid of other fishermen. A boat was launched from which he dived repeatedly, searching further and further out to sea. The tide was turning dangerously and at last, in despair and half-drowned himself, he was brought ashore – only to find his infant son safe in Susan's arms. His relief manifested itself in rage – at his wife for sheltering in the hut when she should have been outside, watching him doing battle with the elements; and with the unfortunate man for not leaving Colin alone. The bewildered fishermen beat a hasty retreat from his shaking fists, but it was in character that, when he had cooled down, he should seek them out one by one and apologize.[21]

This Irish holiday was also memorable for two events of a slightly mysterious nature. Firstly, there was the episode of Harold's shark. This he hooked from a boat some distance out to sea and, though he wished to play it himself, it was clearly no fish for a five-year-old. The fisherman who took over his bending rod, however, placed the boy's hands over his own and together they brought the huge creature alongside. It was hauled into the boat and its head hammered until the lashing tail lay still. The village turned out to see the giant brought in and dragged into an outhouse adjoining the Fleurys' cottage. There the giant-killer inspected it every half hour or so until, on his last visit before bed, he opened the door to see a greyish white upright shape. It was the fish standing on its tail, miraculously still alive. Harold was terrified and ran for help, but his story was not believed until Wilfred too had seen the ghostly apparition. When at last the men came out, Harold suddenly became sorry for the shark and begged his father so passionately to let it go that Tom persuaded two fishermen to help him drag it back, through the darkening village, to the jetty where it had been landed in triumph some hours before. It was restored to its element and sighted in the bay on numerous occasions for many months afterwards.[22]

The second episode was more disturbing and took place the day before their holiday ended. Tom had set his heart on a last walk and led his family off in a direction they had not taken before. After some time they came to the mouth of an avenue flanked on each side by dark woods. Entering this, they suddenly noticed that the sun had gone in. This and the dense foliage of the interlacing boughs over-head gave them the sense of walking down a tunnel. It began to rain.

Then Harold suddenly called out that there was a large animal moving along a branch high above them. Tom and Wilfred, following his pointed finger, saw it also, but a blast of rain struck their upturned faces and when they looked again the dark shape had vanished. Susan was openly anxious to turn back and the children were subdued, but Tom would not hear of it and led them on down the avenue. At its end, they came to an open space.

and were immediately faced with what appeared to be a sheet of water. It was separated from us by about thirty yards of stony foreshore. It did not somehow quite look like real water; instead it had the metallic sheen of polished gunmetal. The whole effect had the eerie quality of a mirage. This was accentuated by a strange high wall of mist which cut across the water in a perfectly straight line. In this way every bit of background was obliterated and in some curious way it seemed that behind this mist there was just nothing at all. The effect was of utter unreality. This dream-like unrealness gave it a weird mystery and some menacing threat of danger that produced in us all a sensation of being warned. So strong was this feeling that we all closed up together and then remained motionless; we did not speak but just stood and stared. I am certain that we remained in this trance-like state for several minutes until my father, shaking himself a little, spoke to us (his voice, I remember, was not quite firm), telling us that this nonsense of being frightened of nothing had gone quite far enough, and throwing some jocular remark that had a merry challenge in it, he started off towards the water. The rest of us were instinctively holding hands and, still under an inexplicable spell of some sort, followed along just behind him. We had perhaps gone half way when we realized that the water and the wall of mist were receding from us at exactly the same pace that we ourselves were moving. The strangeness of this stopped my father – immediately the water and the mist became stationary again, only now the whole scene had taken on a transcendent appearance as if it was not really there at all but super-imposed over the rough open space. . . . My father was anxious now and my mother and Wilfred were trembling violently; we younger ones were, I think, more unhappy than frightened. It was darkening now and there was a chill in the air.

  My father advanced once more and the same thing happened – the water and the mist again went back, only this time the normal background of trees and sedgy grass seemed in a horrid way to be coming through as if they were real and solid and the water and the mist were nebulous. This was too much for my mother and, swinging around, she turned to get away from it. It was as she turned that for the first and only time in my life I heard her give a stifled scream. This spun us all around to see, standing ten yards or so from us, the shadowy figure of a tall man. This strange figure seemed to radiate the same cold incandescent quality that even now was permeating the hallucinatory lake. For some inexplicable reason the whole attitude of this illusionary being diffused a mute declaration of his intention to do harm to us and this, I know, gave us all a quite unreasonable feeling of desperate insecurity.

My father must have recovered himself and at once addressed this sinister looking person, I have no doubt with some apology for our trespass if we were committing one. The sound of my father's voice had the unexpected effect of contorting the man into a frenzy of fury, and he raised the heavy stick he was carrying with such ferocious intent that attack from him seemed unavoidable. The surprise perhaps silenced my father and immediately the figure relaxed to its original stationary position. After a minute of bemused silence my father tried again, only to produce the same silent paroxysm. Perhaps it was the unnatural muteness more than the gesticulating that created the cold fear that now held all of us except my father. The rest of us were motionless and speechless but he was now very angry and belligerent and advanced upon this thing or man, with the astonishing effect of causing it to walk backwards away from my father, keeping an unvarying distance. It seemed as though the two of them were synchronized, every hesitation or movement of my father was repeated in a backward direction by the figure who still faced us. If my father retreated the figure came forward. This marionette movement continued backwards and forwards until my father, his quick temper rising, strode forward with real determination until he came to the very edge of the wood. . . . It was now that my mother's despairing voice cried out so urgently 'Tom, Tom, come back, come back'.

At this instant the figure, which had been clearly there until now, was suddenly not there any longer. . . . Our tightness left us, and freedom once again was all about us. . . . my father with great vigour hustled us together and taking a direction right away from the place, herded us along at a tremendous pace. As he turned us away, we all looked back towards the lake. It was no longer there.[23]

That evening, the fisherman and his wife looked in to say good-night, and Tom and Susan began to recount their adventure. The change in them both was immediate and astounding. Their faces hardened, and Tom, realizing that the subject was not to be pursued, stopped abruptly. After an embarrassing silence, the fisherman and his wife urged the Owens to say nothing about it to anyone.[24]

A happier holiday of a quite different sort took place in August 1903 or 1904.[25] A girlhood friend of Susan's offered the Owens the use of her furnished cottage in the Cheshire hills near the village of Broxton. Tom could not take his own holiday at this time, but realizing that his wife was in need of a change from housework and the worry of unpaid bills, he persuaded her to take Wilfred to the cottage for a week or two. He and the other children went to see them installed. The cottage was small and crumbling, with two low-ceilinged bedrooms upstairs, a living room and a kitchen-larder below.[26] An enormous pig grunted and shuffled in a sty outside. The weather was perfect and, at Wilfred's suggestion, Harold and he gathered harebells and bracken fronds 'like carven croziers',[27] massing them on the living-room table as a surprise for their parents who had gone shopping in the village. Wilfred was fond of picking flowers for his mother. In Ireland he had filled her room with a purple and yellow profusion of wild irises gathered from the bank of a stream, and on occasions, as she rested on a sofa, had covered her with flowers.[28]

On the Sunday evening, Tom, Harold, Mary, and Colin returned to Birkenhead, leaving Susan and Wilfred to long days in the sun, long evenings in the lamplight. They spent many hours reading together, but what books will probably never be known: Keats's *Poems*, perhaps, or the 1903 reprint of Charlotte Brontë's *Shirley*, with its pencil-marked description of Miss Ainley that accorded so well with Wilfred's view of his mother:

> She talked never of herself – always of others. Their faults she passed over; her theme was their wants, which she sought to supply; their sufferings, which she longed to alleviate. She was religious – a professor of religion – what some would call 'a saint', and she referred to religion often in sanctioned phrase – in phrase which those who possess a perception of the ridiculous, without owning the power of exactly testing and truly judging character, would certainly have esteemed a proper subject for satire – a matter of mimicry and laughter. They would have been hugely mistaken for their pains. Sincerity is never ludicrous; it is always respectable. Whether truth – be it religious or moral truth – speak eloquently and in well-chosen language or not, its voice should be heard with reverence.[29]

Marked also in this copy are the passages about William Cowper's 'gift of poetry – the most Divine bestowed on man',[30] and Milton's Eve.[31]

All that is certain is that Wilfred's thoughts were centred – as never before – on poetry,

> at Broxton, by the Hill
> Where first I felt my boyhood fill
> With uncontainable movements; there was born
> My poethood.[32]

The note of Wordsworthian revelation is appropriate, as Harold Owen makes clear in his beautiful evocation of those golden weeks:

> It was in Broxton among the ferns and bracken and the little hills, secure in the safety and understanding love that my mother wrapped about him with such tender ministration, that the poetry in Wilfred, with gentle pushings, without hurt, began to bud, and not on the battlefields of France.[33]

The rest of the family, back in Birkenhead, had a more cheerful time than they had expected, thanks to the boisterous presence of a young Liverpool woman – the daughter and sister of sailors – whom Tom brought in as housekeeper. This Elizabeth (and her tattooed brother) captivated Harold in particular, but Susan was less impressed and, after her return, Elizabeth was seen no more at 51 Milton Road.[34]

In October 1903, Harold started at the Birkenhead Institute. Wilfred, at his most elder-brotherly and unsympathetic, escorted him his first morning and handed him over to Miss Farrell. She took an immediate liking to Harold and in due course he was invited to stay with her for the weekend. This he was happy to do, but he rebelled at her suggestion that he should sleep in her bed. Eventually it was agreed that he should sleep by himself, but he awoke next morning to find her heavy body beside his. Refusing to stay any longer, he was taken home in disgrace.[35] Wilfred was displeased over this incident – making clear that he thought Harold was to blame – and he was even more embarrassed when, shortly after his brother had moved up to the main school, Harold was involved in a playground battle from which he emerged with a bloody nose and a nickname, 'The Birkenhead Bullfighter'.[36] Not long afterwards, he was taken away from the Birkenhead Institute and sent to a Free Church School, but conditions there were so bad that he was shortly removed from this also. His mother decided that she would teach him at home, but her housework left her little free time and Harold's tuition soon ceased altogether.[37]

In February 1903, Mr. Connacher died and was succeeded as head-master of the Birkenhead Institute by Mr. James Smallpage. His son Eric entered the school that year and soon became a friend of Wilfred's. The headmaster's wife had old-fashioned views about the company her son should keep and used to embarrass him by vetting his friends. Wilfred, however, was pronounced to be 'a nice boy from a nice home', and his friendship with her son received her official approval.[38] He had then, and was never to lose, what his less law-abiding brother was to describe as

an assured diffidence. This gravity of approach, which remained always in advance of his years, coupled as it was with his attractive appearance (not to be confused with good looks), his thick dark brown hair and small delicacy of build – perhaps a lack of robustness even – gave him an air of over-adultness. I always think of it as his 'small dark look'. All this was with him at ten years of age and had an unusual attraction for all the masters and mistresses who ever taught him. His hands, too, were expressive and peculiarly indicative: they were always clean, blue-veined, white and delicate looking. I never once saw him with schoolboy's hands. Indeed in all my recollections of Wilfred when he was at school I can never recall any impression of a schoolboy: I can only think of him – even when he was only eleven or twelve dressed in school clothes with a schoolboy satchel on his back – as a student.[39]

This is the impression one receives from the science exercise book he began in January 1904. The handwriting is careful and regular, capital letters having a slightly self-conscious flourish, and the diagrams are painstakingly drawn. Most of these exercises have received full marks. Mr. Smallpage ended his report that January: 'I think his abilities are excellent.'[40]

Life at 51 Milton Road had settled into an ordered and – for the children, at least – not uncomfortable routine. Admittedly, money was scarce. There were not many luxuries to be eaten with the Plas

Wilmot cutlery, but there was a strong sense of family solidarity and they made the most of the simple pleasures of home life. Tom gave 'Sue' an illustrated copy of Bunyan's *Pilgrim's Progress* for her birthday in March 1904, and his nightly reading aloud from this or some children's classic became a family custom. He read, as he sang, well. After the reading was over,

> my father would ceremoniously prepare for us what he liked to call sailors' fo'c'sle food. This ritual was carried out with full seriousness, and only on these occasions. Bowls were produced, the kettle boiled, slices of bread diced into exact squares, a lump of dripping placed in the bowl underneath the bread and the whole covered with boiling water. After a few moments to brew, we would attack it with great gusto and we thought it was the finest food we ever had.[41]

Tom Owen, who had a Welsh passion for music of any sort,[42] arranged for Wilfred to have piano lessons, which from the start were a great success. He was taught by a Miss Taylor, who lived in Liverpool and would come over to Birkenhead in the evening to lead him through his scales and first pieces. She used to stay for supper with the family, delighting them with a fund of amusing and often racy stories. When, in the winter of 1906/7, the Owen finances were so strained that Tom had to tell Miss Taylor he could no longer afford her modest tuition fees, she would not hear of abandoning the lessons. She enjoyed those evenings so much, she said, that she would continue to come for nothing. And she did.[43]

Another welcome visitor to 51 Milton Road was Cousin May, a distant relation of Susan Owen's. She had a tongue even racier than Miss Taylor's and such an abundance of generous vitality that her annual visits were preceded by weeks of excited anticipation. This, for the children, was increased when Susan,

> with lowered voice and conspiratorial solemnity told us that while of course Cousin May was everything that was good and virtuous she *did* paint her face (it was thus described in the early 1900's), which was a very wicked thing to do; equally wicked was Cousin May's predilection for the stage and her constant theatre-going: at this Wilfred and I pricked up our ears. Wilfred immediately demanded to know 'Had Cousin May been an actress'; my mother's horrified emphatic denial made Wilfred look disappointed and me feel so.[44]

The Owens on Scarborough beach, 1905

Mrs. Owen can hardly have approved when Cousin May, not content with painting her own face, set up a clinic for the removal of unwanted hair from the faces of ladies less artful than herself where their complexions were concerned. No doubt Susan Owen saw it as Divine Retribution when one of Cousin May's patients contracted blood-poisoning and the clinic had to close its doors under threat of legal damages. Fortunately, its proprietor escaped with a modest settlement out of court, whereupon biting, as it were, the Hand of Providence, she plunged gaily into speculation on the stock market until, once again threatened with disaster, she decided to invest her remaining savings in a girls' private school at Scarborough. Providence showed its approval by making this venture a success.

She was thwarted, however, in her attempt to introduce Harold and Wilfred to the theatre. Susan Owen would not hear of it. In vain did she promise to choose a suitable play, an educational play, Shakespeare. She even modified her proposal to the extent of suggesting a visit to the circus, but the boys' mother was adamant and Wilfred had to wait for his first taste of the theatre until after the family had moved to Shrewsbury.[45]

In the early summer of 1905 they all stayed with Cousin May in Scarborough. Tom and the boys played cricket[46] and rode ponies on the beach. Wilfred became rather a good horseman,[47] as Alec Paton was to discover when a year or two later he and Wilfred went for a gallop on the sands at New Brighton.[48] When the Owens returned from Scarborough, Alec's parents invited Wilfred to join them on their family holiday at a farm in Glan Clwyd, Rhewl, in Denbighshire. And so, early in August, he set off with Mr. and Mrs. Paton, Alec and his two sisters – Marion aged seven, and Catherine aged five – and an uncle of theirs, Alec Stuart.[49] He described his arrival in a letter to his mother:

At first, before we got to the farm the place was not what I anticipated, we had to go *through*, not along, a dirty, wet, muddy lane. But the farm is fine. I am very happy but I am not wild. We are both kept under great restriction. We got up a ladder on to a haystack in a Dutch Barn. In case you dont know what a D.B. is, I will draw one.

Well, we made little nests on the top, but Mrs. Paton heard us moving the hay and soon called us down. (Mr. P. laughed.) I am asked to thank Mr. Owen for the f. rod. It is useless now! We cannot fish!! No licence!!! Is it not sad!!! Alec's Uncle broke my rod. It is mended now. He was fishing this morning when a river bailiff came up & told him something about how to fish, thinking he had a licence! You have to pay 15 or 16 shillings for 1 to fish, I *think*. This is a filthy letter, all blots. Thank Mary & Colin for their letters. I slept in chair bed 1*st* night but I do not now. I sleep with Alec.[50]

The boys would get up late in the morning, vexing Mrs. Jones the farmer's wife.[51] Then they would climb trees in the orchard, pick plums, or sail paper boats on the little river Clwyd, which flowed through the farmyard. Once, Wilfred fell in trying to recover an errant handkerchief. He told his mother: 'Alec & I found two little streams; his is the "Wiswos", & I call mine the "Fontibell".'[52] On their walks, the same interest in naming things showed in his organizing caterpillar races. The furry contestants were christened, set down on the country road, and cheered towards the winning post. They also played soldiers with nonsensical words of command.[53]

One day the boys climbed Moel Farma (1,823 ft.), the highest hill in the Clwydian range.[54] They fished – furtively and without success, both losing their hooks – and Mr. Jones allowed them to help him drive the cows and pigs from farmyard to field. Every evening, after the oil lamps had been lit, they would all gather in the large farm kitchen and sit in high-backed settles before the open fire. The Jones's three daughters, who could speak almost no English, would try amidst peals of laughter to teach Wilfred and the three Paton children Welsh.[55] They went to bed by candle-light and every night, remembering his mother's injunctions, Wilfred would read himself a passage from his Bible. He wrote to her towards the end of the holiday:

I hope you are all quite well, I am eating tremendously! We went gathering nuts this morning, I have got, altogether, 113. I am going to bring them home for the children you must not tell them please. Mr. Jones has bought 120 sheep today. They are so tired after walking 3 days that some will let me stroke them. I can count up to 10 in Welsh, & have learnt a few expressions. It will soon be time to milk the cows now. I can milk a bit. I drink buttermilk for dinner, & have cream on the stewed fruit. Indeed I fare very sumptuously, & wish Mary was here to eat the plums we get off the tree every day.

There are nine little piggies. You would be amused if you saw them. Their heads are too large for their bodies & their tails are like curly bits of string.

We are having fine weather now. I am very glad of the boots, because in the morning the grass is wet. I have not been to Ruthin yet. When I go I want to buy a little tiny boat to sail down the Clwyd. It is nearly time for the post now.

With love love & kisses always from Wilfred[56]

He was beginning to 'fare very sumptuously' on words.

In 1905 Wilfred won the school's Junior Duke of Westminster scholarship (value £5), which would seem to have further convinced the headmaster and his wife of his suitability as a friend for Eric, in that they invited him to spend a fortnight with them at Waenfawr, on the slopes of Moel Eilio, three miles south of Caernarvon. His own parents were happy that he should go and, after a family holiday in Cornwall,[57] Wilfred set off with the Smallpages. For a fortnight he and Eric played in water-meadows beside a sparkling trout river. They fished but caught nothing, so pursued dragonflies instead, and on hot days bathed in the brooks that fed the river. One afternoon, when they were hacking down thistles to get at a rabbit-hole, Eric was stung by a couple of wasps. Back at the cottage a blue-bag was applied and Wilfred declared that the sufferer was an Ancient Briton wearing woad. On another occasion they went down to the narrow-gauge railway line with Eric's sister and sat on the rails to feel them vibrate as a train approached. The prize for 'last off' was won by the little girl, who received a torrent of Welsh profanity from a frightened engine-driver.

The boys shared a bedroom and last thing at night used to tell each other stories that were meant to be original, but when Wilfred began 'You have often wondered how I came to lose the top of my left ear', Eric recognized one of the tales of Brigadier Gerard and the ensuing pillow-fight had to be quelled by Mr. Smallpage.[58]

Also in 1906 Wilfred went to stay with his aunt Emma and uncle John Gunston, who had just moved into a comfortable suburban house they named Alpina in Clement Road, Wimbledon.[59] John Gunston was by Owen standards well-off, the owner of a chain of butcher shops, and the father of four children: Gordon, Dorothy, Vera, and Leslie, the last of whom was to become Wilfred's closest boyhood friend. Two years younger than Wilfred, he was at Kings College School, Wimbledon, and returning from school would often see a slight figure with short legs crossing the common, hands clasped behind his back, a distinctive domed felt hat on his head. The children knew him as 'the man who makes poetry as he goes along'. The world knew him as Algernon Charles Swinburne, and he was probably the first poet that Wilfred Owen ever set eye upon.[60]

Harold's education was now, unofficially, in the hands of a house-keeper, Mrs. Moore, and she taught him more than any of his previous teachers. Unfortunately, however, it transpired that her kind and capable hands had light fingers. One evening in the autumn of 1906 she failed to return to 51 Milton Road. At length, fearing some accident, Tom Owen informed the police who, recognizing his description, bade him check his household possessions. Almost every piece of Plas Wilmot linen and silver was found to be missing. Some of it was recovered from Birkenhead pawnshops, but Mrs. Moore – to the children's relief – was never caught.[61]

One weekday morning Tom Owen failed to go to the Station, which was unusual enough. He was also in an extremely bad temper, which, on a holiday morning was even more unusual. The children realized that something momentous was afoot when he reappeared after breakfast wearing a morning suit and carrying a silk hat, which he proceeded to brush with great care. That evening he returned jubilant and, taking his wife aside, whispered a few words to her,

after which he demanded that his family should be assembled around him. When we were seated to his satisfaction – he was very fussy about this – he, still standing, proceeded with his delivery of one of his set speeches. The gist of it was that we were to leave Birkenhead almost immediately to go and live in Shrewsbury. He then went on, still in his speechifying manner, to whet our appetites for the delights to come, and in his own excitement and enthusiasm over-gilded the prospects; but we drank it all in and begged for more and he supplied it with visions of life in the country, boating and fishing on a river, early morning excursions, bird-watching, walks and, above all, a better neighbourhood, better house, and more and nicer food, and wound up by thrilling us with the news that he himself henceforward would be a much more important person than hithertofore – his own words those. After making us all very happy with a read from 'Uncle Remus', he took us all into the tiny kitchen and, finding his dripping and bread, he boiled his kettle and proceeded to make celebration for us – and for himself – with his famous lobscouse.[62]

He had been appointed Assistant Superintendent of the Joint Railways,[63] an important post with a salary which, though meagre enough, was nevertheless an improvement on any he had earned so far. Harold was delighted by the prospect of leaving Birkenhead, but Wilfred was not, and Tom went round to ask Mr. Paton whether it might be possible for him to stay behind, during term time, with them. The Patons all welcomed this suggestion, but Susan Owen flatly refused even to discuss the possibility that she might be separated from her favourite son.[64]

Not long after Christmas 1906 – when Susan gave Wilfred a copy of *La Sainte Bible*[65] – the packing began, and one day early in 1907 they were all assembled

in the empty house waiting for the cab. My father was by now in one of his real states of fluster, pulling out his watch every few seconds and openly accusing my mother of not having ordered the cab at all. . . .

Wilfred was hunched up in a corner deep in some book or other, seemingly impervious to the fretted tempers snapping around him. He was dressed in a Norfolk knickerbocker suit, much in vogue among schoolboys at that period, of some brownish material, with stockings and boots, and a narrow stiff white collar with a stringy-looking tie that would never keep closed up to the collar itself. His very dark brown hair was falling untidily but attractively over his forehead: it badly needed cutting. Another source of irritation to my father – of which we three boys were all guilty – was our aversion to visiting the barber often enough to satisfy him. Wilfred had slung over his shoulders his school satchel containing his current exercise and text books from which he refused to be parted. In his hand was the book he was reading and stuffed into his pockets were other books. He seemed unconcerned and calmly indifferent to the event, and only raised his head to admonish one of us if he thought we were making things too difficult for my mother. His preoccupation and air of neutrality was an added friction to my father who would have liked him to have co-operated and shown interest in what was going on. . . .

It was my father squeezing himself into the overloaded four-wheeler that broke the final link with Birkenhead. This epoch was finished . . . all that had happened here was to be left behind . . . as the cab rolled away down the mean street both my father and mother looked back at the small empty house. Mary and I looked forwards . . . in front of us was a new beginning. The little Colin wedged on the floor could look neither way. Wilfred looked at his book.

Tonight we should be in Shrewsbury.[66]

3

SHREWSBURY

They arrived, as in Birkenhead, eleven years before, to the steady drumming of rain on the cab roof. This time, however, they were greeted not by black beetles but by a pair of magnificent white moustaches. Harold

had never seen anything like them before and it was probably my intense interest in them which made me notice other things about the stately old gentleman, his shock of tousled very white hair and his cold icy-blue eyes that I soon discovered were piercing right through me in a most uncomfortable way, and his extraordinarily transparent skin stretched tightly over his prominent face bones. The bones seemed to hold an illumination that glowed through the skin itself so that it made me fearful and unhappy. Presently, he placed one of his bony hands on my shoulder and, speaking to me, broke my spellbound absorption. It was only then that I noticed the really tiny old lady who immediately smiled very sweetly and warmly at me, at the same time handing me a mug of cocoa with a biscuit.[1]

The moustaches belonged to old William Owen in whose small house Tom and his family stayed until they succeeded in renting one of their own. This, 1 Cleveland Place, was in the same road on the eastern side of town as Hawthorn Villa. Wilfred, who had a romantic liking for attics, commandeered the second-floor room under the eaves for himself and Harold. They had to share a bed and if, as was usually the case, Harold was the first to creep between the sheets, he would be ordered to go to sleep, but would be

unable to do so and would lie restless but not daring to move about, looking now and again towards Wilfred, whose dark round head I could see bent low over the improvised writing-table, ceaselessly writing and muttering to himself, the single guttering candle by which he was working throwing a grotesque and huge shadow on the steeply sloping ceiling. I did not mind so much when he was writing but when he was reading I found myself waiting, with held breath, for the turning of each page. From time to time I could lie still no longer; Wilfred without turning or stopping what he was doing would exclaim with savage irritation: 'Oh, do go to sleep, you stupid boy. I cannot work unless you do.' On other nights, he would pace the eight feet or so of the minute room, declaiming aloud or memorizing in a mumble. Hours later would come the painful business as he inserted his cold and shaking body into the bed; his chattering teeth would keep me awake after he himself had fallen into exhausted sleep.[2]

Once they were settled into their new home, the question of schools came up and Tom and Susan discussed the various possibilities, often with the children present. It was thought most important that the right school should be found for Wilfred, and it was decided that, rather than risk sending him to the wrong one, they would wait until they had a clearer picture of the alternatives. Harold's abilities were considered insufficient to justify expense and it was decreed that he should go to a free board school as soon as possible. Accordingly, a few days later he set off, clutching the tuppence required of him each week, to a prison-like building on the other side of town. As in Birkenhead, he had again to endure a baptism of fire. Mauled in the playground his first break-time, he was more savagely set upon after school and only escaped by felling his Goliath with a lucky stone. Returning home bleeding and dishevelled, he was rebuked by his parents and by Wilfred, who were disinclined to believe his story. Only Mary comforted him, giving him her store of chocolate.

Although the reputation of the Birkenhead Bull-Fighter now afforded Harold a measure of protection from physical assault, he hated the school and was troubled in particular by the salacious talk and antics in the latrines. He tried to speak to Wilfred about this, who must in turn have spoken to Susan. She, with her comfortable ability to see only what she wanted – and it was proper – to see, told Harold that since God had ordained that he should attend the school, he must put his trust in Him. The nine-year-old replied 'if God really thought this school was a nice place then he could not know what he was talking about, so I did not see how I could trust Him at all'. At such moments, Susan took comfort from the very different attitude of her first-born, whose letters show an increasing interest in religion, or perhaps an increasing interest in pleasing his mother:

> We went to S. Giles' yesterday, Mr. Roberts[3] preached. 'Lo, I am with you alway, even unto the end of the world.' *Matt.* 28. XX.
> HYMNS 220, 281, 320.
> No Scrip. Union card came, but it is all the better, I had already found my own in the drawer.[4]

Letter after letter to Susan Owen (who was staying with the Gunstons in April 1907) gives the text of the day's sermon, the hymns that were sung, or ends with a pious postscript, as: 'Greet ye one another with a kiss of Charity. Peace be with you all that are in Christ Jesus. Amen. 1 *Peter* V. 14.' Wilfred's early preoccupation with religion for a time equalled and perhaps exceeded his preoccupation with literature, culminating in what was known to the rest of the family as 'Wilfred's Church'.

> Aided and encouraged by my mother, Wilfred would on Sunday evenings arrange our small sitting-room to represent a church. The table would be moved away, all available chairs collected and arranged for pews, an armchair turned backwards making a pulpit and lectern. At first it was all very simple but as his enthusiasm grew and his imagination took wing, it became more and more elaborate and my mother was kept busy making altar cloths, stoles, and a perfectly fashioned small linen surplice, all most beautifully worked, for she was a superb needlewoman. Finally she made a bishop's mitre. This was most extraordinarily effective; it was made from Bristol boards, white and glossy and cunningly enscrolled with gold paint. Wilfred would spend a long time arranging the room, after which he would robe himself and, looking very priestlike in his surplice and mitre, would call us in to form the congregation. He would then conduct a complete evening service with remarkable exactitude and would end by reading a short sermon he had prepared with great care and thought.[5]

Susan, at this time an ardent parishioner of St. Julian's Church, was an energetic worker for the Temperance Society and the British and

Foreign Bible Society. Clergymen were frequent callers at 1 Cleveland Place, although Tom disliked all but one who seemed to be more interested in cricket than the prayerbook.[6]

In the early Spring of 1907, Wilfred started at the Shrewsbury Technical School, a grey stone building on the east bank of the Severn, beside the English Bridge. It was a good school and from the beginning he did well – particularly in French, a subject in which he was receiving special tuition from a Miss Goodwin, who came to give the children piano lessons. 'Goody', as she was known to the family, also ran a small private school in a neighbouring street, and to this Mary and Colin were sent.

Wilfred's interest in poetry and drama commended him to the English mistress, Miss Wright, whose help and encouragement were to be of crucial importance to his development as a poet.[7] His school exercise books provide an index of his reading at this time: in May 1907, *The Faerie Queene*, Book 1, and Macaulay's 'Horatius'; in September, an essay entitled 'Autumn' contains plentiful quotations from Keats's 'Ode', while other essays show him to have been studying *Macbeth* and *Richard II*; in October, it is *Twelfth Night*; in November, *Cymbeline*, *Much Ado about Nothing*, *Othello*, *King Lear*, *The Taming of the Shrew*, *Henry IV*, and *Henry V*. With his taste for drama – already demonstrated in 'Wilfred's Church' – he responded to this new and intensive diet with enthusiasm, marking his texts with loving care: the Penny Poets, the Era Shakespeare and the Everyman Library volumes (price, respectively, 1d, 8d, and 1/– each). It was probably during these months, and in Miss Wright's class, that Wilfred's pencil began to draft a blank-verse poem on the inside cover of his (1907) school edition of *A Midsummer-Night's Dream*:

> ~~Wh~~ Within those days
> ~~About~~
> When glossy celandine forgets to flower,
> And bugle blooms where hyacinth hath been
>   sweet moods and mystery dawn
> And those ~~things~~   ~~which~~ least
> Men need a poet's tongue to tell them of,

I made a wayward journey, through new paths.
~~Alone I went, as is my mournful~~ fate
I went ~~to~~ in quest of healing for a body tired
~~Partly to~~
  ~~And new~~ enthusiasm for a soul
  ~~Too~~
               love
~~To~~ Grown faint in ~~praise~~ of beauty and of truth
      more
        ~~as~~
And further~~more I half~~ I half-forknew,
           some for
Some vision waited me, even ~~to~~ me
As ~~unto~~ those old dreamers on May Morn
  When
~~In~~ England's muse was young.[8]

Wilfred's school exercise books of this period reveal almost as much about his thinking as his reading. An essay on 'The imagined effects on the Country of a Strike among the Railway Workers' shows him – and presumably his father – more concerned for the welfare of the country, and for those other workers dependent on the railways, than for the members of the Amalgamated Society of Railway Servants threatening to strike. Writing on 'The Force of Example', he declares with prophetic irony that 'the example of a great death has often been more powerful than a great life'. An essay on 'Value of Poetry' states that 'rules for metre and versifying are taught by act, & acquired by study; but the force & elevation of thought which alone makes poetry of any value, must be derived from Nature'. In accordance with this prescription, Wilfred was to be seen every night framed in his attic window, working by candle-light at his books.[9]

With the approach of summer, Tom Owen began to think again of those outdoor delights he had so enthusiastically prophesied that evening in the kitchen at Birkenhead. On fine mornings he would get up at 5.30 or earlier, wake Harold and see that he washed in cold water, then prepare a simple breakfast for them both.

After the tea and bread and butter, we would steal quietly out of the house and set off for the fields and river which were no distance away. . . .

   The country around was heavy with uncut hedges and small clumps of
bush and trees, and in the nesting season my father would find – and mark
down for watching – many different kinds of birds' nests and was always
seeking to add new species to our list. In the breeding season we would go
out almost daily and if a nest was expected to hatch out, would return in
the evenings to mark progress. Sometimes we would take one particular
nest for watching and, hiding ourselves in the bushes nearby, would stand
motionless for long periods watching the parent birds rearing their young.
Other times on warm sunny mornings we would walk straight down to the
river, my father looking for two suitably secluded alcoves in a hedge.
Having selected these, he would repair to his and get into his bathing
costume. I would go to mine and put on short swimming trunks. My father
was always very particular about all this and although I was so young would
never let me bathe in the nude.[10]

Tom clearly enjoyed these expeditions, but no sooner was he home
again than the patient bird-watcher became the impatient father,
asking why breakfast was late, why Wilfred was not up. Finally, he
would stride briskly out of the house muttering to himself and
twirling his walking stick like a windmill. Sometime later, Wilfred
would follow him down Underdale Road, his right shoulder sagging
under the weight of a book-crammed satchel.

   As a result of his elder brother's increasing self-absorption, Harold
turned more and more to the seven-year-old Colin for companion-
ship. Both had outdoor interests, and within months of arriving in
Shrewsbury they had explored most of the surrounding countryside.
One one of these midsummer walks, they crossed the green acres of
the Severn Valley to where the river bends sharply south under the
high bank from which the village of Uffington looks back towards
the roofs and spires of Shrewsbury.[11] Not having sufficient pennies
for the ferryman's fee, they turned back, resolving to save their
pocket money: Wilfred at that time received 6d a week, Mary 3d,
Harold and Colin 1d each.

   A fortnight later, armed with the necessary tuppence each (a penny
each way), they retraced their steps and shouted for the ferryman.
Having hauled them across the river, he charged them only a
ha'penny each because they were so small. All day they explored the
village in a daze of heat and happiness and, at supper that evening,
gave the rest of the family a lyrical account of the ferry, the mill, the

The Uffington ferry

hump-backed bridge over the canal, and the little church. Tom enquired about the prospects for fishing and must have been satisfied with the reply for he proposed a family picnic his next free Saturday. This proved a great success, though Wilfred was disappointed in the church and particularly its stained glass,[12] which was surprising, as some of it dated from the fifteenth, sixteenth, and seventeenth centuries.

In general, however, the family were delighted with the Church of the Holy Trinity, Uffington, and decided to go to it regularly rather than to St. Julian's in Shrewsbury. The idea was Tom's and, frequently in the summer, he would take one or more of the children with him to evensong. The walk was somewhat too long for Susan, although occasionally she would come with them, having travelled in a hired carriage to within two or three fields of the ferry. Harold, in particular, loved these expeditions and never lost the explorer's proprietary feeling that the village belonged to him.

On one of these summer-night returns from Uffington church, when we were walking through the last of the meadows before we reached the lane, I had fallen back behind the others as I was sometimes wont to do – I was fond of slowly dragging my feet through the cool wetness of the grass. When I was climbing over the stile leading into the lane I noticed in the half-darkness that my boots looked strange and peering more closely I saw that they were completely covered with buttercup petals; in the darkness they glowed like gold. I was immediately intrigued with this and called out to the others that I had feet of gold, but they were a long way up the lane, the mist was muffling my voice, and they could not hear me properly, so I did not persist and presently I heard Wilfred walking back to see what I was calling to them about. When Wilfred reached me he too was fascinated with the strange luminous effect. While we were still looking at them we heard my father's footsteps turn and come towards us. He was softly calling out as he came to ask if we were all right and I was just about to call back through the darkness when Wilfred gently pressed my arm for silence – hesitated a moment and then called quietly back, 'Harold's boots are blessed with gold'.[13]

And so that echo of the Vicar of Uffington's blessing at the close of evensong passed into the poet's subconscious, to emerge, eleven years later, in 'Spring Offensive'.

> And the far valley behind, where the buttercup
> Had blessed with gold their slow boots coming up.[14]

Although Wilfred fell less under the spell of Uffington than Harold, he was at this time developing outdoor interests of his own. With his cousins Vera and Leslie Gunston he formed an Astronomical, Geological and Botanical Society (of three members), writing to them on 15 November:

On thinking over the Rules, (for which I believe I have never yet thanked you) a new subject came into my head, that of Mountain Climbing. It is, as you will see, an almost essential branch of each of our studies, and mountaineering is also to the ambitious & strenuous outdoor naturalist, not only the noblest but the most insatiable of all *noble* sports. I propose that the aims of the movement shall be:

(1) The promotion of scientific study & exploration of certain glacial regions.
(2) ★The cultivation of Art in relation to mt. scenery.
(3) The Christian education of the inhabitants to an appreciation of their mt. heritage.
(4) The encouragement of the mt. craft, & the opening of new regions as a national playground.
(5) The preservation of the natural beauties of the mt. places, & of the fauna & *flora* in their habitat (with special reference to V.)

  ★It is hoped that you, V. will become the Photographic Representative, for what is Astronomy without its sister-art Photography? & some pictures showing strata, etc. would be invaluable to me.[15]

This rather selfconscious letter he signed – it would seem for the first time – with a monogram   ⓦ ,   based most probably on the monogram of the Great Western Railway.

The winter of 1907/8 made possible skating expeditions which delighted Tom Owen above all others and galvanized Wilfred into rare high spirits:

if my father gave the word that ice was holding somewhere he would jump and rush about, cracking his fingers, laughing and working himself up into a fine and infectious joy, calling out to all of us for hurry and speed. It was, perhaps, the only thing for which he would readily and immediately drop his books – and, with them, his serious and abstracted air. . . .[16]

Most of all they enjoyed skating at night, and it is hard to believe that Wilfred, who early in 1908 received full marks for an essay contrasting 'the school of Wordsworth' with 'the school of Pope', did not on these occasions have running through his head the famous passage from 'The Prelude' beginning:

> And in the frosty season, when the sun
> Was set, and visible for many a mile
> The cottage windows through the twilight blaz'd,
> I heeded not the summons: – happy time
> It was, indeed, for all of us; to me
> It was a time of rapture: clear and loud
> The village clock toll'd six; I wheel'd about,

> Proud and exulting, like an untired horse,
> That cares not for his home. – All shod with steel,
> We hiss'd along the polish'd ice, in games
> Confederate, imitative of the chace
> And woodland pleasures, the resounding horn,
> The Pack loud bellowing, and the hunted hare.[17]

In April 1908, Wilfred once again stayed with the Gunstons at Alpina in Wimbledon, seeing the Tower and the Cup Final;[18] and in June fulfilled one of his principal ambitions when his father took him to France for a week's holiday in Brest.[19] His mother was told they had a 'rough passage', a description at which Tom would no doubt have snorted. It is easy to imagine the Assistant Superintendent reasserting his seaman's authority, refurbishing his nautical vocabulary, rediscovering his sea legs on the ferry's pitching deck, expelling from his lungs the smoke of the Shrewsbury shunting yards, and delightedly inhaling the salt wind from the deep. While he communed at the rail with ghosts from the good ship *Benalder*, his landlubber son was – no less delightedly – practising his French on 'a charming French young lady'. Fulfilling the omens of that auspicious beginning, the holiday was a great success. 'Everything is delightful – hotel magnificent', Wilfred reported, adding: 'It is a pleasure to speak to the people here they are all so affable. I am easily understood, but can make nothing of what they say.' He must have enjoyed impressing his father, who must have enjoyed being impressed, for Tom was a generous parent with all too few opportunities for indulging his proper pride in his scholarly son. On this and their few subsequent holidays together, Tom's boyish exuberance reasserted itself, narrowing the gap between father and son. His passion for 'expeditions' led them down the long straight streets of Brest to the naval dockyards overlooking the wide indented bay, and no doubt under Wilfred's direction they climbed to the castle on the cliff top facing the open sea.

At about this time, Harold, who had endured a disheartening succession of unsatisfactory schools, suddenly found himself or, to be exact, was found – by Mr. Weaver, Principal of the School of Art. This was housed in the Technical School building and there,

The canal at Uffington, a water-colour by Harold Owen

under Mr. Weaver's kindly eye, he discovered his vocation as a painter with something of the same excitement that was kindling Wilfred at his books. Their father, alarmed at the thought that 'here was another son of his pursuing the arts',[20] resolved once again to try boat-building as a corrective distraction. Together with Harold he built a full-rigged, four-masted ship, the *Mary Millard*. Wilfred was no more interested in this than he had been in the *S.S. Susan*.

One day in the autumn of 1908, Harold and Colin were sailing their new vessel on the Severn when Colin fell in and all but drowned before his desperate brother could drag him ashore. Having got him home, Harold was further terrified to be told by Wilfred that Colin would surely catch pneumonia and die on the eleventh day.

The pneumonia idea and his over-eagerness to entertain the suggestion of death sprang from a concern for and an unhealthy absorption in his own state of health. This was beginning to grip him dangerously and his violent outburst towards me was possibly only an outlet for his own suppressed anxiety. Keats was ever-present in his mind, and he was given to this absorption in the life and work of men in all the arts who had died young;

he was also wont to compare the histories of these talented short-lived lives with his own plans for his writing of poetry. He could never divest himself of the parallel this comparison implied. I know that Wilfred was beginning to be convinced, and deeply convinced, in his own mind that high attainment and the expected period of life were impossible to combine, and he was inclined when working well to fear it denoted early death; and when feeling robust and healthy to fear that this was a signal of lack of talent and a negation of all his hopes for literary achievement.[21]

Susan Owen, who herself had hypochondriac tendencies, encouraged Wilfred's belief in the delicacy of his constitution – subconsciously, no doubt, because she enjoyed pampering him. His letters to her show an excessive concern with their minor ailments, their coughs, their aches and pains.

Although the Owens' Shrewsbury neighbourhood was, socially, a considerable advance on any they had known in Birkenhead, the habit of keeping themselves to themselves was not easily lost. Wilfred formed no school friendship as close as that with Alec Paton. The boys that came to the house, Maurice McNaught and John Ragge, found more in common with Harold and Colin. In 1909, Wilfred and Harold squired a little girl, Dorothy Iles, to the Central Hall Picture House and Wilfred gallantly gave her a brooch of gilt wire scripted into the letters of her name.[22] At a children's party he dressed up as a schoolmaster in cap and gown and taught his guests to sing 'The Siamese National Anthem': 'O Wa Ta Na Siam'.[23]

Generally speaking, however, one has the impression that Wilfred at this time enjoyed the company of his contemporaries less than the contemplation of the long dead. As his botanical interests had led him on to the study of geology, so this in turn led him to archaeology. In August 1909 he wrote to his mother that, 'After seeing you off I repaired to the Museum & found two priceless objects of whose presence there I was formerly unaware. The museum & Haughmond* are my only consolations.'[24] Those objects were parts of a

---

* Either Haughmond Hill or Haughmond Abbey, which was founded about 1135, as a house for Augustinian canons, at the edge of a wooded escarpment, looking out towards the spires of Shrewsbury and the Welsh mountains beyond. It was rebuilt some fifty years later, and there remain now the foundations of that enlarged church and the handsome ruins of cloister, chapter house, kitchen, infirmary hall, and abbot's lodging.

capital from one of the columns of the basilica at Uriconium, the Roman city at Wroxeter, on the Severn, east of Shrewsbury. Having long pored over the Roman weapons, shards, mosaic fragments, and household objects in the Shrewsbury Museum, that August he paid the first of many visits to the actual site of the excavations. Later, Harold would go with him down

the long, dusty road to Uriconium, pedalling away on the wreck of a bicycle that Colin and I shared, Wilfred on his new and shining one, for a day among the Roman remains. This, of course, would be one of Wilfred's special days; I would have gone along ostensibly as an assistant to help him in his search for fragments, with always the coveted possibility of finding coins. I had no interest whatsoever in these muddy bits of shard but I had first-class eyes and was very quick at spotting a gleam or an unusual shape. I was really much better than he was at this, as I soon found out, but never said so for fear of lessening any triumph of Wilfred's. He would sometimes ask me to go with him on these expeditions. I was always eager to do so for I enjoyed these days alone with him and it was pleasant bicycling along through the woods and villages. I was quite content, as we rode along, to listen to his discourses as he furbished up or arranged his knowledge of antiquities. I liked especially his unusual display of eagerness on these jaunts and as anticipation of what he might find lit up his face, transfiguring it from rather serious gloom into bright-eyed, boyish expectation, he would spurt on like mad, calling over his shoulder, 'Hurry, Harold, hurry. Think what we may be missing – the greatest find of the century.'[25]

Wilfred made a friend of the curator of the site, and a number of his finds were of sufficient interest for them to be added to various museum collections.

Christmas 1909 found him staying with the other members of the AGBS at Alpenrose,[26] a house that his prosperous uncle John Gunston had built for his early retirement the year before, at Kidmore End in south Oxfordshire. It stood in eight acres of land, on which were kept cattle, pigs, and poultry, and became a favourite holiday place for all of what John Gunston called 'Souza's Band'. On this occasion, Wilfred and the Gunston children went to Reading Museum to see the Roman remains from the excavations at Silchester[27] and, after dark, looked at the stars through Leslie's telescope, identifying the constellations with the help of Sir Robert Ball's *Story of the Heavens*.[28]

William and Mary Owen's Golden Wedding, 24 January 1909
Back row: *Wilfred Owen, Tom Owen, Emma Quayle, Edward Quayle, Cecil
Quayle, William Owen, John Taylor.* Middle row: *Susan Owen, Kenneth
Quayle, Mary Owen, Margaret Quayle, Anne Taylor.* Front row: *Mary Owen,
Harold Owen, Colin Owen, Edith Taylor*

In January 1910, Souza's Band found themselves moving house to
71 Monkmoor Road. Two hundred yards away from 1 Cleveland
Place, their new home had been built in 1905 by a Mr. Knight who
rented it to them for £1 a week.[29] Tom Owen insisted on naming it
'Mahim' – despite the disapproval of his wife and Wilfred – after a
salubrious suburb of Bombay 'which held pleasant recollections for
him'; he would not be more specific.* This house like their last was
three-storied, but its rooms were larger and lighter than any the
family had known since leaving Plas Wilmot. It was set back some
way from the street and had a pleasant little garden at the back,

---

* A clue to this minor mystery is perhaps to be found on p. 148 of Samuel T. Sheppard's
Bombay (Bombay, 1932): 'The Boat Club has had particularly strange vicissitudes, moving
from Apollo Bandar to Mahim and, in 1892, to Bandra before finding a home on the
shor of Back Bay.'

dominated by a pear tree and a small grove of sweet-scented syringa bushes.

In this house Wilfred had been given one of the rooms in the topmost story for a bedroom-study, again by his own choice, to secure for himself quietness and seclusion and to satisfy in him that harping dramatic urge for an attic. This particular one was ideally built to suit him, for the good-sized window projected over the roof, giving average ceiling height for a tiny square inside; this space just took his bookcase-writing-desk, leaving room for his chair. In this way, he had an excellent light to work by, while leaving the rest of the attic in romantic gloom. The roof itself formed one side of the small place, so that the wall came back almost from floor level at an angle of about forty-five degrees. It was not possible to put an ordinary bed under this but a camp-bed was fixed up for him, which added to the garret-like effect he so much cultivated.[30]

Mahim: the house on the extreme left

Perhaps the most attractive feature of this room was its uninterrupted view over the Shrewsbury Racecourse and the fields beyond to the majestic hump of the Wrekin. Away to the right he could see Lord Hill's Column, then the largest doric pillar in the world, erected in 1816 to commemorate the achievements of the Peninsular General.

Tom Owen's third sister, Anne, had married a widower, John Taylor, who in 1905 opened a bookshop at the front of their large house in Torquay. There, at 264 Union Street, Harold and Wilfred spent a happy fortnight in August 1910, playing on the beach with their fifteen-year-old cousin Edith or wandering about the town. They liked its terraced heights and the shock-headed palms fronting the sea. Wilfred was drawn, as by a magnet, to the offices of the local newspaper and one morning said bitterly: 'You know, Harold, if Mother and Father would only help me, I might be editor of that newspaper – no, no, not that one, a London paper – one day, but I must have help and I just can't get it.'[31] On the beach they made friends with the son and two daughters of an eminent American geologist, Ralph Stockman Tarr, who had organized the Cornell Greenland Expedition that went north on Peary's ship in 1896. The boy, Russell, shared Wilfred's interest in geology and further impressed him with his superb and daring swimming and diving.[32] However, what made the holiday memorable for Wilfred was his discovery that the novelist Christabel Rose Coleridge, granddaughter of the poet, was living only 'a few furlongs away'.[33] One afternoon, when Russell was out riding with a rich friend, Wilfred set off in search of this literary relic with Harold in dutiful attendance. Although she was not at home when first he rang her bell – 'after about fifteen minutes of indecision' – he subsequently found her in, and she and her brother Ernest Hartley Coleridge inscribed their names in his copy of *The Golden Book of Coleridge*.[34]

Their holiday ended on a good note. At Wilfred's suggestion, he and Harold spent their last evening on the cliffs overlooking Tor Bay in which the fleet was at anchor and brilliantly lit up. Reviewing their past fortnight, they spoke of the Tarrs

and wondered, not very hopefully, if we should ever see them again. Wilfred showed his only sign of discontent when he said how much he would like to see America, but added with characteristic haste, 'not of course until I know France and Italy better than I know England'. Rather timidly he asked me if I would mind if he recited some poetry and was pleased and encouraged by the warmth of my agreement. Later he talked of painting, telling me if I really wished to be a painter I must study all the Old Masters, as he did the poets.[35]

It is not known, and will probably never be known, when he began writing poetry. The answer almost certainly lay in the sack of papers that Susan Owen, on her son's strict instructions, burnt at his death.[36] Of the poems and fragments that survived the flames, the earliest, other than the lines pencilled in his copy of *A Midsummer-Night's Dream*, is probably 'To Poesy', an ironical beginning for a poet whose most famous manifesto was to declare: 'Above all I am not concerned with Poetry.' The handwriting of 'To Poesy' suggests that it was written in 1909–1910 after a strong diet of Keats. In 'The Fall of Hyperion', the poet in Saturn's temple hears the priestess Moneta say:

> 'If thou canst not ascend
> These steps, die on that marble where thou art. . . .'
> 'None can usurp this height, . . .
> But those to whom the miseries of the world
> Are misery, and will not let them rest. . . .'
> 'Are there not thousands in the world,' said I,
> Encourag'd by the sooth voice of the shade,
> 'Who love their fellows even to the death . . .?

With these lines ringing in his ears, Wilfred begins:

> A thousand suppliants stand around thy throne,
> Stricken with love for thee, O Poesy.
> I stand among them, and with them I groan,
> And stretch my arms for help. Oh, pity me!
> No man (save them thou gavs't the right to ascend
> And sit with thee, 'nointing with unction fine,
> Calling thyself their servant and their friend)
> Has loved thee with a purer love than mine.

He hymns her name, he says,

> Nor yet because thou know'st the unseen road
> Which leads into the awful halls of Fame, ...
> No more is this my fervent, hopeless quest –
> To stand among the great ones there, to meet
> The bards of old and greet them as my peers.
> O impious thought!

In what follows, however, he engagingly half-contradicts himself:

> Show me then the task,
> That shall, as years advance, give power and skill,
> Firm hands, an eye which takes all beauty in,
> That I may woo thee thus, if thus thy will.
> Ah, gladly would I on such task begin
> But that I know this learning must be bought
> With gold as well as toil, and gold I lack. . . .
> In divers tongues my thoughts must flow out free;
> And, in my own tongue, with no word amiss,
> For all its writers must be known to me.
> My hand must wield the critics weapons, too,
> To save myself, or strike an enemy.
> Oh grant that this long training ne'er undo
> My simple, ardent love!

He urges her to 'give Thyself to me/At last', promising to guard her good name:

> Loath would I be to show my exceeding bliss
> Even to closest friends. But all unseen,
> And far from men's gaze would I feel thy kiss;
> No witness save the speechless star-lamps keen
> When thou stoop'st over me. No eye
> But Cynthia's look on us when through the night
> We sit alone, our faces pressing nigh,
> Quietly shining in her quiet light.

If 'To Poesy' was written by candlelight, moonlight, starlight in a Shrewsbury attic, 'The Rivals' would seem to have been composed in an Oxfordshire garden, when Wilfred was staying with the

Gunstons at Kidmore End.[37] His one manuscript is dated '1910 Dunsden'; and he first visited this neighbouring village, that was to be the scene of a later act in his life, with his aunt and uncle, who preferred the Dunsden church services to those of their local church at Kidmore End.

The pastoral poet tells his no doubt imaginary Maid that she has a rival in Nature, whose charms he sensuously describes:

> Many a slim tree, dark of tresses,
> Whispering, gives me strange caresses.
> Steadfast shines Narcissus' eye
> When I would his beauty try.
> And he loads my sighs with scent,
> Not with frowns of discontent.
> Water lilies all tranquil lie
> When their secrecies I spy.
> Ruddy pout the mouths of roses –
> More I kiss, more each uncloses.

This description of Nature in terms of the human body, conventional though much of it is, yet suggests the first stirrings of that sense of the indivisible union of all living things that was to become one of his dominant themes. In 'A Palinode', also written almost certainly in 1910, he describes an interesting transition:

> Some little while ago, I had a mood
> When what we know as 'Nature' seemed to me
> So sympathetic, ample, sweet, and good
> That I preferred it to Society.

Finding that 'men and minds . . . Disturbed without exciting', he retreated from them:

> But if the sovereign sun I might behold
> With condescension coming down benign,
> And blessing all the field and air with gold★
> Then the contentment of the world was mine.

★ See p. 44 above and 'Spring Offensive', discussed on pp. 274–5.

With stanza 8 the poet's withdrawal turns to melodramatic misanthropy:

> I said I had no need of fellows more,
> I madly hated men and all their ways.

He tries to close 'The book of human knowledge',

> But in my error, men ignored not me,
> And did not let me in my moonbeams bask.
> And I took antidotes; though what they be
> Unless yourself be poisoned, do not ask.
>
> For I am overdosed. The City now
> Holds all my passion; these my soul most feels:
> Crowds surging; racket of traffic; market row;
> Bridges, sonorous under rapid wheels;
>
> Pacific lamentations of a bell;
> the smoking of the old men at their doors;
> All attitudes of children; the farewell
> And casting-off of ships for far-off shores.

In the last two stanzas, and particularly the line – four from the end – that was later incorporated in the poem 'All Sounds have been as Music',[38] one hears the first, tuning note of the mature poet.

In April 1911, Wilfred again stayed with the Taylors in Torquay, and it was perhaps in his uncle's bookshop that he bought the copy of Sidney Colvin's *Keats*[39] that occasioned a fragment entitled 'Before reading a Biography of Keats for the first time':

> With doubt as well as thirst I come to drink
> Thy store of Knowledge fresh, O unknown Book!
> From seeing Keats through thee I long did shrink
> Lest cold clear changeless records mar the look
> Of heroic beauty that he seems to wear.
> I now behold him through a glimmering mist,
> The glittering rain of his own words,
> How like a god on high uprist, . . .

Wilfred Owen came to Keats as Keats to Chapman's *Homer* and grew to worship him in an almost religious sense. This is made explicit in a letter to his mother written in 1912. He has been reading W. M. Rossetti's *Life and Writings of John Keats* and says: 'I never guessed till now the frightful travail of his soul towards Death; . . . Rossetti guided my groping hand right into the wound, and I touched, for one moment the incandescent Heart of Keats.'[40]

He began reading Colvin's biography 'with fear and trembling'. His careful underlinings enable us to see Keats as his disciple saw him. He has marked, for example, the word *Celtic* in the sentence: 'In the gifts and temperament of Keats we shall find much that seems characteristic of the *Celtic* rather than the English nature.'[41] Attempting to account for this, Colvin mentions that 'His father was a native of either Devon or of Cornwall; and his mother's name, Jennings, is common in but not peculiar to Wales.'[42] Wilfred, who was proud of the Celtic origins proclaimed by his own name, Owen, was delighted to read that Keats, too, had a mother who was devoted to him, and he underlined the statement that she 'humoured him in *every whim of which he had not a few*'[43]; also the key-word in the sentence: 'But beneath this bright and mettlesome outside there lay deep in his nature, even from the first, a strain of powerful *sensibility* making him subject to moods of unreasonable suspicion and self-tormenting melancholy.'[44] Again, his indelible pencil marked Colvin's quotation from the reminiscences of Edward Holmes: '*He was a boy whom any one from his extraordinary vivacity and personal beauty might easily fancy would become great – but rather in some military capacity than in literature.*'[45]

One Friday in April,[46] Wilfred took the train from Torquay to Newton Abbot and along the widening estuary to Teignmouth. There, head down and collar up against 'soft buffeting sheets and misty drifts of Devonshire rain',[47] he went in search of the house where Keats had lived from March to May 1818. He found it, 20 Northumberland Place (formerly 20 the Strand), and gaped at its bow windows regardless of the people inside, 'who finally became quite alarmed'. Returning, he wrote

Sonnet, written at Teignmouth,
on a Pilgrimage to Keats's House.

Three colours have I known the Deep to wear;
'Tis well today that Purple grandeurs gloom,
Veiling the Emerald sheen and Sky-blue glare.
Well, too, that lowly-brooding clouds now loom
In sable majesty around, fringed fair
With ermine-white of surf: To me they bear
Watery memorials of His mystic doom
Whose Name was writ in Water (saith his tomb).

Eternally may sad waves wail his death,
Choke in their grief 'mongst rocks where he has lain,
Or heave in silence, yearning with hushed breath,
While mournfully trail the slow-moved mists and rain,
And softly the small drops slide from weeping trees,
Quivering in anguish to the sobbing breeze.

               W. E. Owen.

Mahim,
Monkmoor Road,
Shrewsbury.

Wilfred was now eighteen and having to consider what he should do next. He had left the Technical School, but its staff kept their interest in him. When he joined the Wyle Cop School as a temporary Pupil Teacher and found the work heavier than he had expected,[49] one of his former masters, Mr. Edwards, volunteered to ask the headmaster of the Wyle Cop whether Wilfred could not have more time for his own studies. And, as he wrote to his mother, the wife of his former headmaster called on a surprising mission:

to warn me against the Teaching Profession (Elementary). Her husband could not candidly do this, she said, but she thinks it 'wicked' that young people should enter it without a fair premonition of the hopelessness of their fate, and without knowing of the profound dissatisfaction among all who are now teachers.

Civil Service is her cry, and I am to see Mr. Timpany about it one of these evenings. I wish you were here to approve or condemn this good lady's counsel.

Have you ever asked Uncle John's opinion on these matters?

Really, indecision is rapidly turning into distraction. When I begin to eliminate from my list all those professions which are impossible (seemingly) from a financial point of view, and then those which I feel disinclined for – it leaves nothing. But is my inclination to matter after all? Yet what I do find so hard to distinguish between is aimlessly drifting, and waiting upon God.[50]

Mr. Timpany, knowing Wilfred's ambitions, recommended journalism[51] but, with summer approaching and his head full of poems, he was in no mood to make practical and unpalatable decisions.

He was staying at Alpenrose that June and, finding him still undecided about his future, the Rev. Herbert Robson, Vicar of Kidmore End, also gave him some advice:

to become the 'assistant' of some hardworked or studiously inclined parson, helping in parish work, correspondence etc. and being generally companionable to a lonely country-sequestered bachelor, such as himself. *Not* to him actually, however, one reason being – that it would never do to have one *with relations in the parish*! He had heard, however, that 'Wiggan of Dunsden' wanted help in the parish this winter, and suggested applying to him, especially as his views coincide with ours.

For we must be most careful as to the kind of parson I go to. Some would keep me trotting round the parish all day: some, (who have no servant perhaps) would require me to scrub floors. He knows of one priest, moreover, who celebrates Mass daily, and requires some one to say 'amen' in the consecration prayer since it is uncanonical to have no congregation.[52]

Although it would seem from Wilfred's letters of this period that his religious ardour had somewhat abated, Mr. Robson's scheme appealed to him in that the right 'kind of parson' would give him coaching for the university entrance examination in return for help with his parish work. On 23 June Wilfred went over to Dunsden to meet Mr. Wigan, and, standing in the neo-Gothic porch for the first time, tugged the cast-iron bell-pull, shaped like a huge inverted lily, that rang its muffled chime behind the kitchen's green baize door. The day was a success, he stayed to lunch, and pronounced his host 'a most delightful parson'.[53] Nothing definite was decided, however, and he returned to Shrewsbury and his preparation for the London Matriculation exam in September.

He was working long and hard in his high room overlooking the Wrekin, but the lure of cornfields and dusty lanes was not to be resisted indefinitely. On 15 August he joined his mother and Harold on a grand picnic at Pontesbury, organized by some friends. After a 'ripping lunch' in a green hollow known as 'The Happy Valley', the eighteen younger members of the party played games until it was time for the Shrewsbury contingent to catch their train home. On the station platform, before the green flag fell, they sang 'Auld Lang Syne'.[54]

Then there was the day of the fair. Wilfred and Harold had been persuaded to go, by their mother, rather against their will – for it had been organized in aid of some religious charity and promised to be more decorous than a fair should be. They set off, however, cheered by the pleasant jingle of small change in their pockets, and followed the more raucous music of the fairground to a green Border valley ablaze with coloured awnings and flags, paintwork and brass-work brilliant under the August sun. Harold spoke of painting the scene, and was commanded by his brother to set his 'impressions in pigment' immediately they got home. At the shooting gallery their father's training in marksmanship – he had been a first-class shot in his GIPR Volunteer Rifles days – brought them each an armful of prizes.

It was when the sun was setting that the fair came into its own and – the church element having discreetly withdrawn – threw off its last vestiges of religious make-believe, really opened up its booths and side-shows, and produced as if by magic all the monstrosities, from the tattooed woman to punch-drunk boxers. The noise and tempo of the steam organ increased as the crowds of country people poured in. Wilfred and I began really to enjoy ourselves and milled amongst the sweating excited throng with enormous gusto, getting caught up in the jostlings of red, shining-faced young men and women as they pushed from one side-show to another.[55]

Finally, a little intoxicated by the striptease of a female tightrope-walker, they turned for home. After they had walked in silence for some way, Wilfred suddenly asked Harold what he had thought of her. The younger boy had no idea how to put his sensations into words, and felt resentfully that he was being analysed under a microscope.

Wilfred noticing my silence did not press me although in his usual way he could not resist muttering to himself something about 'oafish avoidance of discussion'. I must have said something in reply – and remembering how quick we were to fly verbally at one another, I have no doubt it was something pretty provocative. I was sorry things had gone like this for I had enjoyed my afternoon with him and did not want it to be spoilt now. It may have been the gentleness of the evening and the pleasantness of walking through the darkling lanes that broke our threatened ill-humour for presently, simultaneously, we turned to each other and smiled.
    'It's funny, Harold, how petulant we get with one another.'
    'Yes, it is, we don't seem to be able to help it, do we? Perhaps after all it doesn't matter much.'
    'No, I don't think it does really.'
    'No.'
    After a few more minutes of quietness, Wilfred said, 'Harold, if I were you I should try and do that painting of the fair. I think it might be important, especially if you use ordinary paint and not my wretchedly ridiculous "pigment".' This set us off laughing together. . . .[56]

On 9 September Wilfred went up to London to sit his exam and took a room at 38 Worple Road, Wimbledon. Under the eye of 'a pompous old Rajah of an Examiner – gorgeous in his silken hoods –'[57] he wrote an essay on 'The Ideal English King';[58] 'did a really excellent paper in French; and a *most satisfactory* in History'.[59] He had hopes of getting a 'first' and, to celebrate, went off to the British

Museum, where he spent some hours in subdued ecstasy gazing at Keats's manuscripts. Delightedly he wrote to his mother:

his writing is rather large and slopes like mine – *not at all* old fashioned and sloping as Shelley's is. He also has my trick of not joining letters in a word. Otherwise it is unlike anybodies' I know, and yet I seem to be strangely familiar with it. It is none too precisely formed – a proof that he is thinking of nothing but the matter and not of himself and his pen. The letters are to Fanny (i.e. the *sister*) but, poor fellow, he can't keep the name of Brawne out of it! I was highly jealous of other people seeing this at first, but was nevertheless gratified when various *French* visitors seemed familiar with his name![60]

Another day he made his pilgrimage to Keats's house in Well Walk, Hampstead,[61] and afterwards attempted a poem on the subject.* He saw *Henry V*, *Macbeth*, and *The Tempest*, before leaving London for Kidmore End. On 28 September he walked over to Dunsden and played croquet with the Vicar, who pressed him to join him as a lay assistant and pupil. Wilfred, however, preferred to leave matters open until he knew his matriculation results.

The long-awaited embossed envelope reached him one morning after he had returned to Mahim. He seized it from Harold and, trembling violently, tugged out the letter. A few seconds of silence and then, with a despairing sigh, he slumped back on to his bed and burrowed under the blankets. He had gained a pass, but not the first-class honours of which he had dreamed.[62]

With a heavy heart, he wrote to the Vicar of Dunsden accepting his offer.

---

* This unfinished and unsatisfactory fragment begins:
There is a set of men today who deal
– Or think they deal – with spirits of the past.

4

DUNSDEN AND AFTER

The Reverend Herbert Wigan, who met Wilfred Owen at Reading Station on 20 October, was a man of medium height, who moved and spoke in a measured, dignified manner. A bearded bachelor of forty-nine, he had been brought up in a tractarian rectory in Kent, and until middle age was an 'advanced' exponent of that school of thought. As a young man, he had a bout of 'Roman fever', of which he was cured by a trip round the world.[1] The labyrinthine vicarage to which he brought his new lay assistant and pupil had been built in 1870. Its rooms had a sombre air, largely on account of the dark yew hedges that kept the garden from prying eyes, and a fine Spanish chestnut and a copper beech then carpeting the sunken croquet lawn with leaves. The young man was shown to a bedroom on the first floor, looking out over gently sloping fields towards the distant smudge of Reading. As he wrote to his mother three days later:

Mysterious ministering spirits keep the room in order, for surprising things happen, though I have never seen a living wight therein. Thus – every night I find my pyjamas scrupulously laid out upon the coverlet in exactly that position in which it is easiest to put them on!

At seven every morning a meek voice announces to the noble sir that his shaving water waits outside. . . . At the stroke of the awe-inspiring gong, he takes a large chair on one side of the fire, in the dining room, with Mr. Kemp on the other, the Vicar at the table, and the domestics sitting in respectful admiration in a row at the end of the room. After prayers the said admiring domestics withdraw, and breakfast is taken, when (as in all meals) his noble highness brandishes the breadknife, and dispenses his cuttings as required.

Left alone, and with something of my gravity thrown off, I then set to work at a bureau-bookcase in the dining room till lunch.[2]

The Rev. Herbert Wigan

Alfred Saxelby-Kemp, the Vicar's other lay assistant and pupil, Wilfred found 'very pleasant indeed; thoroughly enjoying his parochial work, if not so much his studies'.[3] He had twice failed his entrance examination for St. John's Hall, Highbury, the London College of Divinity, and was preparing for a third attempt in December. He, for his part, liked Owen. The Vicar he thought rather lordly and rather dull, 'always bringing out the same three standard jokes at dinner when anyone came to stay'.[4] Owen soon

Dunsden Vicarage from the croquet lawn

came to much the same opinion, but his first impressions were much more favourable:

> he talked of literary people at dinner today. He is a sixth cousin of the great William Morris! has heard Ruskin lecture!! was introduced to Holman Hunt!!!
>
> Furthermore, is thoroughly at home in Dickens' country in Kent!! read Romola *in Florence* overlooking Ponte Vecchia!! was acquainted with the original of Sam Weller! and other Characters![5]

This seemed to augur well for Owen's tuition, and he launched into his literary studies with renewed energy. On 30 October he went into Reading to hear Sir Walter Raleigh give a lecture on Charles Lamb, and there spent some of his five-shillings-a-week pocket money on books recommended by the University Correspondence College,[6] with which he had enrolled. His parish duties he took seriously, writing to his sister in November:

> I addressed the Children's Service in the Parish Hall on Sunday Afternoon. I am also booked for the Scripture Union on Thurs. I enjoy speaking very much. I use no notes, and spend no great time in preparation; but I use no high falutin' words, but try to express myself in simple, straightforward English. I believe the children are impressed for the time being. I hope they will really benefit, for, of course, I give them the Messages, with one Purpose, and not with any idea of displaying my own bumptiousness.[7]

In the same letter he speaks of 'the wretched hovels of this Parish, . . . the crazy, evil-smelling huts of the poor', and a note of genuine compassion becomes audible above the self-conscious echoing of Shelley:

> Numbers of the old people cannot read; those who can seldom do so. Scores of them have passed their whole lives in the same stone box with a straw lid, which they call their cottage; and are numbed to all interests beyond it. Those who have within them the Hope of a Future World are content, and their old faces are bright with the white radiance of eternity. Those who, like the beasts, have no such Hope, pass their old age shrouded with an inward gloom, which the reverses of their history have stamped upon their worn-out memories, deadening them to all thoughts of delight.[8]

Although the style of Owen's Dunsden letters to his mother is often tiresomely arch and affected, his sympathy for the poor of the parish becomes increasingly evident as when, the following March, he writes:

I am holding aloof from the short-breads; and I mean to give some to a gentle little girl of five, fast sinking under Consumption – contracted after chickenpox. Isn't it pitiable? She is going to a hospital (weeks hence *of course*), and may be beyond the reach of doctors by that time. She can't take unappetising food, poor Violet;[9] but how is aught to be provided her; when the Father is perennially out of work, and the Mother I fancy half-starving for the sake of four children. This, I suppose, is only a typical *case*; one of many *Cases*! O hard word! How it savours of rigid, frigid pro-fessionalism! How it suggests smooth and polished, formal, labelled, mechanical callousness![10]

His compassion at this time is more often extended to the young, for whom he had a special sympathy, than to the old. He enjoyed the company of his 'children', as he called them, and particularly that of his two 'protégés', Milly Montague and Vivian Rampton.[11] He went for walks with Vivian,[12] gave him piano lessons,[13] and smuggled him in to tea at the vicarage.[14]

    Nothing, however, was allowed to distract him for long from poetry. In November, he won second prize – 'a *leather-bound* N. Test. *& Psalms* in Latin'[15] – in a *Bible Society Gleanings* competition for the translation of a hymn from the Latin,[16] and one warm day in December wrote a verse-letter 'from somewhere in Oxford-shire':[17]

To North
Are hills where Arnold wandered forth
Which like his verse, still undulate in calm
And tempered beauty.
           And the marriage-psalm
Was sung o'er Tennyson, small space away.

This rhyming letter has something still more intimate, for, towards its close, Owen declares his longing for a new great poet – for all of us, and himself:

Let me attain
To talk with him, and share his confidence.

Dunsden Church. Today in its graveyard lie Tom Owen (1862–1931), Susan Owen (1867–1942), and Mary Owen (1896–1956)

His loneliness as a young poet breaks out; he may read even Keats and 'still', he appeals, 'I am alone among the Unseen Voices'.

> Full springs of Thought around me rise
> Like Rivers Four to water my fair garden.
> Eastwards, where lie wide woodlands, rich as Arden,
> From out the beechen solitudes hath sprung
> A stream of verse from aerial Shelley's tongue,
> While, as he drifted on between the banks
> Of happy Thames, the waters 'neath the planks
> Of his light boat gurgled contentedly
> And ever with his dreams kept company.
> To-day, the music of the slow, turmoiling river,
> The music of the rapid vision-giver,
> To me are vocal both.
>   To eastward, too,
> A churchyard sleeps, and one infirm old yew,
> Where in the shadows of the fading day,
> Musing on faded lives, sate solemn Gray.
> There to majestic utterance his soul was wrought,
> And still his mighty chant is fraught
> With golden teaching for the world, and speaks
> Strong things with sweetness unto whoso seeks.
> Yet can I never sit low at his feet
> And, questioning, a gracious answer meet.
> For he is gone, and his high dignity
> Lost in the past (tho' he may haply be
> Far in Futurity as well).

Shortly after Christmas, which he spent at Mahim, he discovered

that Shelley lived at a cottage within easy cycling distance from here.[18] And I was very surprised (tho' really I don't know why) to find that he used to 'visit the sick in their beds; kept a regular list of the industrious poor whom he assisted to make up their accounts;' and for a time walked the hospitals in order to be more useful to the poor he visited! I *knew* the lives of men who produced such marvellous verse could not be otherwise than lovely, and I am being confirmed in this continually.[19]

His quotation is from John Addington Symonds's *Shelley*, which he had been reading. As with Colvin's *Keats*, in the same English Men of Letters Series, Owen's markings and underlinings show him identifying himself with the poet. They also show something more interesting: a six-line quotation marked as follows:

> Eagle! why soarest thou above that tomb?
> To what sublime and star-y-paven home
>   Floatest thou?
> I am the image of swift Plato's spirit,
> Ascending heaven: – Athens does inherit
>   His corpse below.[20]

In January 1912 he was noting the possibilities of half-rhyme.

He had now been at Dunsden for three months without his letters once making mention of any coaching from the Vicar. No doubt there was a little of this, but the greater part of his time was spent out in the parish, visiting the sick and the needy, making arrangements for baptisms, marriages, and funerals. On Sunday mornings he would assist at Holy Communion, Matins, and Bible Class; take Sunday School after lunch; and in the evening attend one of an endless succession of church meetings in the so-called Parish Hall, a large room built on to the vicarage; 'not that they themselves are in any way disagreeable,' he told his mother, 'but that I want to be *reading*. The time I am at Book and Pen seems to be growing smaller and smaller'.[21] A fortnight later, he is lamenting that 'the isolation from any whose interests are the same as mine, the constant, inevitable mixing with persons whose influence will tend in the opposite direction – this is a serious drawback'.[22] It did not prevent him from writing, however.

In poem after poem he describes, often luxuriantly, the beauty of the human body and, with hardly an exception, it is the male body that is celebrated. This fact must not be overlooked, for it is relevant to a proper understanding of the later poems, but neither must it be overemphasized. Instilled with the principles of a dominant and puritanical mother, Wilfred recoiled from everything covered by her definition of uncleanness, and sublimated his natural sexuality, as do most boys at some time or other, into the admiring contemplation of 'clean' male beauty. A sense of sin, frequently associated with such an upbringing, may perhaps account for the masochistic note to be detected in certain poems of this period. In the 'Lines Written on my Nineteenth Birthday', for example, he imagines himself in the throes of an almost Christlike suffering that has unmistakable sexual overtones:

> . . . there have been revealed
> Heart-secrets since the coming of this day,
> Making me thankful for its thorn-paved way.
> Among them this: 'No joy is comparable
> Unto the <u>Melting</u> – soft and gradual –
> <u>Of Torture's needles in the flesh.</u> To sail
> Smoothly from out the abysmal anguish-jail
> And tread the placid plains of <u>normal ease</u>
> Is sweeter far, I deem, than all the glees
> Which we may catch by mounting higher-still
> Into the dangerous air where actual Bliss doth thrill.'★

The 'dangerous air', to quote from another poem of this period,[23] was that of a place

> . . . called the World, and lo! the name
> Of him, the unapparent spirit, was
> An evil Angel's; and I learnt the name
> Of that strange, regnant Presence as the Flesh.
>   ⎧maid
> It bore the naked likeness of a ⎨boy
>   ⎩

That bracketed alternative becomes the more extraordinary in the light of what follows:

> Flawlessly moulded, fine exceedingly,
> Beautiful unsurpassably – so much
> More portraiture were fond futility
> For even thought is not long possible,
> Becoming too soon passion: and meseemed
> His outline changed, from beauty unto beauty,[24]
> As change the contours of slim, sleeping clouds.

★ The italics in this poem are WO's own.

His skin, too, glowed, pale scarlet, like the clouds
Lit from the eastern underworld; which thing
Bewondered me the more. But I remember
The statue of his body standing so
Against the huge disorder of the place
Resembled a strong music; and it triumphed
Even as the trend of one clear perfect air
Across confusion of a thousand chords.
Then watched I how there ran towards that way
A multitude of railers, hot with hate
And maddened by the voice of a small Jew
Who cried 'Away with him!' and 'Crucify him!'

It seems probable that Owen did at some point mount briefly
'Into the dangerous air where actual Bliss doth thrill'. A sonnet,
portentously entitled 'The Peril of Love', declares not altogether
convincingly:

So I, lightly addressing me to love,
Have found too late love's grave significance.
A fierce infatuation, far above
The zeal for fame or fortune, like a trance,
Exhausts my faculties.

This is schoolboy stuff. Less finished, but more intimate, is a passage
from a fragmentary 'Ballad of a Morose Afternoon', written most
probably some time after he had left Dunsden:*

And many of my thoughts were given to him
And many of his hours were given to me . . .
We two were friends while two short years outran
        suffered that grand,
The while he ~~underwent the~~ *crucial change,*
The inalterable change, from boy to man.
And metamorphoses not less strange
        ~~created and annhihilated~~   ~~turn by~~ turn

* The manuscript is written in pencil (represented by *italic* type) and a later ink (represented by roman).

>   or
>   ~~and~~ would it after all
> Be better if I had not ~~touched y hand~~
>   known my voice not for me
> ~~Be better if I~~
> Or heard my heart? And would it ~~after all~~
> Be better ~~if I had not seen his face?~~
>   never to have ~~seen~~
>   to have looked on him?

This would seem to indicate an adolescent infatuation for another boy, but when and for whom it is not possible to say. Nor is there any indication that the other recognized, let alone reciprocated, his feelings.

Probably the first person outside Owen's immediate family circle to know of his poems was his cousin Leslie Gunston, who was himself writing poetry at this time. Having left Kings College, Wimbledon, when his parents moved to Alpenrose, he was now at the Kendrick School, Reading,[25] and a frequent visitor at Dunsden Vicarage. One day in the early summer of 1912, Owen – influenced perhaps by the competition that produced Shelley's 'Ozymandias' – proposed that they should each write a poem on the same subject. And what should that subject be? Looking out of the window at a dark flash of wings under the eaves, he suggested 'The Swift'. Gunston agreed and their poems were written, Owen's a markedly Shelleyan Ode, ending:

> O that I might make me
>   Pinions like to thine,
> Feathers that would take me
>   Whither I incline!
> Yet more thy spirit's tirelessness I crave;
> Yet more thy joyous, fierce endurance.
> If my soul flew with thy assurance,
> What fields, what skies to scour! what Seas to brave!

His scientific and his literary interest in natural history continued side by side. He did 'a little Botany when travelling round the Parish',[26] and on 29 February bicycled down the country lanes into Reading for an interview with Dr. Childs, Principal of University College. He wanted, he said, to sit for the 'Inter[mediate] Arts' degree in English, Latin, Botany, French, and History in 1913. As they talked, Dr. Childs jotted down: 'May come next Term for Lat. Bot (& possibly Fr.) Fees to be about 3/5 × £11 for Term.' Six weeks later, he was back in University College arranging to attend botany classes for six hours a week.[27] He spoke to one of the Lecturers, Miss Rayner,★ and reported to his mother that

she seems very nice indeed. Premises and all appurtenances are *admirable*. The lady, with her satellites was photographing the eclipse† when I interviewed her. I was riding home at *12.10*; the sky was clear; and very weird the universe seemed; the atmosphere dulled as if charged with volcanic dust, especially on the horizon.

On 6 May he told his mother:

> 'Mr. K. left this morning.
>   "Toll for the Brave!
>   Brave Kemp in felt is gone!" '‡

His hopes that he might inherit the now vacant 'den' that had served Kemp as a study came to nothing. He finished a blank verse retelling of Hans Andersen's 'Little Claus and Big Claus',[28] and was understandably dissatisfied with it, for its ponderous pentameters are packed with discordant archaisms.

Kemp's departure meant that Owen had more parish work than formerly and even less time for his own studies. As he wrote home on 12 June, he was also beginning to tire of theology:

★ Miss M. M. C. Rayner was Lecturer in Botany at University College, Reading, 1908–13, and was one of those to whom WO later planned to give a copy of his collected poems after the War. See p. 265 below.

† 16 April 1912. It began at 10.51 a.m. and reached its maximum at 12.11 (as WO was riding home). It was the largest solar eclipse seen in the British Isles for fifty-four years.

‡ Toll for the brave –
  Brave Kempenfelt is gone . . . .
    His sword was in the sheath,
  His fingers held the pen,
    When Kempenfelt went down
  With twice four hundred men.
        William Cowper, 'Loss of the Royal George'

I definitely abandon the *thought* of Divinity Training *till* at least an Arts
Degree is won. Such at present is my resolve. All theological lore is growing
distasteful to me. All my recent excursions into such fields proves it to be a
shifting, hypothetical, doubt-fostering, dusty and unprofitable study. Such
a conclusion at my time of life is not to be wondered at. It may change
hereafter. All I can do now is to groan with Meredith:

> '*Ah what a dusty answer gets the soul*
> *When hot for certainties in this our life.*'[29]

Clearly, too, he was growing critical of Mr. Wigan:

I am increasingly liberalizing and liberating my thought, spite of the
Vicar's strong Conservatism. And when he paws his beard, and wonders
whether £10. is too high a price for new curtains for the dining room, (in
place of the faded ones you saw); then the fires smoulder; I could shake
hands with Mrs. Dilber who stole Scrooge's Bed-Curtains; and was
affronted that old Joe[30] was surprised, or questioned her right! From what
I hear straight from the tight-pursed lips of wolfish ploughmen in their
cottages, I might say there is material for another revolution. Perhaps men
will *strike*, not with absence from work; but with arms at work. Am I for
or against upheaval? I know not; I am not happy in these thoughts; yet
they press heavy upon me. I am happier when I go to '*distribute dole*

> *To poor sick people, richer in His eyes,*
> *Who ransomed us, and haler too than I*'.[31]

It is significant that, no matter what the subject of his letters, he
cannot keep his mind off poetry for more than a few lines at a time.
In June, his botany lecturer at University College discovered his
literary interests and sent him on to the Head of the English Depart-
ment, Miss Edith Morley, who found him an 'unhappy adolescent,
suffering badly from lack of understanding . . . and in need of
encouragement and praise'.[32] These she gave him, together with
some useful advice about the technicalities of poetry, and at her
recommendation he read Ruskin and Milton on his free afternoons
and evenings in the gloomy vicarage.

July brought him a welcome change of scene. Armed with the free
railway passes that Tom Owen usually managed to secure for his
family, he set off on Monday the 8th for Scotland. It was a brilliant
day and, having changed trains at Edinburgh, he arrived after supper
at Kelso, to find the rest of the family comfortably settled in Pringle

Bank, the spacious eighteenth-century house owned by 'Aunt Nellie' Bulman who, as Nellie Roderick, had been Susan's favourite governess at Plas Wilmot thirty years before. The widow of a prosperous builder, she had three children in their early twenties, John, Blanche, and Bill, and knowing the Owens' straitened circumstances, they had determined to give them the holiday of their lives. Tom Owen was introduced to golf and in no time was 'fearfully keen'.[33] They played croquet and held shooting matches on the lawns of Pringle Bank. With Walter Forrest, Blanche's fiancé, they fished for salmon in the Tweed and the Teviot, which join to the south of Kelso, and bicycled into the surrounding countryside. Wilfred was delighted with Kelso, its square so reminiscent of a Flemish market town, the horseshoe in Roxburgh Street cast by Bonnie Prince Charlie's steed in 1745, the ruined abbey and castle, all seen under a cloudless sky. On 17 July he made a pilgrimage to Abbotsford, Sir Walter Scott's house, and the following day set off with Blanche for Flodden field. They took the train to Coldstream and then bicycled to the battlefield. For once, a bitterly cold wind was blowing and Blanche was impatient to get back, but Wilfred was in a state of high excitement and would not be shifted. He read all the guidebook and part of Scott's *Marmion*, sketching the battle-field on the fly-leaf of this.[34] Then, making Blanche represent one army and himself representing the other, he

proceeded to reconstruct and carry out the proposed manoeuvres until in his mind he had the battle alive and taking place. He himself all the time walked about rapidly without seemingly tiring as he adjusted the imaginary armies. . . . while he was doing this he would be very voluble, explaining to Blanche his theories, exhorting her to follow his reasoning or perhaps asking her to take up a position at some distant point the better to illustrate his argument.[35]

Not until 9.20 did they arrive back at Kelso.

The next time he left for Keswick, where an Evangelical Summer Convention run by Anglicans and Free Churchmen had been held every summer since 1875. None of the theological discussions made an impression on him equal to that of

a Northumberland lad who works in the pits, whose soul-life and Christi-

Wilfred Owen aged nineteen

anity is altogether beyond my understanding. He has absolute peace of mind; faith before which mountains not only sink, but never become visible; and most other virtues of which the Keswick Platform speaks. The watching of his conduct, conversation, expression of countenance during meetings, bids fair to speak louder to my soul than the thunderings of twenty latter-day Prophets from their rostra upon these everlasting hills.

While your sleek Thomas, Hopkins, Dixon, Holden, Scroggie,* and the rest of these double-barrelled guns, whose double-barrelled names I refuse to write, while they, I say, *preach* that *preaching* is no witness of a Christian Soul, your scar-backed mining-lad *acts* that acting *is* efficient. Scar-backed, I say, through running along subterranean 'roads' four feet high, and scraping against its jagged roof. And while my guide to Edinburgh would calmly send people to the Devil for no greater provocation than say having an ugly face, this youth lets no profane word pass his lips, tho' pricked with piercing pain and surrounded by the grossest human mud that ever sank to a pit's bottom.[36]

Clearly audible in this is the mingled anger and compassion, the accents of the later lieutenant on the Somme.

In August he was back at Dunsden, alarming his mother with a melodramatic account of a minor bicycling mishap[37] and, in September, with the news that he needed glasses, having 'pronounced Astigmation, Hypermetropia and all the rest'.[38] After his appointment with a London optician, he went on to the British Museum and there, or at Keats's House, saw the relic that prompted his poem 'On Seeing a Lock of Keats's Hair', which ends:

> It is a lock of Adonais' hair!
> I dare not look too long; nor try to tell
> What glories I see glistening, glistening there.
> The unanointed eye can not perceive their spell.
> Turn ye to Adonais; his great spirit seek.
> O hear him; he will speak!

Influenced perhaps by Keats's dictum, quoted by Rossetti in his *Life and Writings of John Keats*, that 'A long poem is a test of Invention, which I take to be the polar star of poetry, as Fancy is the sails, and Imagination the rudder',[39] he embarked upon a verse rendering of Hans Andersen's fairy tale 'The Little Mermaid'.[40] It is not difficult to see why he chose this particular tale. A romantic story of sacrificial love and acute bodily suffering nobly borne, it offered some scope for those painterly descriptions of physical beauty that he so enjoyed.

---

* Dr. W. H. Griffith Thomas, the Rev. Evan Hopkins, Dr. J. Stuart Holden, and Dr. W. Graham Scroggie were eminent in Evangelical circles, and regular speakers at the Keswick Convention.

A mermaid heroine would have appealed to an admirer of Keats's 'Lamia', and he chose the 8-line stanza of 'Isabella'. The texture of the verse is markedly Keatsian, but it moves with ease and assurance through its seventy-seven stanzas. Thus the description of the mermaid's treasure-seeking:

> Her sisters joyed to find such curious things
> As foundering ships let fall to their domain;
> But she cared not for showered coins or rings,
> And claimed no share of all that precious rain
> Except a marble statue – some boy-king's,
> Or youthful hero's. Its cold face in vain
> She gazed at; kissed; and tried with sighs to thaw;
> For still the wide eyes stared, and nothing saw.

So Isabella had tended Lorenzo's severed head:

> She calmed its wild hair with a golden comb,
>   And all around each eye's sepulchral cell
> Pointed each fringed lash; the smeared loam
>   With tears, as chilly as a dripping well,
> She drenched away: – and still she comb'd, and kept
> Sighing all day – and still she kiss'd, and wept.

The Little Mermaid falls in love with her prince and follows his ship into the storm that is to sink it. Owen's description of this contains an image that astonishingly anticipates his poems from the Western Front:

> It is late. Starry lamps and fierce fusees
> Fade out. The stunning guns are dumb. All ears
> Hark to a grumbling in the heart of the seas.

It is hard to believe that 'The stunning guns are dumb' was written in 1912 and not 1917. An early version of that sentence was 'The stunning cannons speak', and its revision is paralleled by the development of two lines in another, fragmentary, poem written long before the outbreak of war and entitled 'Nights with the Wind. A Rhapsody':

And ~~then the~~
   now it was the thunder of gruff guns
The growl of ~~gunnery and the roar of~~ bombs.
   cannon, and cloud-cleaving

Perhaps it was the naval gunnery practice at Spithead, which on occasions would rattle the windows at Alpina, that gave Owen this foreknowledge of the eardrum-pounding concussion of an artillery barrage.

On 18 September, he wrote an inflated piece entitled 'The Dread of Falling into Naught'. A month later, on 15 October, there took place in Dunsden churchyard the double funeral of Alice Mary Allen and her four-year-old daughter, Hilda Agnes.[41] Owen's reaction to this village tragedy moved him to a more direct and genuine poetic utterance than any hitherto.★

DEEP under turfy grass and heavy clay
They laid her bruised body, and the child.
Poor victims of a swift mischance were they,
Adown Death's trapdoor suddenly beguiled.
I, weeping not, ~~but~~ as others, but heart-wild,
Affirmed to Heaven that even Love's fierce flame
Must fail beneath the chill of this cold shame.

So I rebelled, scorning and mocking such
As had the ~~unthinking~~ callousness to wed   *|ignorant*
~~Even on steps~~ long frozen by the touch   *|On altar steps*
Of stretcher after stretcher of our dead.
Love's blindness is too ~~I said~~ terrible, I said;
I will go counsel men and show what bin
The harvest of their homes is gathered in.

But as I spoke, came many children nigh,
Hurrying lightly o'er the village green:
Methought too lightly, for they ~~all did lie~~   *|came to spy*
~~To look~~ into their playmate's ~~cot~~ terrene.   *|bed*
They clustered round; some wondered what might mean
Rich-odoured flowers so whelmed in fetid earth;
While some Death's riddle guessed ere that of Birth.

★ There is one typescript of this poem. WO's manuscript corrections are printed in italic.

And there stood One child with them, whose pale brows
Wore beauty like our mother Eve's; whom seeing
I could not choose but undo all my vows,
And cry that it were well that human Being,
And Birth and Death should be, just for the freeing
Of one such face from Chaos' murky womb.
For Hell's reprieve is worth not this one bloom.

The rebellious note in the second stanza is sounded more clearly in an untitled poem:

Nov. 6. 1912

Unto what pinnacles of desperate heights
Do good men climb to seize their good!
What abnegation from all mortal joys,
What vast abstraction from the world is theirs!
O what abuses ~~of health~~ insane, desperate pangs,
Annihilations of the Self, soul-suicides,
They wreak upon themselves to purchase ─ God!
A God ~~who shall obsess through temper~~
to guide through these poor temporal days
Their comings, goings, workings of the heart,
Obsess, indeed, their natures utterly,
~~And to prepare meanwhile~~ Meanwhile preparing, as in recompense,
Mansions celestial for their endless bliss.
And to what end this Holiness; this God
That arrogates their intellect and soul?
─To ~~no~~ nonsight end! Their offered lives are not so grand,
So active, or so sweet as many a(n) ones
That is undedicate, being reason-swayed.
And their sole mission is to drag, entice
And push mankind to those same cloudy crags
Where they first breathed the madness-giving air
That made them feel as angels, that are less than men.

Few stranger poems can have been written in an Anglican vicarage, but this explains why on 12 December Owen tells his mother that his nerves 'are in a shocking state, and no mistake. My breast is continually "too full". Just as if one had been over-long in a putrid atmosphere, and had got to the advanced stage of being painfully conscious of it.'[42] Susan considered writing to the Vicar to express her concern for her son's condition and rashly told Wilfred of this. 'Do you want to "do for" me completely?' he replied. 'You could not do more harm than by such an action.' The handwriting of this letter shows signs of considerable agitation,[43] and his return to Shrewsbury for Christmas came as a welcome escape.

There were other tensions, however, at Mahim, for Tom had just told Harold that he must

give up all thought of any career in the Arts and set about finding . . . a job. . . .

My father having got this off his chest immediately became very cheerful and hustling me out of the bedroom called out lightheartedly through the house that we must clear the dining-room and have a family game. . . . we always had a current favourite; so much so that we would usually run the same one for weeks until we had exhausted it. We were very competitive over these and quite often tempers would be lost; but this only increased our tremendous enthusiasm. Sometimes it would only be a simple board game with hooks and rubber rings, other times Snakes and Ladders and always of course the dearly loved Happy Families with the beloved Mr. Potts the Painter and Bill Bones the Butcher. We included many games, and were never at a loss. If we tired of our repertoire we would make up our own, especially guessing ones. Scores were always meticulously kept, not for the evening only but from week to week. Charades, dumb and dressed up, were our particular favourites, but these were kept for special occasions. Both my father and Wilfred were uncannily good at these and with the smallest aids would turn themselves into characters from Dickens or other classics.[44]

Over Christmas, the possibility of Wilfred leaving Dunsden was discussed and, on 28 December, he went up to Birmingham to meet the Rev. John Morgan, who was looking for a young man to help him in his new parish of St. Patrick's, Bordesley. Evidently they took to each other, but Owen confessed 'that I did not consider myself a fit person to dare to undertake such work, and revealed to him my state of mind'.[45] In a mood of deepening depression he returned to Dunsden and, on 4 January, wrote to his mother a crucial but now tantalizingly incomplete letter.★ The first page is missing. The second begins:

The furor [*several words missing*] now abated in the Vicarage, thank Mnemosyne; but I hope that I, who 'discovered' him something over a year ago, may [*half page missing*] but the Vicar's presence (taciturn instead of wontedly gay) symbolic of my stern Destiny, sat heavy on my soul the night. I have already braced myself to one important interview; the upshot of which was that he begged me to spend the next morning upon Tracts! Others will follow.[46]

One can only guess at the events described in these pages, but in that Owen was himself able to describe them to his extremely prudish mother, they cannot have been very shocking. Could the furore have been caused by Wigan finding Vivian Rampton smuggled into the vicarage? Wilfred, it would appear, had 'discovered' him something *under* a year before, but this was hardly a moment for chronological exactitude. It is possible to see some support for this theory in the wording of a subsequent passage from the same letter:

Murder will out, and I have murdered my false creed. If a true one exists, I shall find it. If not, adieu to the still falser creeds that hold the hearts of nearly all my fellow men.

Escape from this hotbed of religion I now long for more than I could ever have conceived a year and three months ago. . . .

★ See the Editors' Introduction to the *Collected Letters*, p. 5:
[In 1957], when it was first decided to transcribe the letters preserved by Susan Owen, certain words and phrases, and some short passages, were inked out, rubbed out, or pencilled over, in the originals. This was done by [Harold Owen], in good faith, and without a realization of the difficulties that might arise later. The intention was to remove trivial passages of domestic news of the kind that would certainly be left out in any volume of selected letters – something that was at that time contemplated; to remove names of people whose families might have been upset by some particularly scathing reference, or simply by the unexpected appearance of their names in print; and to remove words or expressions that seemed displeasing or unworthy. . . . In addition, . . . a few short passages, publication of which was felt more strongly not to be necessary, were scissored out of the originals and destroyed. Fortunately, there were few such passages: probably not amounting altogether to more than half a dozen printed pages.

To leave Dunsden will mean a terrible bust-up; but I have no intention of sneaking away by smuggling my reasons down the back-stairs. I will vanish in thunder and lightning, if I go at all.

The phrase 'smuggling my reasons down the back-stairs', whether used consciously or unconsciously, lends further support to the theory; and the whole passage has interesting points of resemblance to a sonnet that would seem to relate to this time and, in its first draft, read:[47]

The ~~End~~   To EROS.

(To Eros)

In that I loved you, Love, I worshipped you.
In that I worshipped well, I sacrificed.
All of most worth I bound and burnt and slew:
Old peaceful lives; frail flowers; firm friends;
                                    and Christ.

I slew all false loves; I slew all true,
That I might nothing love but your truth, Boy.
~~And~~ My Fair fame cast ~~off~~ away, as bridegrooms do
Their wedding garments in their haste of joy.

But when I fell upon your sandalled feet,
~~To kiss them, oh!~~ You loosed my lips; you rose;
I heard the ~~flaunting~~ singing of your wings' retreat;
Far-flown, I watched you flush the Olympian snows,
Beyond my hoping.   Starkly I returned
To stare upon the ash of all I burned....

The first, melodramatic title, 'The End', would accord with a resolution to 'vanish in thunder and lightning'; the theme of Christ sacrificed for Eros applies, or one can see Owen believing it applied; and there is the verbal echo of 'falser creeds'/'falser loves'.

While it is quite possible to hear Owen telling the Vicar to his face that he cannot accept his ruling as to the suitability of his friends, one should not overlook the accumulated evidence that the real point at issue between them was Christ rather than Eros. For months Owen had been coming to the conclusion that the Christ of the Gospels, whom he never ceased to revere, had no place in the institution served by Mr. Wigan. As he wrote to his mother on 8 January:

I have had further talks to the Vicar; and our relations are taking more definite shape every day. The very crux to which events have been tending for months and months is now upon us. It is very meet and right that you should be near at hand.[48]

She came to Alpenrose for a few days to be near him and when, at her departure, he watched her train pull out of Reading station, he had a premonition that they would not be long apart.[49] On 4 February, he broached the subject of his leaving Dunsden to the Vicar and found it was not unexpected. 'He had only been waiting for me to be first in the matter. Unless I "get right", I pack off this very week, – about Friday perhaps.'[50] He ended this letter with a ringing (and unacknowledged) quotation from Keats: 'I have not the slightest feeling of humility for anything in existence, but the Eternal Being, the Principle of Beauty, and the Memory of Great Men.'[51]

He did not 'get right' and, on 7 February, shook the theological dust of Dunsden off his feet. There remains among his manuscripts – scribbled between a quotation from 'The Eve of St. Agnes' and a verse fragment of his own – notes for a letter:

To Vicar – solely on the grounds of affection. I was a boy when I first came to you, and held you in the doubtful esteem that a boy has for his Headmaster. It is also true that I was an old man when I left. . . . The Christian Life affords no imagination, physical sensation, aesthetic philosophy. There is but one dimension in the Christian religion, the strait line upwards whereas I cannot conceive of less than 3. But all these considerations [?] are nothing to the conviction that the philosophy of the whole system as a religion is but a religion and therefore one Interpretation of Life & Scheme of Living among a hundred, and that not the ~~best~~ most convenient.

The wildness of the handwriting suggests that this may have been written from the sickbed to which he retired, with congestion of the lungs, on his escape from Dunsden. In this way, his brother believed, 'his bodily succumbing to the physical illness which seized him immediately after he had returned home acted as a safety-valve; it came just in time to prevent a nervous breakdown'.[52]

Harold himself, having left Art School, had at last agreed to embark on the career of his father's choosing. Wilfred was still ill in bed when, on Friday 13 March 1913 – by superstition a day unlucky three times over – his fifteen-year-old brother in a midshipman's uniform came to say goodbye:

raising himself to a sitting position he hailed me with , 'Lo. Enter the man.' He was in a cynical mood and not really pleased at being disturbed. . . .

Wearily, for he seemed to be possessed with a sad tiredness, he quietly gazed at me, then turning away his face on the pillow whispered in his almost inaudible way, 'If I can't please Father and I never seem to be able to – at least I should think you must be doing so, now.' Then springing upright with one of his sudden movements, with a quick change of mood, he put on his tutorial manner and hectored me about not missing my opportunities for observation and mental enlargement when I visited Italy and the many other lands which would so soon be familiar to me. His mind was working enviously now and irritably he told me how much more profitable it would be for him to be going instead of me and, with some rhetoric said, 'Give me only Italy – and you may have the rest.'

. . . As I was closing his bedroom door, he called out to me to remind me how atrocious my English still was, and barked at me that if – when we met again – he found that I had the slightest trace of a Liverpool accent, he would disown relationship for ever.[53]

In mid-April Wilfred himself left Mahim, to recuperate at the Taylors' house in Torquay. He could not resist a second pilgrimage to Teignmouth,[54] and retraced his steps to 20 Northumberland Place where, on a similar day ninety-five years before, Keats had written to his friend Bailey:

Midshipman Harold Owen and family

you may say what you will of devonshire: the truth is, it is a splashy, rainy, misty, snowy, foggy, haily, floody, muddy, slipshod County – the hills are very beautiful, when you get a sight of 'em – the primroses are out, but then you are in – the Cliffs are of a fine deep Colour, but then the Clouds are continually vieing with them.[55]

Having made his devotions at the shrine of his patron saint, Owen went in search of a ghost – only two years older than himself – along the Promenade, where

> the wide sea did weave
> An untumultuous fringe of silver foam
> Along the flat, brown sand. . . .[56]

'How happy-melancholy I was', he wrote to his mother afterwards, 'I will not relate. To be in love with a youth and a dead 'un is perhaps sillier than with a real, live maid.'[57] With the turn of the tide came the rain. He 'could see no poetry in its tears, *this* year', and caught the 4.30 train back to Torquay.

As spring drew into summer, it seems likely that he made further expeditions to Uriconium on his 'magical Sturmey-Archer',[58] with George Fox's *Guide to the Roman City of Uriconium* in his pocket and, perhaps, Housman's lines in his head:

> The gale, it plies the saplings double,
>   It blows so hard, 'twill soon be gone:
> To-day the Roman and his trouble
>   Are ashes under Uricon.[59]

In Fox's *Guide*, he read

that the city and its inhabitants perished by fire and sword. Everywhere, when the earth which covers its remains is turned over, it is found to be black from the burning, and plain traces of the massacre of the citizens showed themselves when the ruins, amongst which the visitor strays, were excavated. Skeletons of men, women and children lay amongst the blackened walls. In their terror some of the unhappy people had sought refuge in the hollow floors of the baths. The skeleton of an old man, near whose hand lay the little treasure he hoped to save, was discovered crouched between the pillars of the hypocaust of chamber 5, and not far from him were also the skeletons of two women. The dark and narrow hiding place did not avail to save the fugitives, for the beams of the blazing roofs in their fall blocked all way of escape, and they perished stifled by the smoke of the burning buildings.[60]

Fox refers to an old Welsh poem, ascribed to a bard named Llywarch Hen, which 'describes, in vivid language, the destruction of a city on the Welsh border, and the slaughter of the chief to whom the city belonged'.[61] This mention of a poem supposedly 'the death song of Uriconium' may have given Owen the idea for a poem of his own. Perhaps, too, he was influenced by Colvin's description of the genesis of Keats's 'Ode on a Grecian Urn': 'The sight, or the imagination, of a piece of ancient sculpture had set the poet's mind at work, . . . conjuring up the scenes of ancient life.'[62] In something of the same spirit Owen sat down to write 'Uriconium/An Ode'. Striving to

catch his reader's attention, his voice at first is self-consciously
rhetorical:

> It lieth low near merry England's heart
> Like a long-buried sin; and Englishmen
> Forget that in its death their sires had part.
> And, like a sin, Time lays it bare again
>   To tell of races wronged,
> And ancient glories suddenly overcast,
> And treasures flung to fire and rabble wrath.

As the twenty-year-old poet warms to his subject, the archaic diction
falls away and is replaced by a rich particularity. He is able to invest
objects under glass in the Shrewsbury museum with a dramatic
vitality:

> For here lie remnants from a banquet-table,
> – Oysters and marrow-bones, and seeds of grape –
> The statement of whose age must sound a fable;
> And Samian jars, whose sheen and flawless shape
>   Look fresh from potter's mould.
> Plasters with Roman finger-marks impressed;
> Bracelets, that from the warm Italian arm
>   Might seem to be scarce cold;
> And spears – the same that pushed the Cymry west,
> Unblunted yet; with tools of forge and farm,
> Abandoned, as a man in sudden fear
> Drops what he holds to help his swift career:
> For sudden was Rome's flight, and wild the alarm.
> The Saxon shock was like Vesuvius' qualm.

Those 'Bracelets . . . from the warm Italian arm' probably owe
something of their warmth to Keats: Colvin had particularly admired
the 'warmed jewels' that Madeline unclasps on the Eve of St. Agnes.
Even so, in this one stanza alone, the Samian jars 'fresh from potter's
mould', 'Plasters with Roman finger-marks impressed', the bracelets, and the spears 'unblunted yet' all reveal an intensity of sensuous
perception uncommon in so young a poet. The reference to 'Vesu-
vius' qualm' derives from his reading of E. L. Bulwer's *The Last
Days of Pompeii*,[63] perhaps in January 1909 when he wrote a lurid

school essay on the subject of 'Earthquakes'. His Ode ends on a high rhetorical note:

> Above this reverend ground, what traveller checks?
> Yet cities such as these one time would breed
> Apocalyptic visions of world-wrecks.
> Let Saxon men return to them, and heed!
>   They slew and burnt,
> But, after, prized what Rome had given away
> Out of her strength and her prosperity.
>   Have they yet learnt
> The precious truth distilled from Rome's decay?
> Ruins! On England's heart press heavily!
> For Rome hath left us more than walls and words,
> And better yet shall leave; and more than herds
> Or land or gold, gave the Celts to us in fee;
> E'en Blood, which makes poets sing and prophets see.

One wonders whether Lieutenant Owen, sorting through his manuscripts, ever perceived the prophetic ironies of that stanza.

Probably within weeks of completing 'Uriconium' he started another Keatsian ode, entitled, 'Written on a June Night (1911)'. His imagination, clearly in a state of ferment, threw up images of physical violence that have little apparent connection with each other or with the sunset that is the poem's avowed theme:

> Who feeleth not, when June bereaves our land
>   Of easeful Night,
> Some weariness, some fear, some hate
>   Of evening Light,
> Hot light, both earlier and more late,
> Beneath our eyelids thrusts a flaring brand?

The poet listens to the birds, 'As might a sick man mid a boistrous crew', while

>   . . . a guilty mystery
>   Hangs in the air
> As if the sun had slackened his march
>   To spy and stare
> (His solemn face love-flushed and arch)
> Upon his sister Night incestuously.

The sun sinks and, in the fifth stanza of his ode, Owen introduces an image strangely prefiguring his later style and subject-matter:

> And so her holy works are left undone,
>   And new day glares
> On the armies of forced-marching men,
>   From prayers to cares
> Hurried before they reach the amen;
> Mercilessly driven by the tireless sun.

Images of bereavement, physical violence, incest, and war are succeeded, in stanza six, by one of murder:

> O never will the western brilliance die?
>   As it might chance
> A murderer murdering in a dream
>   The victim's glance
> Though checked, will not close down its gleam,
> And the body will not cool, nor the spirit fly; . . .

This hectic and unsatisfactory poem would seem to be basically an unconscious expression of frustrated sexuality.

In early June, Harold returned from his first voyage, a frail shadow of the sturdy boy that had left home three months before; but he was lucky to be alive at all, having survived a fearsome attack of heat apoplexy in Calcutta.[64] To celebrate his return, his father decreed that they should 'burn out' an old oak tar-barrel for Susan to use as a wash-tub. Wilfred, with characteristic lack of tact, declared:

'You know, Father, if you try to fire that thing you will burn the house down.' And he proceeded to give us all a little lecture upon the extremely volatile combustibility of burning tar. This was all that was needed to cause my father not only to throw away caution but to become instantaneously highly combustible himself; and with irate looks and many snorting trumpetings thrown towards Wilfred, he immediately proceeded to hop around collecting newspapers and other dry rubbish exclaiming as he did so, 'Can't find a spark of pluck in this family, everybody frightened of anything I try to do. . . .' He would at that moment have preferred to set the house on fire rather than be thwarted and, pouring in a great can of paraffin – 'for luck, and just to show us' – lit his paper torch and tossed it in.

At first, nothing much happened; then smoke came up, thickening all the time until great clouds and twisting spouts of oily blackness poured up. This seemed harmless enough, and my father was looking jubilant again, until, with a crackle, the mass burst into orange flame. The eddying wind whipped this about in all directions but mostly towards the house. My father frightfully red in the face, was prancing about like an intoxicated bantam cock, throwing water about in all directions and shouting to us in no uncertain way to do the same. Actually, he was enjoying himself immensely, and now that there was no room for arguments so were all the rest of us. All at once the whole thing seemed extremely comical, so that we could hardly run for laughing. Wilfred was enjoying it all, too, and shrieking instructions with the best of us as we rushed in and out to the tap for water with tremendous agility and infectious excitement. When the trellis work caught alight, it was he, Wilfred, who concentrated on the flames and subdued them. When the paintwork on the house door and windows began to blister and sizzle, my father, grabbing hold of me, yelled: 'The clothes props – the props! We must get the props and tip it over and roll it away from the house!'[65]

The house was saved but not the barrel. However, the incident left them all in the gayest of spirits. Their strong sense of family unity was reaffirmed next day when Tom once again led them over the fields, over the ferry, to Uffington Church.[66]

Wilfred had decided to sit for a scholarship to University College, Reading, and a few days after Harold's return the two brothers hurried to Shrewsbury Station. Just as his train was about to leave, Wilfred leant out of the carriage window and said:

'Harold, in spite of your disgusting pronunciation of famous cities, you have provided me with a problem which I propose to solve before I get out at the hated Reading. Here it is: Is it better to stop in England and learn to pronounce place-names with perfection, and never see the cities themselves, or is it better to go and see the places and never be able to pronounce the names of them properly? I don't know which is best to do.'

The train was slowly drawing out now, and walking along level with him, I called out: 'You do what you like, old idiot! I'm going to do both.'

He was pulling away from me rapidly, but I had time to see the surprised look on his face and to hear his voice come back with: 'You have given me the answer! – Out of the mouths . . .'[67]

He failed to win the scholarship, considered returning to Dunsden to assist Mr. Hulcoop the village schoolmaster,[68] abandoned the idea, and went to stay with his prosperous uncle Edward Quayle and his family.[69] Not long afterwards he succumbed to another of his bronchial attacks. His mother nursed him devotedly, insisting – despite the doctor's insistence to the contrary – that he was pre-disposed to TB, if not already suffering from it.[70] By a happy chance, one of Owen's long-held ambitions found a sympathetic echo in his doctor's recommendation that a winter in the South of France would do him good.

He was offered part-time employment as a teacher of English in the Berlitz School in Bordeaux; his father, touchingly, promised him a small allowance to supplement his salary; and in mid-September he stood at the rail of a steamer filling his lungs with the rich air of France.

5

FRANCE

Arriving in Bordeaux, he rented a small room in the Rue Castel-moron for one franc a day, but that proved more than he could well afford, and he stayed there only a few weeks.* On 28 September he moved into a room at 95 Rue Porte Dijeaux, which combined 'the qualities of cheapness, nearness to the school, tranquility and a large window, *overlooking a "garden"*!!'[1] There was one other English *professeur* at the school, called Tofield, with whom Owen had little in common. As he wrote scornfully to his mother, he

smokes much and saves little, has to obtain Remittances from home. He was a student of Nottingham College, but failed to pass Inter-Arts, and now at 22, is spending his time in France, awaiting a Civil Service Exam. in Spring.

I don't particularly like him. He is tall, & something of a gawk, easily enraged; and of limp principles, (I should imagine). Neither have I yet discovered that he has any interest in life.[2]

By contrast, he liked most of his pupils. One after another they were ushered into his presence by a *chasseur*, the procedure being 'more like a doctor's consultation than a school'. For some weeks he supplemented his income, to the welcome tune of four francs a

---

* The franc was worth 9½d. in 1913. He paid £1. 4s. 6d. a month in his first lodgings; 16s. 2d. in his second. His monthly salary from the Berlitz School was 130 francs, or £5. 2s. 11d.

night, by lecturing in French from eleven o'clock until midnight on 'the working of a *Ballon dirigeable à distance* by Wireless'. Afterwards, he told his mother,

we usually sit drinking (syrops) in a Café till one or two o'clock. Syrops, mind, for my friend the Inventor neither drinks nor smokes and is in all respects a most amiable and estimable fellow (little older than myself, I should think.) Now, he is so pleased with the manner in which I show him off, and generally with my knowledge of French, command of English, and inklings of Wireless Telegraphy, that he had made me a proposition to the effect that if I should like to travel with him, he would give me 200 f. a month (£96. a year) – as well as travelling expenses paid. He speaks bad French and worse English, and consequently needs an interpreter and secretary while in Paris (November) and America – Mexico of all marvellous places! (next spring.)[3]

It would seem that Owen's first letters home from France, which have not survived, must have been a good deal less cheerful, dwelling at length on his coughs and colds and on headaches caused, he was convinced, by deteriorating eyesight. His mother at first urged him to see a doctor, then to come home. He would not hear of this and so his parents decided that, in place of the family holiday which would be abandoned, his father should go to Bordeaux. Wilfred, seeing himself as a Chattertonian figure, consumptive and impecunious in an attic, had probably depicted his general condition as rather worse than it was. Certainly, Tom found him in early October much better than he had expected. His relief and Wilfred's delight at seeing him put them both in a festal mood. This was almost destroyed their first evening together by a not-untypical misunderstanding. Wilfred had a confession to make that he found difficult to put into words. His mumbling and stammering led his father to the wrong conclusion. Realizing this, he tried

to retract from the conversation altogether; but it was too late, and seeing Father's panicky look and his quick glances around the apartment as if at any moment he expected some sweet little French damsel to come pirouetting out from one of the closets, Wilfred threw up his hands in despair and flopped into a chair; my father full of contrition, very red-faced and with a startled attitude of real alarm spreading over him, exclaimed: 'My dear Wilfred, the very last thing I wish to do is to cause you embarrassment . . .

I did not come over for that but you must let me out of here at once . . . it is too awkward . . . when you have arranged things, I will come back.'

He continued with frantic exhortations to Wilfred not to say any more . . . that affairs like this came to every young man – and the less said about them the better – that for his part he refused to listen further to anything he had to say. Purple-faced now with his own embarrassment he leapt up and charged for the door. Wilfred with great speed rushed after him and nipping in front of him somehow turned him around and clutching his arm managed to propel him into the room again; astonished over Wilfred's unexpected agility, my father demanded immediate explanation. Wilfred with the eloquence of desperation managed with cool lucidity now to convey to him that all that he had been trying to tell him was that he – my father – had now become invested with a title and that in his – Wilfred's – circle of friends he was, unfortunately, very well known as 'Sir Thomas Owen'.[4]

The unsuspecting knight fell back in astonishment into a fortunately placed chair and, recovering himself, demanded that this misapprehension be remedied forthwith. His sense of humour, however, soon reasserted itself and father and son went off for dinner. As this was ending, a young student – whom Wilfred had long been eyeing with some unease – crossed the restaurant and made an elaborate speech heavily spiced with 'Sir Thomases'. Tom courteously invited him to take a glass of wine with them, and so charmed his guest that Wilfred later teasingly accused him of relishing the situation as much as he had himself. For the rest of Tom's happy stay in Bordeaux Wilfred called him 'Sir Thomas' whenever they were alone, which released them both from the inhibiting constraints of their formal father and son relationship.[5] It is significant that they were never more at ease with one another than on this occasion and their two earlier holidays in France. At home it would seem that, subconsciously, they competed for Susan Owen's attention and that she made as little secret of her disappointment in the course of her husband's career as in her hopes for the future of her son.

Despite the alarm caused at Mahim by his earlier account of his ailments, Owen continued to treat his mother to a catalogue of his minor disorders: on 19 October he has a painful throat,[6] on 6 November it is 'a slight *grippe*',[7] five days later he is 'obstinately c–nst–p–t–d'.[8] On the Feast of All Saints he stayed in bed with a

headache and was somewhat dismayed when Mme. Dubo, his
landlady,

hied to the Cemetery . . . to tend the Dead, and left the living to fend for
itself. . . . I boiled water for my tea, and cooked egg and toast. With one
knife, one plate, one spoon, and only half a stomach, imagine me taking
this repast in the dismal evening gloom, – perhaps at the same time that
you were round your cheerful table, and the twilight was pleasant over
Haughmond, and Autumn spoke not of sadness; nor the evening bells of
death. But, at this moment, are slowly tolling the most sepulchral-throated
bells I ever heard. Tonight every family in France turns its thoughts to its
dead.[9]

Dr. Maurice Aumont, the Director of the Berlitz School at Bordeaux,
looked after him in an efficient and kindly way and Owen liked him
at first. However, he soon came to see him as a hard taskmaster. On
5 December he told his mother that one day he had to give seven
lessons in eight hours;[10] a fortnight later it is 'Ten lessons tomorrow'.[11] That month a Miss Hewitt joined the staff as 'Prof.
Anglais II' and there was some suggestion that a third *professeur*
might be coming to share their load, but this turned out to be a
myth invented to boost their morale.[12] As at Dunsden, Owen was
soon complaining that he had insufficient free time for his own
studies. Teaching English by the direct method all day did nothing
for his French, and Aumont refused to make it possible for him to
attend the free courses at the University.[13] Despite these dis-
appointments, however, he had 'no reason to regret having come
to France', and Christmas 1913, found him sustained by his mother's
gingerbread and in good spirits.

   In the middle of January M. Langholz, the Sub-Director of the
School, asked him whether he would be interested in becoming
Director of a small Berlitz School in the north of France. 'There
would be plenty of work in winter; hardly any in summer; and clear
profits of 4,000 francs a year.'[14] He was attracted by the idea,
especially when he learnt that the School was the one at Angers then
under the direction of M. Aumont, who had installed an inefficient
lady manager. Profits had fallen, but even so, Langholz told him,
'Aumont is asking 4,500 f as the price of its sale'. Unless, therefore,

Owen wrote to his father, 'some Rich Uncle is prepared to advance some 5000 f, the thing will be impossible';[15] and he must have known his father well enough to be certain that Tom would never countenance a request for such a loan from his brother-in-law, 'the Merchant Prince' Edward Quayle. Wilfred went on to say that, even if the necessary £200 could be raised, he would rather see it invested in college fees, because 'an English Degree admits one to a French University, where one does a little English Instruction, while following Courses for French Degrees'. His father must have winced to read Wilfred's apologia:

> If I have shirked the idea of Shop, or Office, or Elementary School, it is only because I am more clear-sighted than another; and see that once fixed in a low-level Rut one is ever-after straightened there; – straightened intellectually and socially as surely as financially.
> Neither am I under any delusions as to Literature as a means of livelihood.[16]

He was writing nothing at this time,[17] being caught up in 'a whirl of lessons' to the point where he finally complained to M. Aumont. This had some effect, but three weeks later things were as bad as ever and he 'had a grand bust-up' with the Director and told him there was enough work for three English *professeurs*. Aumont agreed, but explained that he was unwilling to engage another because there was certain to be a slackening off at Easter.[18]

On 18 March Wilfred Owen was twenty-one. Delighted with his mother's gift of a Waverley fountain pen and Shelley's *Complete Works* from Mary, Harold, and Colin, he went out to dinner at the house of a friend and pupil, Pierre Berthaud.[19] The Berthaud parents were both primary school teachers and over the coming months Owen was to have many happy meals under their roof. He was also a frequent visitor at 12 rue St. Louis, the home of M. and Mme. Lem and their son Raoul, and on Easter Sunday accompanied them on a picnic to Castelnau in the heart of the Médoc. He set off

> inside my old green suit, old boots, old tie, sans cuffs, gloves or hair-parting; prepared for a rare escapade in the country; so was a little abashed to find Raoul in his very best, cuffs protruding shirt-front bulging; all prognosticating that either we were going to a fine family or that some member of it

had fine eyes. The first member we saw at Castelnau put me at ease – an ancient man, in wooden boots, corkscrew trousers, and a coat twice as ancient as himself. But lo! waiting for us at the station-gates, stood the young lady I already knew in costume as modern as her grandfather's were antique; and with her a superb specimen of human beauty, the younger sister of sixteen![20]

This was Mlle. Henriette Poitou, and Raoul and Wilfred were soon competing for her attention. At lunch Wilfred was gratified to see 'the marvellous eyes' looking in his direction four times a minute, and afterwards he and she went for a walk arm in arm. As he later wrote to his sister Mary,

I could scarcely have been happier. *Raoul* might clearly have been happier than he was; but it was hardly *my* fault. And the memory of those moments will remain sweet to me, chiefly, my dear Sister, chiefly because I took no *advantage* of that young and ardent nature, neither even said what I thought of her 'appas', but left the compliments, with the vows, to Raoul. Perhaps I listened with too much sympathy to her plaints of captivity: how she is watched and warded everywhere: not even allowed to visit people in Bordeaux; but has no gayer, nobler, or [more] learned companions but the grandmother, everlastingly regretting her grandson; the little villagers; the father forever lauding his wines; and a professor who prepares her for an examination.[21]

That night the rivals shared a bedroom, but the nightingales or the scent of the pines or the image of Henriette kept Wilfred awake. On Easter Monday he was taken on a tour of the vineyards and, after lunch and a game of *cache-cache*, caught the train back to Bordeaux where he wrote fifty lines of poetry in as many minutes and got 'better results out of a piano than much practice could give'.

 Six weeks later, in a long letter to his mother, he writes of 'the call of an Art':

I certainly believe I could make a better musician than many who profess to be, and are accepted as such. Mark, I do not for a moment call myself a musician, nor do I suspect I ever shall be; but there! I love Music, Violin first, Piano next, with such *strength* that I have to conceal the passion, for fear it be thought weakness. . . . But it is as extravagant of me to think of Music now as it would be for, say, Father to think of training as a sea-captain. . . .

Yet wait, wait, O impatient world, give me two years, give me two *free months*, before it be said that I have Nothing to Show for my temperament. Let me now, seriously and shamelessly, work out a Poem. Then shall be seen whether the *Executive Power* needful for at least one Fine Art, be present in me, or be missing.[22]

As the famous summer of 1914 unwound its slow procession of bright days, Owen had further thoughts of directing a Berlitz school[23] and of taking a special course of French for foreigners at the University of Bordeaux,[24] but in the middle of June these were swept aside. An elegant Parisian pupil of his, Mme. Léger, asked him if he would like to spend a month in the Pyrenees with her and her husband and their eleven-year-old daughter Nénette. Madame managed an interior decorating business in Bordeaux and Paris and was planning a tour of Canada in October, by which time she was anxious to speak English.[25] The proposal attracted Owen immediately and everything was swiftly and satisfactorily settled. Not for years had the future seemed to hold such promise, but on *le quatorze juillet* he observed a strange portent of the darker future that was to take him and so many others unawares. He had been watching a firework display in the Place de Quinconces,

when a ferocious storm broke. The noise of hundreds of thousands of feet and voices surging back into the town was a noise not to be forgotten. It re-awoke all the mysterious terrors which one feels for the first time in reading the *Tale of Two Cities*. And then such a pandemonium of thunder claps to finish – or rather never to finish! For they lasted till six this morning and awoke me half a dozen times in the night.[26]

He saw Raoul off on his way to England for a holiday at Mahim* and set about preparing for his own sojourn in the Pyrenees. On 31 July he left Bordeaux early in the morning and was met at Bagnères-de-Bigorre by M. Léger and Nénette. In their donkey-cart he rattled through the little town and up a steep and secluded lane to the Villa Lorenzo. Sheltered from the north wind by the brow of the hill on which it stands, it commands a magnificent view south-

* This was not a success. See *JFO*, III, pp. 62–8.

ward to snow-capped mountains. Owen drew his mother a plan of the house

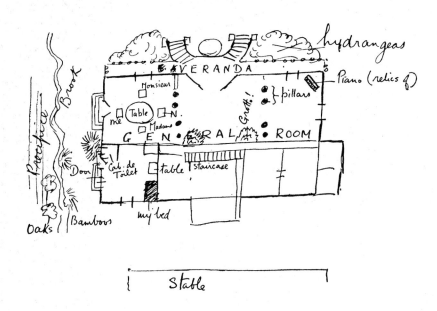

and sent her a description of his 'excellent friends':

Monsieur Léger was educated in a Paris Engineering School, but 'abandoned the Sciences for Dramatic Art' (so saith a short notice I have read on him.) He played Comedies, I think; and the mere stamp of his countenance is enough to confirm it. He is quite small, but his bearing is notable, and his head typically dramatic: no hair on top to speak of, deep, dark eyes under prominent and moustache-like eyebrows, broad mobile mouth, clean shaven. Head beautifully poised, a little leaning-back. Voice agreeable – (but I have not yet heard him recite.) There is nothing *stagey* about him, absolutely nothing in manner of speech, gesture, or idea; and that is remarkable considering. But the most mysterious thing is his age. In some lights, whether regarded, entire or in part, behind, before, or aside, he looks just thirty. At other times he is an old man, a grandfather. As a matter of fact, he is over fifty.

Madame is much younger. She is elegant rather than *belle*; has shapely features luxuriant coiffure, but is much too thin to be pretty. Probably she has been very pretty indeed. She is obviously of the same opinion herself. Her toilette, even for driving in donkey cart, is unimpeachable.

Yesterday she pointedly told me she could not stand plain people. *Je les déteste* were her words. I felt uncomfortable. You, who may take the inference in a sense more complimentary to myself, may be uncomfortable in another way. She has even confided to me that she doesn't love her husband excessively. This is all very amusing for me – and nothing else.

But I am immensely happy to be in the company of Nénette. I am enclosing a picture, with the warning that it is not very like, is not complimentary, and must be seen *through a lens*. Nénette, (not a nice name, *tant pis*) is perfectly a child, and, with that, is almost a perfect child. Papa prefers that she should not be educated in a town school, where they learn a great deal, but *not* of studies. So she goes to school with the peasants, and makes great progress. This is at the sacrifice of her accent, which is an important thing to a father like Mons. Léger. But *that* can be cured. The result of living out here is that Nénette's physique is magnificent. As far as I can judge, she has also more than her share of intellect. Anyhow she began to compose dramas at nine years of age. Some of her writings are astonishing. I said that our piano was atrocious: hence I dont know whether she can play with sense or not; but she goes through her exercises admirably.[27]

This letter is dated 1 August, but it must have been finished some days later when the magnified echo of the pistol shots in Sarajevo had reached even to Bagnères-de-Bigorre.

The news of War made great stir in Bagnères. Women were weeping all about; work was suspended. Nearly all the men have already departed. Our household is one in a thousand. Mr. Léger, who doesn't look his age, and I, who look French, are objects of mark at present. I had to declare myself, and get a permit to remain here; where I must stay still under penalty of arrest and sentence as a spy – unless I get a special visa for emigrating. I don't know how this state of things will affect my Courses in Bordeaux. Our food is already much dearer, and we are all getting ready to live on bread and maize-soup. If need be, Monsieur & I will undertake the harvest between us. Nobody is very gay.

By contrast, in most of the capital cities of Europe there was a good deal of hysterical gaiety as demonstrating crowds shouted 'To Paris' or 'To Berlin'. In England there were

The Villa Lorenzo, about 1914. The figure on the left may be Madame Léger

Those long uneven lines
Standing as patiently
As if they were stretched outside
The Oval or Villa Park,
The crowns of hats, the sun
On moustached archaic faces
Grinning as if it were all
An August Bank Holiday lark. . . .[28]

A week later, as conscripts and volunteers were rallying to their flags
and the troop trains rolling across Europe, Owen reported that most
of the men of the village have gone, the women pass their time
knitting in the streets, and 'I continue meanwhile to be immensely
happy and famously well.'[29] On 10 August he confessed – not
altogether convincingly – in a letter to Colin:

I feel shamefully 'out of it' here, passing my time reading the Newspapers
in an armchair in a shady garden. Numbers of Bordeaux ladies are going
to the Armies as Nurses. The only thing I could do, so Madame Léger says,
would be to serve as stretcher-bearer, on the battlefield. After all my years
of playing soldiers, and then of reading History, I have almost a mania to
be in the East, to see fighting, and to serve. For I like to think this is the last
War of the World![30]

It is difficult to plot with any precision Owen's reactions to the
War, as they appear in his poetry, because he seldom dated his manuscripts with more than the year of their composition, and frequently
not even with that. Probably the first poem to be started after the
outbreak of war was that originally entitled 'The Ballad of Peace
and War'. Retitled 'The Ballad of Purchase-Money/s',[31] it shows
as great an ignorance of the issues involved as anything from the
pen of the maligned Rupert Brooke:

O meet it is and passing sweet
    To live in peace with others,
But sweeter still and far more meet
    To die in war for brothers.

This sentiment was to be dramatically reversed in the more famous conclusion of 'Dulce et Decorum Est'. 'The Ballad of Purchase-Money' ends on a Housmanic note:

> Fair days are yet left for the old
>> And children's cheeks are ruddy,
> Because the good lads' limbs lie cold,
>> And their brave cheeks are bloody.

It is hard to imagine how this could come from the same hand, and in the same year, as '1914':

> War broke: and now the Winter of the world
> With perishing great darkness closes in.
> The foul tornado, centred at Berlin,
> Is over all the width of Europe whirled,
> Rending the sails of progress. Rent or furled
> Are all Art's ensigns. Verse wails. Now begin
> Famines of thought and feeling. Love's wine's thin.
> The grain of human Autumn rots, down-hurled.[32]

The apparent echo of Rupert Brooke's 'red/Sweet wine of youth' is probably fortuitous. His sonnet, 'The Dead' was not published until December 1914,[33] and one of the drafts of '1914' is dated 1914.

More interesting is the 'world'/'whirled' rhyme of lines 1 and 4. On the back of a draft of another poem, 'The Imbecile',* almost certainly written in Bordeaux, Owen listed pararhymes for a poem apparently to be entitled 'Nocturne':

land	Ardour
learned	Odour
leaned	~~Harder~~
lined	Eider

brays	toll
browze	toil
breeze	tool

---

* Although the subject of this poem is probably 'the poor Idiot girl of Bray's' [*CL*, p. 149] in Dunsden, the paper and ink of the mss suggest that they were written in France. On the back of a 4-stanza version of the poem in French there are jotted notes about pupils – Maurel, Mll. Cille, Côté – in the same pencil as listed the pararhymes.

There is an unpublished poem called 'Nocturne' among his papers, but its rhymes are conventional. The word 'nocturnes', however, appears with six of the rhyme words listed here in a poem written two years later, 'Has your soul sipped?'[34] An even longer period of gestation was to produce the more confident pararhyming of 'From my Diary. July 1914'.[35] Writing this in July 1917, he may have forgotten that he did not reach Bagnères-de-Bigorre until the afternoon of 31 July. In his letter of 10 August he told Colin:

one fine morning I went forth, pretending I was going to herborise; and finding, as I knew I should, an enchanting stretch of water in an alder-glade, I was not long in 'getting in.' So now I go down every day, and I know, when I vaunt my coolness and freshness, the others would be green with envy, if they were not so infernally red with heat.[36]

Three years later, in his little room in Craiglockhart War Hospital, he was to remember

> Boys
>   Bursting the surface of the ebony pond.
> Flashes
>   Of swimmers carving thro' the sparkling cold.
> Fleshes
>   Gleaming with wetness to the morning gold.

The stars that, in the same letter, are said to be 'twice as brilliant than I have ever seen them before', take their place in the poem's luminous conclusion:

> Stars
>   Expanding with the starr'd nocturnal flowers.

The 'maid/Laughing the love-laugh with me' must be Nénette, an enchanting creature for whom, Owen told his sister, 'I draw, play the piano, make boats, act comedy, invent stories, play hide-and-seek, bury dolls, etc.'[37] She is 'The Sleeping Beauty', who

> lay not blanketed in drowsy trance,
> But leapt alert of limb and keen of glance,
> From sun to shower; from gaiety to ruth;
> Yet breathed her loveliness asleep in her:

> For, when I kissed, her eyelids knew no stir,
> So back I drew tiptoe from that Princess,
> Because it was too soon, and not my part,
> To start voluptuous pulses in her heart,
> And kiss her to the world of Consciousness.[38]

Nénette's mother was no stranger to the world of consciousness. She told Owen 'that she could do what she liked with her men friends'[39] and evidently hoped to number him among them. He became aware that she had developed a considerable liking for him 'both in a physical and intellectual sense',[40] a liking which, he was quick to reassure his mother, he could only reciprocate in the latter sense. Susan was clearly growing alarmed at the course of her son's friendship and wrote to warn him against the contagion of the Stage. He asked Mary to tell her that Madame had never had any connection with the theatre (other than by marriage, he might have added), but admitted that his mother's suspicions about her attitude to him were more or less correct. 'But I dont care two pins, so let her be tranquillised'.[41] Susan Owen had no reason to doubt her monopoly of her son's emotions. To a similar maternal warning six months before he had replied:

> You ought not to discourage too hard.
> If you knew what hands have been laid on my arm, in the night, along the Bordeaux streets, or what eyes play upon me in the restaurant where I daily eat, methinks you would wish that the star and adoration of my life had risen; or would quickly rise.
> But never fear: thank Home, and Poetry, and the FORCE behind both. And rejoice with me that a calmer time has come for me; and that fifty blandishments cannot move me like ten notes of a violin or a line of Keats.
> All women, without exception, *annoy* me, and the mercenaries (which the innocent old pastor thought might allure) I utterly detest; more indeed than as a charitable being, I ought.[42]

When Owen wrote to acquaint his mother with 'a piece of personal news which makes my heart bound', her heart must have bounded in another direction to hear that Madame had asked him to accompany her on a business trip to Canada in October.[43] This plan came to nothing and he was shortly to be able to tell his mother that 'The Affair Léger is "settled".'[44]

By this time another figure dominated his horizon, that of the French poet and writer Laurent Tailhade, who in the middle of August gave two lectures in the Casino at Bagnères-de-Bigorre. Madame Léger invited him to lunch at the Villa Lorenzo on the 28th and Owen looked forward to this with some excitement.

Wilfred Owen with Laurent Tailhade, September 1914

Unfortunately, Tailhade was 'suffering from his heart' that day and they had little real conversation.[45] His hostess suggested, however, that he might prefer to stay with them than at his hotel and he gladly accepted. Next morning Owen called on him to know when he would like to move and found him

at his window in shirt-sleeves, mooning. He received me like a lover. To use an expression of the Rev. H. Wigan's, he quite slobbered over me. I know not how many times he squeezed my hand; and, sitting me down on a sofa, pressed my head against his shoulder. [*two lines illegible*] It was not intellectual; but I felt the living verve of the poet . . . who has fought *seventeen duels* (so it is said).[46]

Tailhade, who was then a portly fifty-nine, had like Owen been intended for the Church, but had revolted against Christianity. He was now a confirmed pacifist and the author of two pamphlets, *Lettre aux Conscrits* (1903) and *Pour la Paix* (1909), which had caused a considerable stir. At a later stage in their friendship, when Owen's thinking had been much influenced by the older man's ideas and ideals,[47] he would not have written as he did to his mother at the end of August:

I can do no service to anybody by agitating for news or making dole over the slaughter. On the contrary I adopt the perfect English custom of dealing with an offender: a Frenchman duels with him: an Englishman ignores him. I feel my own life all the more precious and more dear in the presence of this deflowering of Europe. While it is true that the guns will effect a little useful weeding, I am furious with chagrin to think that the Minds which were to have excelled the civilization of ten thousand years, are being annihilated* – and bodies, the product of aeons of Natural Selection, melted down to pay for political statues. I regret the mortality of the English regulars less than that of the French, Belgian, or even Russian or German armies: because the former are all Tommy Atkins, poor fellows, while the continental armies are inclusive of the finest brains and temperaments of the land.

With the start of September, wounded soldiers began to arrive in Bagnères-de-Bigorre and when, at the end of the month, Owen wrote to Harold, he no longer spoke of 'this deflowering of Europe', still less of 'a little useful weeding'. Under Tailhade's good influence, he rediscovered the natural compassion he had shown for the poor and the suffering at Dunsden.

I went with my friend the Doctor Sauvaître to one of the large hospitals one day last week, where he is operating on the wounded. The hospital is in the buildings of the Boys' *Lycée* and appliances are altogether crude.

---

* He first wrote 'snuffed out'.

First I saw a bullet, like this  cut out of a Zouave's★ leg. Then we did the round of the wards; and saw some fifty German wretches: all more seriously wounded than the French. The Doctor picked out those needing surgical attention; and these were brought on stretchers to the Operating Room; formerly a Class room; with the familiar ink-stains on floor, walls, and ceiling; now a chamber of horrors with blood where the ink was. Think of it: there were eight men in the room at once, Germans being treated without the slightest distinction from the French: one scarcely knew which was which. Considering the lack of appliances – there was only one water-tap in the room – and the crowding – and the fact that the doctors were working for nothing – and on Germans too – really good work was done. Only there were no anaesthetics – no time – no money – no staff for that. So after that scene I need not fear to see the creepiest operations. One

 poor devil had his shin-bone crushed by a gun-carriage-wheel, and the doctor had to twist it about and push it like a piston to get out the pus. Another had a hole right through the knee; and the doctor passed a bandage thus:

Another had a head into which a ball had entered and come out again.

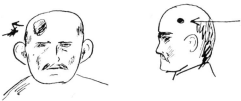

This is how the bullet lay in the Zouave. Sometimes the feet were covered with a brown, scaly, crust – dried blood.

I deliberately tell you all this to educate you to the actualities of the war.[48]

★ Member of the French light-infantry corps, originally formed of Algerians and retaining their uniform.

The transition recorded in the letters of this period, from ignorance to some understanding of the horrors of war, makes its first appearance in his poems with 'Long Ages Past', written on 31 October:

> Long ages past in Egypt thou wert worshipped
> And thou wert wrought from ivory and beryl.
> They brought thee jewels and they brought their slain,
> Thy feet were dark with blood of sacrifice.
> From dawn to midnight, O my painted idol,
> Thou satest smiling, and the noise of killing
> Was harp and timbrel in thy pale jade ears:
> The livid dead were given thee for toys.[49]

The 'good lads' of 'The Ballad of Purchase-Money', whose 'limbs lie cold', are now more accurately seen as 'The livid dead'.

As a farewell present, on 7 September Tailhade gave Owen inscribed copies of Flaubert's *La Tentation de Saint Antoine* and Renan's *Souvenirs d'Enfance et de Jeunesse*[50] and, in return, Owen gave '*son vieil ami*' his old fountain pen.[51] Ten days later, he returned with the Légers to their house in the rue Blanc Dutrouilh and set about looking up friends, reading French literature, and looking for pupils to teach after Madame Léger's departure for Canada. She left for Le Havre on 11 October and Owen at once moved into the house of his friends the Lems.[52] His room had no writing-table, no wardrobe, no drawers, no armchair, and its window overlooked streets loud with the noise of lorries from six a.m., so he was glad to find a quieter room *chez* Veuve Martin, 31 rue Desfourniels. He moved there on 19 October and described it delightedly to his mother:

fine old house – looking on a little square – out of reach of tram-noises, but two minutes from trams – my rooms form a corner – a great window each way – room well carpeted – four armchairs – Louis XV (genuine) bureau – Louis XV Wardrobe – second wardrobe with mirrors modern, Louis XVI, – bed and night-table to match – fine marble fireplace – thirty (supportable) pictures – and – a piano, out of tune, but with-out tone. A Dressing Room leads out of the Chamber: no lack of mirrors and shelves & cupboards – and even a gas-jet is fixed up for my hot-water. This window faces east as every dressing room should, and is blessed with a delightful morning sun. Suppose I help your imagination with a few lines – [53]

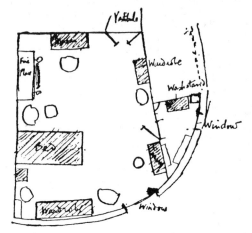

There was some talk of him returning home, but he was now attending free courses at the University and enjoying teaching his own pupils, who ranged from a French Viscount and a Russian professor of mathematics to two boys of eleven and twelve.[54] On 6 November he wrote to his mother:

I heard that Tailhade, together with Anatole France, is shouldering a rifle! Now I *may* be led into enlisting when I get home: so familiarise yourself with the idea! It is a sad sign if *I do*: for it means that I shall consider the continuation of my life of no use to England. And if once my fears are roused for the perpetuity and supremacy of my mother-tongue, in the world – I would not hesitate, as I hesitate now – to enlist.[55]

His hesitations were reinforced by the news of the increasing success of German submarines in the Channel.[56]

Then, on 29 November, he heard of a lady looking for a tutor for her nephews and, going in search of her three days later, took the tram to Mérignac, some miles outside Bordeaux. The aunt, Miss Anne de la Touche, was unfortunately out, but he met the two little boys, Johnny and Bobbie de la Touche. The sons of an official in the Chinese Maritime Customs Service, they and their younger twin brothers Charles and David had been staying with their aunt in her little house at Mérignac when war was declared, and were unable to get back to England. Bobbie and Johnny should have returned to Downside for the autumn term and their aunt, having sent them to the École Ste. Marie in Bordeaux and found it unsatisfactory, was looking for a tutor to succeed a '*ridiculously* English' lady, Miss Patterson.[57] Owen liked the four boys and described them to his mother:

The eldest is thin; but it is his features rather than his health which are delicate. He is pretty rather than handsome. The second is neither; but equally intelligent, and more sensible. The third is David, who gives the appearance of fatness without being so; and bears a really close resemblance to *Harold* at his age – 10 or so. The youngest*is temporarily crippled. One brother threw him down in play, fracturing the pelvis: – $2\frac{1}{2}$ hours operation! Justifies the fragile appearance of the lads. In spite of their speaking French at will, they are all from top to toe, English schoolboys. The jargon they kept up was delicious for me to hear. The good Aunt questioned me about these weird words and their meaning, not having the faintest notion of what means 'clout', topping, etc. etc.[58]

With unconscious irony, in the same letter reviewing the possibility that he might enlist, he tells his mother that what would hold him together on a battlefield would be 'the sense that I was perpetuating the language in which Keats and the rest of them wrote'.

Susan, who had been hoping that he might be back in England for Christmas, was disappointed when in the middle of December he announced his decision to defer his departure for another four weeks. He had been giving lessons to the elder de la Touche boys, but as yet had made no settled arrangement with their aunt. She wanted him to live in Mérignac and look after Bobbie and Johnny in the afternoons, but he was loth to leave Bordeaux and uncertain whether, on the terms offered, he could afford to come into town every day to take his other pupils in the morning. There was the added uncertainty of when the Channel crossing might be pronounced sufficiently safe for Bobbie and Johnny to return to England. At last it was decided that he would live in Mérignac and tutor the boys before returning to England with them on 19 January. Writing to tell his mother that he was to move the following Saturday, he said he was waiting 'to talk over my Future, first with You; and then with a Professor or a Recruiting Sergeant'.[59]

On 19 December he piled his belongings into a four-wheeler,

---

* Charles.

Le Châlet, Mérignac

which half an hour later deposited him in front of the little white-washed bungalow in Mérignac. This had one garret-like upstairs room to which, appropriately, Owen was shown. His window overlooked a spacious garden, with plums, greengages, peaches, and figs, running back to a small wood.[60] Le Châlet itself was far from spacious. It had four principal rooms downstairs: a bedroom for the four brothers, a second bedroom for Miss de la Touche, a dining-room, and a drawing-room which also did service as a bedroom for an invalid, Mlle. de Puységur. There were four servants who lived in an outbuilding, so Owen was able to report to his mother that 'all the good traditions of an English country-house are fully observed'. He would rise at 7.30, when the one man-servant brought him hot water for his bath, and go down to 'a double-egg breakfast, with the boys and their Aunt, who have already been to Mass'. He then took a tram into Bordeaux and, about 9 o'clock, began the day's lessons which lasted the morning and sometimes extended into the afternoon. After these he would return to Mérignac and, fortified with tea and toast, give Bobbie and Johnny their lessons from five o'clock until seven, when dinner was served by the two maids. 'The cook knows her trade,' Owen reported to his mother. 'Magnificent coal-fires warm the cockles of my heart. Moreover a gold box of finest Turkish cigarettes are at my disposal'.[61] After the last boy had been tucked in around nine-thirty, he would have 'a somnolent smoke till about ten with Miss de la Touche, and after that . . . reach out for the nearest book, and ruminate over a few ideas' until bed.[62]

On Christmas Eve he went to Midnight Mass with the family and found it a piquant experience,

all mixed up with candles, incense, acolytes, chasuble and such like. If I didn't *bow*, I certainly *scraped*, for there was an unholy draught. How

Family group at Mérignac, 5 July 1915
Back row, left to right: *the Castéjas girl, Charles, Johnny, Bobbie, Wilfred, David.* Front row: *Mlle Puységur, ? Miss Hall, Miss de la Touche, unidentified, the Castéjas boy*

scandalized would certain of my acquaintance and kin have been to see me. But it would take a power of candlegrease and embroidery to romanize me. The question is to un-Greekize me.[63]

It was three o'clock before they went to bed and lunchtime before they got up on Christmas morning. As he slept, only 500 miles away on the Western Front the guns were silent and carols, their words in English and in German, rose mingling out of the frozen mist. And here and there a Christmas tree spired, like the ghost of some shell-splintered stump, on the battered parapet of a trench. Round these frail symbols of a hope so soon to be extinguished men in domed helmets and spiked helmets drank together and clapped their chilblained hands against the cold.

Unaware of this strange truce, Owen on Christmas afternoon took his charges into Bordeaux to see 'the Soldiers' Christmas Tree' and visit their old school. Meanwhile, the debate about their return to England continued. Early in January, Miss de la Touche asked Owen to stay another three months, but the very next day her brother cabled from China: 'SEND BOYS DOWNSIDE'.

this was a bolt from the Celestial Land which knocked us all on the head. The Aunt is more afraid of going against her brother's will than she is afraid of mines and bombs. Still people here all counsel her to continue the present arrangement, and exaggerate the dangers of crossing.[64]

She wrote to the Headmaster of Downside: 'I have decided to send them by rail via Boulogne–Folkestone accompanied by Mr. Owen. . . . If any sea-trouble arises before the 17th, I have made arrangements with Mr. Owen who will remain here and teach the boys.'

After telling his mother of these developments, Owen turned to a topic that must have surprised her. A businessman friend of his, M. Peyronnet, had called his attention to a recent request by the French Minister for War 'for Tin Articles, since an enormous number of pots and pans are needed for the new recruits', and suggested that this might be a profitable market for a British businessman.

Poor Peyronnet is a Manufacturer of Perfumes, and is mad that Eau de Cologne is not strictly necessary in the trenches. His friends, the Bootmaker, the Bicycle-Maker, etc. having Gov. Contracts, are making piles.

Why not his friend the nephew of the English Metal Merchant. Let Father act *immediately*: repeating my words to Uncle.[65]

The 'Merchant Prince' Edward Quayle evidently found this a resistable proposition and his nephew was spared the indignity of becoming a War Profiteer.

One of his pupils, 'The Marine Insurance Agent', told him on 13 January 'that twelve Zeppelins were careering over the Channel, while sixteen Aviatiks were about to spring across the Straits'.[66] He took this news to Miss de la Touche and, at her request, went again to ask the advice of Mr. Rowley,[67] the British Consul, as to whether or not the Channel crossing ought to be attempted. Understandably, Mr. Rowley was not prepared to commit himself either way, but one piece of advice he did offer: that Owen should consider entering the consular service.

He says it would mean a coach, and a sojourn in Spain (for another language), but that the appointments really depended on a '*Tea-Party Examination*' with the Foreign Secretary or one such. Mr. Rowley himself has £600. a year. This must be considered, as the age limits are something like 23–28. What must no longer be considered is the Assistant Elementary Certificated or Un-Certificated Schoolmaster. One of the wisest steps in my life was the one I didn't take (I am with Irish people) in 1911, namely hanging back from what the P.T.'s called 'College'. 'What you want' said John Bulman to me, 'Is a course in the University of Life'. I have taken that Course, and my diplomas are sealed with many secret seals. . . .[68]

He must have realized how perplexed his parents must have been by his continually changing plans and, early in February, his departure again postponed, he wrote to reassure his mother:

I seem without a footing on life; but I have one. It is as bold as any, and I have kept it for years. For years now. I was a boy when I first realized that the fullest life liveable was a Poets. And my later experiences ratify it.[69]

He was, however, painfully aware of having little so far to show for his six months in France.

As for Poetry, I have let the cares of this life, Indolence, Time, and 'No-Time' do their worst. All winter, all last year and longer I have read no poetry, nor thought poetically (at least not by act of will). Neither have I reasoned seriously, or felt deeply on 'matters of faith'. Thus have I sown my wild oats, that my harvest of poppies may be the more abundant, poppies wherewith many dreams may be fed, and many sores be medicined. . . .[70]

His letters of this period show no great interest in the progress, or lack of progress of the War, except insofar as it affected the crossing of the Channel. As 'the stunning guns' pounded the waterlogged trenches of the Western Front, Owen and the boys were shooting game in the grounds of the Château Foucastel, near Mérignac,[71] or studying the Roman Occupation of Britain.[72] He taught them English, History, Arithmetic, Geography, and Latin, and it is clear that he taught them well, if in the authoritarian manner against which Harold had rebelled. When his pupils gave him trouble, he would give them 'lines' or send them to bed,[73] and on one occasion beat David with the flat of a ruler for disobeying his instructions not to touch the fruit in the Orangery of the Château du Parc.[74] Miss de la Touche thought the method and manner of his teaching were 'most interesting', and the boys' father wrote to her in April:

J'ai reçu il y a quelques temps le rapport de Mr. Owen, rapport montrant que c'est un garçon qui voit juste et clairement. Avec cela, étant un garçon encore très jeune, il manque d'indulgence dans son appréciation. C'est une qualité qui vient avec l'âge. Les jeunes gens jugent sévèrement parce qu'ils manquent d'expérience. En somme son rapport et fort juste. . . . Mr. Owen blame Johnny de préférer de guetter un moineau sur un arbre que de s'appliquer à sa leçon.[75]

As befitting his fatherly role, he read the boys *Uncle Remus* and in their games they called him Brer Fox.★

On 13 March he went down with what was first diagnosed as influenza and then as 'Diphtheric Throat', but was better by Easter Sunday, when he accompanied his 'darling little acolytes'† to 'High Mass: real, genuine Mass, with candle, with book, and with bell, and

---

★ See above, p. 35. Charles La Touche still has the Mérignac copy of *Uncle Remus* by Joel Chandler Harris (1848–1908).

† *CL*, p. 311; c.f. line 10 of 'Maundy Thursday' below.

all like abominations of desolation'.[76] Shortly afterwards, he again retired to bed, this time with Roseola, or Scarlet Rash, and once more treated his Mahim audience to a colourful account of his symptoms. From this, too, he recovered quickly; and when Miss de la Touche, 'supported by a French Admiral, her brother, her sister, her solicitor, all her Friends, and the whole population of Mérignac',[77] again decided to defer the boys' departure for England, he realized that he must return by himself. She was still pressing him to stay, but he was anxious for some time at home in which to devote himself to

certain writings. . . . For this a month or so of seclusion is indispensable. Gardening, sketching, photography, writing for magazines may very well thrive on spare effort in odd times; but a Poem does not grow by jerks. If it is to be worth a place in Human Time, it must be worth more than fag-ends of the Poet's time. A patch-work counterpane or a ship full-rigged – in a bottle, may be perfectly fabricated off-an'-on, between-whiles, casual, like. But Poetry, 'coming naturally as leaves to a tree',[78] grows as incessantly and as delicately. And as trees in Spring produce a new ring of tissue, so does every poet put forth a fresh, and lasting outlay of stuff at the same season.[79]

On the afternoon of 15 April he met and interviewed a genial Welsh 'public school man', Mr. Bonsall, and in due course it was arranged that, while Owen was in England, Mr. Bonsall would take Bobbie and Johnny for Latin and Greek three times a week.[80] And so, on 18 May, he at last crossed the Channel and took the train to London, where he booked a room at Cranston's Waverley Hotel in Southampton Row. Rupert Brooke and Julian Grenfell had died almost certainly without his having heard their names, but he thought he saw Rudyard Kipling at a meeting in the Guildhall organized by the Central Committee for National Patriotic Organizations. He spent the best part of a week in London discharging a commission for M. Peyronnet, the scent manufacturer, at the British Industries Fair, and then returned to Shrewsbury and the comforts of Mahim: days at his desk in the attic, evenings round the family fire.

We have no way of knowing whether in those weeks of seclusion, his poetry came 'naturally as leaves to a tree', but it would seem possible that he then wrote one of the most striking of his early poems:

Maundy Thursday.

Between the brown hands of a server-lad
The silver cross was offered to be kissed.
The men came up, lugubrious, but not sad,
And knelt reluctantly, half-prejudiced.
(And
(These kissing, kissed the emblem of a creed.)
                                          had
Then mourning women knelt; meek mouths they ^,
(And
(These kissed the Body of the Christ indeed.)
Your
And? children came, with eager lips and glad.
(These kissed a silver doll, immensely bright.)
Then I, too, knelt before that acolyte.
Above the crucifix I bent my head:
The Christ was thin, and cold, and very dead:
And yet I bowed, yea, kissed - my lips did cling
(I kissed the warm ~~soft~~ hand that held the
              live   thing.)

The opposition of the Christ figure, 'thin, cold, and very dead', with 'the warm live hand', and the final dismissive noun 'that held the *thing*', give this sonnet a brilliantly shocking conclusion. Its tone and general level of sophistication suggest a date later than the Dunsden period, to which the editor of the *Collected Poems* tentatively assigned it.[81] Moreover, the Roman Catholic service it describes, 'the Veneration of the Cross' (on Good Friday, incidentally, not Maundy Thursday,) is most likely one that Wilfred attended with the de la Touche boys the previous Easter.

He was back in London again, to lunch with Leslie Gunston, on 11 June and two days later crossed in fine weather from Folkestone to Le Havre. He 'had time for an evening promenade in Paris',[82] and arrived in Bordeaux early enough on the 14th to find himself 'a spacious, high-ceilinged apartment, with a balcony overlooking the Cathedral'.[83] His Mérignac room was wanted, but he was happy to exchange it for this at 18 rue Beaubadat with its

wardrobe, marble mantelpiece, & handsome mirror, hanging-curtain-wardrobe, a vast writing-desk, beautiful old round table, marble washstand, two armchairs, desk-chair, etc. wall-paper an unfortunate colour; & in design like ten thousand cabbages, over-boiled, and partly digested: – clean, however.

A few days later, he moved to another room one floor lower and, in a letter to his mother, returned to a theme that was to recur with increasing frequency over the coming months:

I noticed in the Hotel in London an announcement that any gentleman (fit etc.) *returning to England from abroad* will be given a Commission – in the 'Artists' Rifles'. Such officers will be sent to the front in 3 months. . . . I don't want the bore of training, I don't want to wear khaki; nor yet to save my honour before inquisitive grand-children fifty years hence. But I *now do* most *intensely want to fight.*[84]

M. Peyronnet, who was pleased with Owen's work at the British Industries Fair, was anxious for him to travel in the East as representative of his perfume company, but realized that such a tour could not be undertaken until the Dardanelles campaign, launched on 25 April, had come to an end. Wilfred hoped that 'things there will last out as long as the war, which will be through the winter'. Reading Hilaire Belloc's *Hills and the Sea* ten days later, he came upon

this passage of De Vigny: *If any man despairs of becoming a Poet, let him carry his pack and march in the ranks.*[85]

Now I don't despair of becoming a Poet: 'Before Abraham was, I am'
so to speak [*one line illegible*]
    Will you set about finding the address of the 'Artists' Rifles'. . . .[86]

Amid his martial reflections he had time to write a peaceable poem,
which he sent to his cousin Leslie:

Now, let me feel the feeling of thy hand —
For it is softer than the breasts of girls,
And warmer than the ~~fat~~ pillows of their cheeks,
And richer than the fulness of their eyes,
And stronger than the ardour of their hearts.

Its shape is subtler than a dancer's limbs;
Its skin is° coloured like the twilight Alp,
And odoured like the ~~large~~ pale, night-scented flowers,
And fresh with early love, as earth with dawn.

Yield me thy hand a little while, fair love;
That I may feel it; and so feel thy life,
And kiss across it, as the sea the sand,
And love it, with the love of Sun and Earth.

An anticipation of 'From my Diary',* this would seem to be
addressed to a man, whose hand 'is softer than the breasts of girls',

* See below, p. 211.

and it is interesting to see how the decorously veiled sentiments of the poem are at variance with language as specifically physical as Keats's. Long before he was horror-struck by violent death and mutilation in the trenches, he was strongly aware of hands, breasts, cheeks, eyes, hearts, limbs.

Though he was no longer living at Mérignac, Owen was continuing to give Johnny and Bobbie lessons; as was Mr. Bonsall, who was 'rather too lax with their discipline; and generally works under the plum-trees of the garden'.[88] The boys, it is clear, preferred the more genial, easy-going older man, although their aunt declared that 'he had no manners'. The well-mannered Owen was at this time increasingly preoccupied with his own affairs, notably the question of enlistment. At one moment he contemplated joining the French Army and Harold recalls a letter, which has not survived, that read something like this:

If I do decide my only proper course is to fight, or more likely in some sleepless dawn a cock starts crowing and with it I commence denial (something which will not be easy to live with) I shall have no compunction about enlisting in the French Army, if they will have me. This I should like much better, I would at least escape the English Sergeants. Everything, even insults (my inefficient fumblings with a rifle will surely bring these down upon me) will be much more bearable in French – after all they will even increase my vocabulary – I shall remain here until I decide what I must do. I have the feeling that France will help me to know what I ought to do, and from her soil I shall receive the conviction, that I so much wish for, that to stay out of it all will be wrong. But I am determined to think for myself and act only when I know which road I must take. Thank goodness Colin is only fourteen – or shall we end by enlisting children?'[89]

In mid-July he had decided against the French Army but, concerned that a Commission in the Artists' Rifles 'might be a long time in coming',[90] he was thinking he would 'like to join the Italian Cavalry; for reasons both aesthetic and poetical'. Italy, after much bargaining with the Allies and the Germans, had declared war on Austria–Hungary on 23 May. Owen soon cooled towards the idea of the Italian Army, as towards that of the French, and gradually he warmed to a vision of himself in the Artists' Rifles: 'Lord Leighton,

Millais, Forbes Robertson', he told his mother, 'were in Artists' Rifles!!'* Even now, however, the War seemed very remote:

I want to visit the battlefield of Castillon, where, in 1453 Talbot Earl of Shrewsbury suffered the defeat which lost Guienne and Bordeaux to the English for ever.† I can't understand it, but this battlefield will interest me as much as the field of the Marne; – and I am reading a tale of the Punic Wars with more interest than the Communiqués.[91]

At the same time he told Leslie Gunston:

I don't imagine that the German War will be affected by my joining in, but I know my own future Peace will be. I wonder that you don't ply me with this argument: that Keats remained absolutely indifferent to Waterloo and all that commotion.[92]

Meanwhile, the brilliant weather continued unbroken. He was stunned by the blazing heat as by strong music; he read *The Prisoner of Zenda*,[93] roamed the woods of Mérignac and remembered Broxton;[94] and went to an open-air performance of Jean Richepin and Xavier Le Roux's opera *The Tramp*.[95] On 12 August he received from his mother a copy of *War Poems from the Times*, a supplement published by *The Times* two days before. It contained 'Wake up, England' by Robert Bridges, Poet Laureate; 'Song of the Soldiers' by Thomas Hardy; 'For all we Have and Are' by Rudyard Kipling; 'For the Fallen' by Laurence Binyon; 'The Battle of the Bight' by William Watson; 'Called Up' by Dudley Clark; 'Gods of War' by A.E.; 'Into Battle' by Julian Grenfell; 'The Trumpet' by Rabindranath Tagore; 'Resolve' by F. E. Maitland; 'The Search-Lights' by Alfred Noyes; 'The King's Highway' by Henry Newbolt; 'Invocation' by Robert Nichols; 'Happy England' by Walter de la Mare; 'Expeditional' by C. W. Brodribb; and 'August, 1914' 'by the

---

* Frederic, Baron Leighton (1830–96), President of the Royal Academy 1878–1896. Sir John Everett Millais (1829–96). Originator in 1848, with Holman Hunt, of the Pre-Raphaelite Movement; President of the Royal Academy in the year of his death. Sir Johnston Forbes-Robertson (1853–1937), actor and theatrical manager.

† The English army under John Talbot, 1st Earl of Shrewsbury (*c.* 1388–1453), heavily outnumbered, was defeated and its commander killed at Castillon, thirty miles east of Bordeaux. This was the last campaign of the Hundred Years War.

author of *Charitessi*'. Each poem was framed by a drawing by Joseph Simpson. In a postcard to Leslie Gunston Owen commented: 'Newbolt's and Clark's splendid! Watson, Binyon all right! Tagore interesting. But who on earth are Maitland, de la Mare etc?'[96]

With that supplement in his luggage and Bobbie and Johnny in tow, he finally, on 14 September, after numerous last-minute changes of plan, took leave of his friends in Bordeaux and boarded a Channel ferry.

6

TRAINING

Arriving in London, Wilfred Owen booked rooms for himself and the boys at the Regent Palace Hotel in a blacked-out Piccadilly. The following day they went to Paddington but, finding there was no connection from Bath to Downside, returned to the hotel and in the evening walked round Whitehall and Westminster looking for Zeppelin raiders. None however appeared. Next day Owen saw Bobbie and Johnny off to Downside and himself caught a train to Shrewsbury. There, for a month, he worked in his attic room and enjoyed his last days of freedom while, across the Channel, the last convulsions of the battle of Loos claimed 50,000 British casualties in 21 days.[1]

In the middle of October he took leave of his parents, Colin, and Mary (Harold was at sea), and made the familiar journey to Reading and Kidmore End. There, on 15 October, Olwen Joergens, the daughter of an artist neighbour of the Gunstons, came to tea. A slight, dreamy girl of nineteen, she too was a poet and, indeed, was to see her work between printed covers before either of the cousins.[2] The following day, Owen visited the office of Mr. Cummings, the architect who designed Alpenrose and to whom Leslie was now articled; and that afternoon had another literary tea, this time with Professor Edith Morley, whose advice and encouragement had meant so much to him when he was at Dunsden. The following week he was back in London where, on Wednesday 20 October, he made his way to the Headquarters of the Artists' Rifles in Duke's Road to undergo a second medical examination (the doctor having failed to sign his papers the first time), which he passed. He must have been pleasantly surprised that no fault was found with his sight. That afternoon he spent looking for lodgings, and was delighted to find a room – for 35s. a week and only two minutes from Duke's Road – in 'a French Boarding House, where Guests, Conversation, Cooking and everything else is French'.[3] '*Les Lilas*', as it was called, was in Tavistock Square, 'a replica of every other Bloomsbury Square; wadded with fog; skeletons of dismal trees behind the palings; but the usual west-end pervasion of ghostly aristocracy'. Another more companionable ghost haunting the railings of this square was that of Dickens, who had lived in Tavistock House from 1850 to 1856 and there written *Bleak House* and *Hard Times*.[4]

After lunch on Thursday 21st he returned to the Duke's Road Headquarters and, with two other recruits, was sworn in. They had to read the oath together. The others, he told his mother, 'were horribly nervous! and read the wrong Paragraph until the Captain stopped them! "Kiss the Book!" says Captain. One gives it a tender little kiss; the other a loud smacking one!!' He was then given a number – 4756 – and a typhoid inoculation, and left the building in high spirits at the prospect of three and a half days sick-leave and the entertainment he had in mind for that evening. After dark he walked through Bloomsbury to Devonshire Street, a narrow cutting off Theobalds Road. It was a slum district which the police paraded in pairs, but outside number 35, keeping the street's three pub-signs company, swung the sign of the Poetry Bookshop. Opened by Harold Monro almost three years before, it occupied the ground floor of a three-storied building crowned by a classical pediment, with two dormer windows peering over the top.[5] *The Poetry Review* had its offices on the first floor, the second was used for poetry readings, and at the top of the house were two small attics, which were rented to needy artists and writers. Behind the shop's old-fashioned window, its small panes filled with poetry books and broadsides, lay a large room. Monro had

called in Romney Green to provide bookshelves, tables and settles in his characteristic style – massive but finely proportioned furniture hewn from great baulks of oak. It added to the homeliness of the shop, and with its

Harold Monro and customer in the Poetry Bookshop

flavour of *rus in urbe* suggested the character of the proprietor. Literary reviews were spread on tables, the bookshelves were unglazed. . . . A coal fire in winter and, later, the occasional presence of Monro's cat and Mrs. Monro's dogs completed the impression of intimacy and domesticity.[5]

There, or in one of the comfortable panelled rooms upstairs, a poetry reading was held in the evening of 21 October. A week later Harold Monro himself read and Owen, recovered now from the effects of inoculation, talked with him afterwards.[6]

By then he had had his first taste of drill under the eye of a sergeant whom he immediately liked and respected, and soon afterwards was writing to his mother:

I have scarcely seen an officer. All our instruction is done by sergeants, who are as chummy between times as they are smart on parade. Impossible to get them out of temper. One is a rare wag, and gives plenty of exercise to the Risible Muscles. I never felt devotion, and not much respect, for any authority or individual in this world since I left the 3rd form of the Institute; but I am beginning again under these fellows. Astonishing what a changed meaning has a Captain or a Colonel for me. If a Major-General approached me I think I should fall down dead. We had to practise Salutes (on Trees) this very morning.[7]

Though he was bored by the constant polishing of badges and buttons, and nauseated by having to fill his boots with Castor Oil (to soften the leather), he had already rediscovered his schoolboy pleasure in dressing up when, on 2 November, he wrote to his mother:

If only this Life went on indefinitely I should be well pleased. It is really no great strain to strut round the gardens of a West-end square for six or seven hours a day. Walking abroad, one is the admiration of all little boys, and meets an approving glance from every of eld. I sometimes amuse myself by sternly contemplating the civilian dress of apparent Slackers. They return a shifty enough expression. When I clamp-clump-clamp-clumped into the Poetry Bookshop on Thursday, the poetic ladies were not a little surprised.[8]

The reading on that occasion was from the works of Rabindranath Tagore, 'by a lady without much insight into the Hindu spirit'. Harold Monro was there and smiled sadly at Owen's khaki.

It had become clear by this time that 35s. a week was more than he could afford on a private's pay and, at the beginning of November, he took a room – at 5s. 6d. a week – opposite the Poetry Bookshop at 21 Devonshire Street. He had barely moved in, however, before his battalion★ was posted to Hare Hall Camp, Gidea Park, Essex, and he had to exchange the comfort of his candle-lit room for a rowdy barrack hut. The work was hard but, for the most part, he enjoyed it and insisted that he was 'splendidly well! and happy (after 4.30 p.m.)'.[9] Soon he was talking of Christmas leave, but here his hopes were dashed. Christmas Day found him in a hut festooned with decorations, where '"it snowed of meats and drinks." One Wiggins, a noted gourmand made all manner of custards & jellies; and

---

★ Unlike other armies, the British Regular infantry fought by battalions, not by regiments. It was not until Territorial and New Army formations entered the field that battalions of the same regiment were frequently to be found brigaded together. A brigade consisted of four battalions until, in 1918, it was reduced to three. In 1914, a battalion consisted of a Battalion H.Q., and four companies, each of four platoons, numbered throughout the battalion 1 to 16. Each platoon consisted of four sections. The fighting strength of a strong battalion was about 800 men.

Donaldson's turkeys were *a point*. Healths *were* drunk but none among us were.'[10] Just as he was cracking his last nut, a Boy Scout friend arrived to take him off to a second Christmas Dinner at his parents' house, after which they all played charades.

He was back with his own family for the New Year and, returning from that leave, was astonished to be offered a commission in the Lancashire Fusiliers, who were on the point of going to France. As he had not yet fired his musketry course, he declined the offer.[11] A fortnight later this course began, but an outbreak of measles then swept the camp, emptying half the beds in his hut. He escaped with nothing worse than a cold but, at a throat inspection early in February, he was told he had 'a granulated pharynx. (2 or 3 lumps on the back wall)' and advised to have them removed. This he did, a few days later.

Shortly before Christmas, Private P. E. Thomas 4229 of the Artists' Rifles arrived at the camp; and there over the coming months, when not giving map-reading lessons on Hampstead Heath, wrote such of his finest poems as 'Rain', 'And You, Helen', and 'Like the Touch of Rain'.[12] It is hard to believe that Edward Thomas and Wilfred Owen never set eye on each other, but virtually certain that they never met. One, however, was aware of the other's existence for, while in Essex, Owen bought a copy of Thomas's *Keats*.

Sometime between the middle of November and the end of February, Harold wrote to ask whether, on one of his short leaves, he might visit Hare Hall camp. Wilfred replied: 'Yes do come . . . a sailor is always welcome among the soldiery',[13] and instructed him with some vehemence not to come in uniform because he wanted to show him round the camp, passing him off as a new recruit. For some time he had secretly envied Harold his experience of living rough in the navy, and was anxious now that he should see 'the state of squalor, unwanted company, and muddy duck-boards in which he had to exist'. It was raining when they met at the camp gates and, after Harold had been shown Hut 6a, he was taken off to lunch in the Mess.

Looking around at the other two or three dozen powerful-looking young men surrounding us in noisy clamour my heart smote me, Wilfred looked so out of place. I noticed as well a constraint and reserve which set him apart from the others. This too bothered me. In the general boisterousness, however, I was relieved to see that this passed without any special notice from the other young soldiers; indeed as the meal went on I found myself admiring tremendously the clever way he was building up a protective barrier around himself but at the same time with great skill avoiding isolation. I cheered up a lot, especially when he and I were being drawn into the general raillery of the conversation, as I saw how competent he was, even witty, when answering back and I was quite delighted when I heard him shouting retorts in the best private's tradition in answer to the inescapable banalities.

Lunch over, Wilfred led me along to the canteen, and here gave me fresh surprise by struggling through the crowd of soldiers, fighting his way to the bar and coming back with two huge mugs of strong beer. I remember so well the mingled look of triumph and diffidence that illuminated his face. The triumph came of course from his successful struggle to get the beer at all, the diffidence came from something different altogether: it sprang from his uncomfortable awareness that his action in procuring the beer, entailing as it did the proposal that we should drink together was, he most uncomfortably knew, a violent rebellion against family tradition. . . .

Seeking each other with our eyes we raised our clumsy canteen mugs and for the first time in our lives silently drank to each other.

When the mugs were empty, Wilfred walked Harold round the camp and astonishing him by saying that he did not expect to pass the 'passing out' examination. His brother, who could not imagine him failing any exam that required nothing more than hard work and commonsense, remonstrated with him and was stunned by his passionate reply:

'What does Keats have to teach me of rifle and machine-gun drill, how will my pass in Botany teach me to lunge a bayonet, how will Shelley show me how to hate or any poet teach me the trajectory of the bullet?' Giving me his twisted smile, he turned and said, 'I must run; or, if I am to pass this bloody exam, I must learn to say double. Be outside the gates at five o'clock.'

Harold returned to find Wilfred in a better humour and agreed to the suggestion that they should walk into town for supper. He was surprised, however, to be lectured all the way on the importance of being a good host. By the time that Wilfred's monologue had traced this subject back to the pre-Christian era Harold was thoroughly bored, but he cheered up when, on reaching the town, his lecturer took his arm and said:

'Now having prepared you well theoretically, I shall at once proceed to give you a practical demonstration of the perfect host: I propose you shall be my guest for dinner this evening. There is quite a reasonable hotel here and from now on, understand, you are in my hands.'

The practical demonstration began well enough. A table had been reserved and the meal, served by a pleasant little waitress, was good. It was eaten, however, to the tune of another topic of conversation not of Harold's choosing – that of his life at sea, which Wilfred assumed to be profligate, and the need for him to save money. With some asperity, Harold told him it was all he could do to live on his meagre pay, and was tempted to add that *he* received no allowance from home. His host, realizing that he was failing to practice what he preached, at once broke off his sermon and called for half a bottle of port. As they were sipping this, he said suddenly:

'D'you remember, Harold, how cross I was with you a year or so ago when we were discussing our ancestry and you told me that you thought Mother, generations ago, must have had a cruel Welsh Puritan preacher in her forbears and that Father, from an equal date, must be descended from a musician – a Welsh harpist perhaps?' . . .

While we were finishing our port we discussed our ancestry further; it was something which absorbed us both in those years. This led us on until we were talking rather naughtily about what fun it would be sometime to get Father out one night and to do him really well and see what the effect would be. . . .

Wilfred signalled for his bill and while he was waiting for it said:

'I am going to cap your puritanical preacher and harpist ancestors, and substitute a buccaneering pirate and an old-maid but that is impossible – or is it – with darling little Mother nothing is impossible no, I think it quite possible – we'll discuss it next time we meet.'

Even the port and his brother's uncharacteristic levity had not prepared Harold for what was to follow: another walk and this time with Helen, their little waitress. It was a fine night and their small-talk, after a slow start, began to quicken as Harold, with his painter's eye for such things, called the girl's attention to the stars set in a silhouette of foliage and reflected in the surface of a stream. He then began to notice that his brother, who had been contributing less and less to the conversation, was lagging behind. He slowed his step to let him catch up. This happened again, and again, until finally Harold told Helen to wait while he went back to see what was wrong. Failing to find him in the darkness, he called out.

Somewhere out of the dark trees Wilfred's voice called back, 'You go on, I am not coming with you.' 'Are you all right?' I called. 'Yes, I am quite all right, but I am going back to the hotel; I must be in Camp by midnight but shall be in the hotel until eleven o'clock if you are back by then.' I called again and yet again but could get no answer. Wilfred had gone.

Angry and embarrassed, Harold returned to Helen and found her, to his surprise, less perplexed and perturbed than he had expected. It emerged that Wilfred, whom she knew only slightly but liked for his quiet ways, had told her of his seafaring brother and asked her if she would go out with them 'to be more cheerful company for [him] than he himself was likely to be'. Harold's anger and embarrassment were hardly removed by this and, after an unsuccessful attempt to resuscitate the topics of their earlier small-talk, he walked her home and hurried back to the hotel. He found Wilfred reading in an armchair and let his pent-up fury thunder round his close-cropped head, to the embarrassment of a gaggle of old ladies who hastily withdrew. Momentarily distracted by their flight, Harold paused in his tirade long enough for Wilfred to interject sardonically something to the effect that he thought sailors liked amusement and feminine company and never missed an opportunity to gain them. Harold replied hotly, asking him whether he thought that someone who had had the run of the brothels of Valparaiso and Buenos Aires was likely to be amused by the entertainment he had provided. His outburst alarmed his brother so much that he asked him to swear that he *hadn't* sunk as low as he had said. When Harold again retorted angrily, Wilfred asked him whether he hadn't realized that this was simply an 'experiment' of his; and was he so ignorant that he didn't know that for centuries in the life of mankind no hospitality was ever complete without the provision of feminine society?

They realized then that the evening was likely to end even more disastrously if they did not hurry, for the bus that was to take

Wilfred back to camp would be leaving in a few minutes. Racing down the street, they reached the bus-stop just in time for Wilfred to undo his coat and tunic, which in his haste he had buttoned up on the wrong buttons, and do them up correctly before clambering aboard. His white face smiled wanly from a window as the bus roared away into the night.

Towards the end of February, to his great delight, he was ordered to attend a ten days' course in London and allowed to find his own lodgings.[14] He headed, like a homing pigeon, for the Poetry Book-shop and was lucky enough to find one of the attic rooms vacant. Although there was barely enough space for the bed, and the sloping ceiling made standing difficult – even for a man only 5 ft. $5\frac{1}{2}$ ins tall – few rooms in London would have pleased Wilfred more. He was glad, too, to be able to introduce Harold to the Poetry Bookshop one evening after supper. They had another meeting in London some-time later, when both had a few hours' leave. It was cold and pouring with rain and they decided to take shelter in a picture palace. Just as Harold was settling down to enjoy the film, he began to notice, with mounting embarrassment, that Wilfred was shuffling his feet in a way that was disturbing his neighbours. He was on the point of giving him a dig in the ribs, when he

noticed he had stopped the awful fidgeting and had got his head down somewhere between his knees; not without genuine alarm now, I investigated more closely and saw with amused horror that he was engaged – most ineptly – in a losing struggle to remove his heavy army boots. Fascinated now, too fascinated even to remonstrate, I could only peer down to try to find out exactly what was happening. Presently off came one boot; carefully putting this to one side he continued his tussle with the other; hypnotized now I could only sit and watch, and wait to see what else was going to happen. With a final wrench, off came the other one. A pause followed this triumph and I was just beginning to think Wilfred was going to settle down and keep still, when stooping down once more he started the fumbling about again. In a second or two I saw gleaming up from the darkness of the floor a bare foot and as another wet sock was dragged off another white foot came to light to join its mate. Straightening himself up once more he proceeded with enormous care to wring out the socks; having done this he put one in each of his tunic pockets. Lifting up one foot and placing the heel of it on the edge of his seat, he pulled out a large khaki handkerchief and with this commenced to dry his ankle, foot, and toes, meticulously adding a little massage from time to time; this process was repeated with the other foot. By now the film had lost its appeal for our immediate neighbours; they like me could only look on with unconcealed astonishment and irresistible attraction. The drying procedure satisfactorily completed, Wilfred rose up, pulled the socks from out of his pockets, turned around, and laid them carefully on the seat. This done he sat down on them and pulled out a packet of Gold Flake. After giving me one with his fingers, he lit one for himself; I could see by the flare of his match that his face wore a bright relieved smile. Settling back in great contentment he was obviously quite prepared to enjoy both his cigarette and the remainder of the film, while his socks dried out underneath him. . . .

Suddenly I knew what it was that worried me so much – Wilfred was afraid. Yet again I was assailed with the unhappy feeling that in spite of his four and a half years' seniority, I was really the elder of us two. . . . A flush of tenderness spread through me as I realized with a pang how physically unsophisticated, almost helpless he seemed. My attention became completely withdrawn from the picture, I could feel only a desperate sort of protective urge towards him, not pity – he never engendered that – but a compelling wish that I might somehow help this hunched-up little figure sitting next to me, so quietly now. . . .

When I saw the picture was coming to an end I nudged Wilfred and pointed to his bare feet. Giving me one of his rare full smiles, with a look of great surprise he peered down at them and then up at me; fumbling about between himself and the seat he brought out the wretched socks, tested them with great care for dryness, nodded to himself as if satisfied and bending down commenced the complicated process of getting them, the boots, and the puttees back again. Glancing down I saw that he was not being very good at this, so I got down on my knees to help him as best I could. We only just managed to secure the puttee ends haphazardly before God Save The King.[15]

To Owen's chagrin he saw nothing of Harold Monro until, at eleven o'clock on his last night in London, Monro came up to the attic and said he was 'very struck' with some sonnets Owen had left for him. He went over them in detail and told Owen

what was fresh and clever, and what was second-hand and banal; and what Keatsian, and what 'modern'.

He summed up their value as far above that of the Little Books of Georgian Verse.[16]

Telling his mother of this important meeting, he added a puzzled afterthought: 'The curious part is that he applauded precisely those phrases which Prof. Morley condemned!'

When he returned to Romford, it was not to Hut 6a but to the Officers' School at Balgores House, which was 'far less comfortable than the Hut'. The house was overcrowded and, although the cadets had such officer-comforts as batmen and 'a Mess Room with table-cloths, properly set out', there was no bathroom and they had to sleep on the floor. The work was hard, their day beginning with drill or a lecture at 6.30 a.m. and ending with a period of cleaning, polishing, and preparations for the next day, from 7.30–9.30 p.m. Army life, he told his mother,

is a curious anomaly; here we are prepared – or preparing – to lay down our lives for another, the highest moral act possible, according to the Highest Judge, and nothing of this is apparent between the jostle of discipline and jest. Again, we turn from the meanest of jobs scrubbing floors, to do delicate mapping, and while staying in for being naughty, we study the abstractions of Military Law.

On the whole, I am fortunate to be where I am, and happy sometimes, as when I think it is a life pleasing to you & Father and the Fatherland.[17]

Despite the fears expressed to Harold, the results of his exams were satisfactory. He did well in musketry, reconnaissance, and drill – for which he got full marks – and only in military law did he do badly. The Drum and Fife Band of the Artists' Rifles he found 'thrilling', and on the night of 1 April was an excited spectator of an enemy Zeppelin's escape from shell-fire and searchlights.[18]

Early in May he sat his final exam, and on the 19th left Romford on 'Leave pending Gazette', which he spent first in London and then in Shrewsbury. On 4 June he was 'gazetted' as 2nd Lieutenant in the 5th Battalion of the Manchester Regiment, which he joined at Milford Camp, near Witley in Surrey, a fortnight later. The next day he gave his mother his first impressions of his platoon:

The generality of men are hard-handed, hard-headed miners, dogged, loutish, ugly. (But I would trust them to advance under fire and to hold their trench;) blond, coarse, ungainly, strong, 'unfatigueable', unlovely, Lancashire soldiers, Saxons to the bone. . . .

My most irksome duty is acting Taskmaster while the tired fellows dig:

The Officers of the 5th (reserve) Manchester Regiment, Witley Camp, July 1916.
Owen is in the front row, second from the right

the most pleasant is marching home over the wild country at the head of my platoon, with a flourish of trumpets, and an everlasting roll of drums.[19]

No sooner had he settled in, than he was despatched on a musketry course to Aldershot, from which he escaped, one weekend, to Reading. On the Sunday he went over to Dunsden, where

the Vicar was as horrifyingly dismal in Church as ever – and as merry at the Porch! 'The war will be over very soon' he proclaimed, just in the Pulpit manner. 'Bray has been called up. Couldn't do without him after all, you see.'[20]

He returned to Witley at the end of July, but a few days later was sent to another musketry camp outside Aldershot, this time in charge of forty-five men from the 5th Battalion the Manchester Regiment and two junior officers. He finished the course a First Class Shot (shades of his father's fairground training) and, in the middle of August, returned to Shrewsbury on leave.

The train that, on the 21st, bore him from Tom Owen's neo-Gothic station, deposited him at Tamworth with an hour to spend before he caught his connection to Romford, so he walked into town to look up his 'old friend Lord Marmion'.* Under 'a low, glamorous Moon . . . [he] found Tamworth Castle, and was informed by the policeman that Lord Marmion had lorded it there'.[21] His new allegiances had not supplanted the old and, seriously though he took his military duties, he was still finding time to read books other than the *Manual of Military Law*. In August he bought Housman's *A Shropshire Lad* and Tennyson's *Tiresias*, and both at Romford and Witley worked on poems of his own.

The earliest surviving from this period would seem to be a sonnet whose one extant manuscript is dated 'May 10, 1916./London':

To —

Three rompers run together, hand in hand.
The middle boy stopped short, the others hurtle:
What bumps, what shrieks, what laughter turning turtle
For Love, racing between us two, has planned
A sudden mischief: shortly he will stand
And we shall shock. We cannot help but fall,
What matter? Why, it will hurt at all,
Our youth is supple, and the ground is sand.

Better our lips should bruise our eyes, than He
Rude Love, out-run our breath; you pant, and I,
I cannot run much farther; mind that we,
Both laugh with Love; and having tumbled, try
To forever children, hand in hand.
The ... is rising.,. and the world is sand.

---

* They hailed him Lord of Fontenaye,
　　Of Lutterward and Scrivelbaye,
　　　Of Tamworth tower and town.
　　　　Sir Walter Scott, *Marmion*, Canto I, 157–9.

This is almost certainly a recollection of a day with the de la Touche boys. He had told his mother in July that he would part 'with three of them regretfully, with two of them sorrowfully, and with one of them very sorrowfully indeed'.[22] Eros who, rather than Venus, is the deity presiding over Owen's early poems of passion suppressed, makes a further appearance in one draft of the sonnet 'Purple':

> Purest, it is the diamond dawn of spring;
> And yet the veil of Venus; whose rose skin,
> Mauve-marbled, purpled Eros' mouth for sacred sin.[23]

This manuscript fair copy is dated 'Sept: 1916', but its diction is so second-hand, its rhythms so clogged with adjectives, that it seems likely that it was begun a good deal earlier than 'To –'. Its 'thunder-throning cloud', however, bears an obvious relation to the more striking opening of a third sonnet, 'Storm', one draft of which is dated 'Oct. 1916.'

> His face was charged with beauty as a cloud
>   With glimmering lightning. When it shadowed me
>   I shook, and was uneasy as a tree
> That draws the brilliant danger, tremulous, bowed.
>
> So must I tempt that face to loose its lightning.
>   Great gods, whose beauty is death, will laugh above,
>   Who made his beauty lovelier than love.
> I shall be bright with their unearthly brightening.
>
> And happier were it if my sap consume;
> Glorious will shine the opening of my heart;
> The land shall freshen that was under gloom;
> What matter if all men cry aloud and start,
> And women hide bleak faces in their shawl,
> At those hilarious thunders of my fall?[24]

That thunder cloud is a fine image for brooding, pent-up passion and we see the poet for the first time facing up to the possibility that the cloud might break and to the consequences of the resulting storm. It is perhaps not too fanciful to detect the presence of Tom and Susan Owen in lines 12 and 13.

Some of these themes recur in a fourth sonnet, which was begun in October 1916 and finished a year later at Craiglockhart War Hospital:

MUSIC

I have been urged by earnest violins
And drunk their mellow sorrows to the slake
Of all my sorrows and my thirsting sins.
My heart has beaten for a brave drum's sake.
Huge chords have wrought me mighty: I have hurled
Thuds of God's thunder. And with old winds pondered
Over the curse of this chaotic world, –
With low lost winds that maundered as they wandered.

I have been gay with trivial fifes that laugh;
And songs more sweet than possible things are sweet;
And gongs, and oboes. Yet I guessed not half
Life's symphony till I had made hearts beat,
And touched Love's body into trembling cries,
And blown my love's lips into laughs and sighs.[25]

The War, audible far off in those 'brave drums' and 'trivial fifes', had made a curiously Brookean appearance in the sestet of 'To a Comrade in Flanders', written in September:*

Let's die back to those hearths we died for. Thus
Shall we be gods there. Death shall be no sev'rance.
In dull, dim chancels, flower new shrines for us.
For us, rough knees of boys shall ache with rev'rance;
For girls' breasts are the clear white Acropole
Where our own mothers' tears shall heal us whole.[26]

The reference to our 'mothers' tears' in the last line introduces a theme found in two other poems that almost certainly date from this period; a theme that bears a significant submerged relation to the

---

* His copy of Brooke's *1914 & Other Poems* was from the thirteenth impression, May 1916. The fact that he had tucked into it a magazine photograph of Brooke's grave on the island of Skyros suggests that he was impressed at least by the legend of the dead poet.

dominant theme of these poems, that of latent or suppressed homo-
sexuality. The first, untitled poem[27] opens cloyingly, the sub-
Keatsian diction of his earlier manner at variance with the
sophisticated half-rhymes and pararhymes:*

> Has your soul sipped
>   Of the sweetness of all sweets?
> Has it well supped
>   But yet hungers and sweats?
>
> I have been witness
>   Of a strange sweetness,
> All fancy surpassing
>   Past all supposing.

By a sort of rhetorical suspension the poet withholds his main clause
for six stanzas of hyperbole:

> Passing the rays
>   Of the rubies of morning. . . .
>
> Sweeter than nocturnes
>   Of the wild nightingale. . . .
>
> Sweeter than odours
>   Of living leaves. . . .
>
> Sweeter than death
>   And dreams hereafter. . . .

The main clause, as revealed in the ninth stanza, introduces a note of
realism that is distinctly disturbing, not to say shocking, in this
luxuriant context:

> To me was that Smile,
>   Faint as a wan, worn myth,
> Faint and exceeding small,
>   On a boy's murdered mouth.

* See WO's listing of some of these rhymes on pp. 105–6 above.

One hardly dares to ask why that smile should have been so sweet to an onlooker. The sexual undertones swell to an audible crescendo in the next stanza:

> Though from his throat
> The life-tide leaps
> There was no threat
> On his lips.

The orgasmic movement is curiously prolonged in a further stanza subsequently cancelled:

> Is it his mother
> He feels as he slips
> Or girls' hands smoother
> And suaver than sleep's?

And so the poem draws to the bland oxymoron of its conclusion:

> But with the bitter blood
> And the death-smell
> All his life's sweetness bled
> Into a smile.

More realistic is another undated, untitled poem in which the poet's contemplation of a handsome 'navy boy' is interrupted by his mention of 'my mother':

> It was a navy boy, so prim, so trim,
> That boarded my compartment of the train.
>   I shared my cigarettes and books to him.
>   He shared his heart to me. (Who knows my gain!)
>
> (His head was golden like the oranges
> That catch their brightness from Las Palmas sun.)
>   'O whence and whither bound, lad?' 'Home,' he says,
>   'Home, from Hong Kong, sir, and a ten months' run.'
>
> (His blouse was all as blue as morning sea,
> His face was fresh like dawn above that blue.)
>   'I got one letter, sir, just one,' says he,
>   'And no shore-leave out there, sir, for the crew.'

(His look was noble as a good ship's prow
And all of him was clean as pure east wind.)
  'I am no "sir",' I said, 'but tell me now
  What carried you? Not tea, nor tamarind?'

Strong were his silken muscles hiddenly
As undercurrents where the waters smile.
  'Nitre we carried. By next week maybe
  That should be winning France another mile.'

His words were shapely, even as his lips,
And courtesy he used like any lord.
  'Was it through books that you first thought of ships?'
  'Reading a book, sir, made me go aboard.'

'Another hour and I'll be home,' he said.
(His eyes were happy even as his heart.)
  'Twenty-five pounds I'm taking home,' he said.
  'It's five miles there; and I shall run, best part.'

And as we talked, some things he said to me
Not knowing, cleansed me of a cowardice,
  As I had braced me in the dangerous sea.
  Yet I should scarce have told it but for this.

'Those pounds,' I said. 'You'll put some twenty by?'
'All for my mother, sir.' And turned his head.
  'Why all?' I asked, in pain that he should sigh:
  'Because I must. She needs it most,' he said.[28]

There is no evidence that the poems of this period, unlike those
written at the Front, were shown to Susan Owen, although, as at all
times, it was to her that Wilfred communicated his hopes and fears
and still the occasional wild scheme. Towards the end of August he
was thinking of applying for a transfer to the Royal Flying Corps,
and told her:

Flying is the only active profession I could ever continue with enthusiasm
after the War.
  Once a certified pilot, the pay is £350. The Training lasts three months.
By Hermes, I will fly. Though I have sat alone, twittering, like even as it

were a sparrow upon the housetop, I will yet swoop over Wrekin with the strength of a thousand Eagles, and all you shall see me light upon the Racecourse, and marvelling behold the pinion of Hermes, who is called Mercury, upon my cap.

Then I will publish my ode on the Swift.[29]

If I fall, I shall fall mightily. I shall be with Perseus[30] and Icarus, whom I loved; and not with Fritz, whom I did not hate. To battle with the Super-Zeppelin, when he comes, this would be chivalry more than Arthur dreamed of.

Zeppelin, the giant dragon, the child-slayer, I would happily die in any adventure against him. . . .[31]

He duly made his application for transfer, but nothing came of it and he seems to have had no lasting regrets. Certainly, he was every inch the Infantry Officer when Harold again visited him, on 14 September.[32] He was looking bronzed and healthy and each was aware of a change in the other.

Gone was our everlasting brotherliness, it had disappeared on that warm summery afternoon; in its place had come enjoyment and appreciation; we could relish one another as persons. In Wilfred I could find no sign of raillery, no sardonic comment, no critical depreciation of me. His eyes were clear of their usual film of intolerant misunderstanding, they remained grave without being sombre, and jumping out from the gravity now and again would come that twinkling naughtiness, a spontaneous burst of gaiety as we laughed together. His eyes looked deeper and calmer – completely calm – the superficial look of strained irritability was no longer in them. I could sense that he was at ease with himself.

After tea he insisted upon taking me all round his unit, especially I must visit the library for which he was responsible. Before we left his room I noticed with what care he adjusted his collar and tie, smoothing his tunic until it fitted and fell perfectly. Opening a drawer he produced a velvet shoe pad with which he gave an extra polish to his Sam Browne. I remarked about the beauty of the richly lustrous leather, I could see that I had pleased him inordinately; giving it a final tweak he took me by the elbow and guided me through the door and along the veranda. Once clear of this he squared his shoulders in a most military manner. We set off walking very smartly.[33]

Wilfred's dark brown hair which, as schoolboy and student, he had worn long, casually parted on one side, a forelock slanting across his forehead, had been cropped by a military barber, brilliantined, and

Officer Cadet Owen in July 1916

scrupulously – too scrupulously, Harold thought – parted down the middle. Wilfred detected disapproval and said:

'You don't like my military hair, do you?'
'No, I don't.'
After a short pause he went on:
'You know, Harold, if I have got to be a soldier, I must be a good one, anything else is unthinkable. I cannot alter myself inside nor yet conform but at least without any self-questioning I can change outside, if that is what is wanted. D'you remember us running along the High Street with my coat

all buttoned up wrong? I can't do that sort of thing now . . . outwardly I will conform . . . my inward force will be the greater for it.' . . . just the same I was glad when having returned to his room he immediately took off his tunic and threw it – just as he would have done at home – in a rumpled heap on the floor and put on an old tweed jacket; with this action he seemed in some way to cast off his role of the efficient soldier and revert again to his more true diffident self. His return to the Wilfred I knew and loved became extraordinarily emphasized for me, as bounding up from the camp bed on which he had thrown himself – suddenly realizing his carefree habit of throwing his clothes anywhere – with an astonishingly boyish look spreading over his face he turned to me and said, 'Dear, dear, Harold, the freedom of thought this hour of your company has given me had demoralized me. Note how I return to old habits, but, oh, how pleasant it is; all the same I must watch my self-imposed discipline for details.' Then with a look almost comical with shamed apology, he rummaged for a coat hanger and picking up the tunic carefully set it to rights and put it away.[34]

They were to meet only twice again.[35]

Two days later, Owen wrote excitedly to his mother that the Battalion was moving to Oswestry on 24 September. A month later they were transferred to Southport, from which he was able to visit the Quayles in their house at Meols outside Liverpool. Early in November he was posted again, this time to Fleetwood on the Lancashire coast, where he was appointed officer in charge of the Brigade Firing Point. A staff officer told him he must have field-glasses, and he asked his father to send him a pair of Zeiss glasses then lying unclaimed in the Lost Property Office of Shrewsbury Station.[36] With some reluctance, Tom Owen agreed to lend them on the strict understanding that they would be immediately returned if their owner called for them. He did appear, Tom sent Wilfred a telegram which reached him on the Range, and the field-glasses were returned. Their leather case, however, was damaged in transit, and only by agreeing to pay for its repair was Tom able to extricate himself from a difficult and embarrassing situation. Wilfred was consoled by 'the good scoring of the men, and this sentence which Major Eaton showed me from a letter from the General: "Owen should be of great assistance to you".'

Rumours that the Battalion was destined, first, for Egypt and, then, for India proved groundless. On 8 December they returned to Southport, and Christmas saw Wilfred back at Mahim on embarkation leave. This ended on 29 December, when he travelled up to London, bought a hat cover and a pen, and had twenty happy minutes with Harold before catching a train to Folkestone. There, in 'a magnificent room' at the Hotel Metropole, he wrote to his mother: 'There is a Boat at 11.30 a.m. More I know not.'

7

THE SOMME

Next morning he watched the white cliffs of Dover sink into the troopship's wake, while the white cliffs to the west of Calais rose to meet them, and then the spires of the ancient seaport. Second Lieutenant Owen's return to France must, in some respects, have resembled the crossing that Private Sam Hardie of the 2nd Manchester Regiment described in his diary three weeks before:

lined up by the quay, we were invaded by french lassies, who tried to sell us fruit, chocolate, etc. we couldn't understand a word they said, some of the chaps took a delight in jesting and flirting with they, they made themselves look like small children instead of soldiers. This went on until we were marched up to the Rest Camp and was put into a hut.[1]

When Owen arrived, he was given a tent to himself and there spent the last night of 1916.

It had been a grim year on the Western Front. The Somme offensive, conceived in December 1915, was launched in the last week of June with a heavy bombardment on an eighteen-mile front that lasted five days. This was intended to break the German wire and pulverize their forward trenches. It left the ground pocked with shell-craters, which the German machine-gunners occupied as their trenches were destroyed. General Sir Henry Rawlinson, the army commander in charge of the offensive, had planned a dawn attack in the wake of the bombardment, but the French on the right of his line wished to see the results of their artillery fire and to attack in full daylight. Rawlinson agreed, and fixed the attack for 07.30 hrs on 1 July.

That morning the sun rose in a cloudless sky, revealing no activity in the German lines that were visible here and there through patches of low-lying mist. The British and French gunfire was intense from the early hours and rose in a furious crescendo shortly before zero hour, when trench mortars joined in with an additional thirty rounds a minute. Under cover of darkness the assault troops had moved into position and cleared the wire from in front of their trenches. Now, with five minutes to go, thirteen divisions of infantry fixed bayonets and waited. The officers, one eye on their synchronized watches, reminded the men of their orders as rifle-bolts were given a last wipe, magazines checked, the loose puttee tied. Over their bowed helmets

The sound was different, not only in magnitude but in quality. . . . It was not a succession of explosions or a continuous roar. . . . It was not a noise; it was a symphony. And it did not move. It hung over us. It seemed as though the air were full of a vast and agonized passion, bursting now with groans and sighs, now into shrill screaming and pitiful whimpering, shuddering beneath terrible blows, torn by unearthly whips, vibrating with the solemn pulses of enormous wings. And the supernatural tumult did not pass in this direction or in that. It did not begin, intensify, decline, and end. It was poised in the air, a stationary panorama of sound, a condition of the atmosphere, not the creation of man.[2]

As all the minute-hands touched 6, the piercing cry of whistles was added to the symphony of the guns, which then lengthened their range. The men scrambled up ladders, doubled through gaps in the wire, and lay down waiting for the line to form up to left and right. Then, at the summons of a second whistle, they stood up and went forward, not at the double but at a walk. Inaudibly, the officers and NCOs shouted 'Keep your extension! Don't bunch! Keep up on the left!' but the troops were hampered by 66 lbs or more of equipment at their backs and shell craters at their feet, and progress was slower than anticipated over the several hundred yards to the first line of German trenches. When the covering barrage lifted at the moment of attack and moved on to the second line of trenches, those Germans who had survived in deep dugouts emerged with their machine-guns and mowed down the first wave of attackers. A second wave and a

third and a fourth were similarly cut down. By early afternoon the
survivors were back in the trenches from which they had clambered
that morning, and the British Army had suffered the heaviest loss
sustained by any army on any day in the First World War: 19,000
men killed and 38,000 wounded.

The French alone had gained their objectives, and with fewer
casualties than they had inflicted. Having gone 'over the top' at 09.30,
they had taken the Germans by surprise and could have advanced
further, but for the fact that this would have imperilled their left
flank where it joined with the British. General Rawlinson ordered
more frontal attacks all along the line and day after day they were
repulsed. At last he obtained permission from General Sir Douglas
Haig to mount a night attack, and at 03.25 on 14 July 20,000 British
troops advanced through the ground mist shrouding No Man's Land
after only a five-minute bombardment. The Germans, many of
them asleep in dugouts forty feet deep, were taken by surprise and
overrun. The Allied barrage lifted again at 15.35 and 16.25, and the
faithful infantry followed it each time. Such of the enemy as emerged
from their trenches to catch the attackers in the rear, as on 1 July,
were themselves caught by advancing support battalions. By midnight, despite gallant German counter attacks, XV and XIII corps
were established on the long-contested Longueval Ridge. But the
cavalry squadrons that, five hours earlier, had swept past their
cheering infantry with jingling harness and bugles sounding the
Charge, were now lying in No Man's Land, cut down by the
German machine-gunners. The great breakthrough had failed.

On 15 September, Haig ordered the first tanks into battle, despite
expert advice that they should be held back until there were more of
them. They fared better than their mounted predecessors and in
places pierced the German line but, with insufficient infantry to
follow and consolidate their gains, the advantage of a surprise attack
was lost. By now the autumn rains had set in and in a few weeks the
Western Front was a stinking quagmire. At the Chantilly Conference
of Allied Commanders on 15 and 16 November, it was decided that
the Allies should be 'ready to undertake combined offensives from
the first fortnight of February 1917, with all the means at their
disposal'.

German dead behind a machine gun post, near Guillemont, September 1916

Preparations were soon in hand, and the general air of expectation had evidently communicated itself to Second Lieutenant Owen when he wrote to his mother on New Year's Day: 'There is a fine heroic feeling about being in France, and I am in perfect spirits. A tinge of excitement is about me, but excitement is always necessary to my happiness.'[3] Something of this excitement was no doubt due to an incident which had taken place that morning: 'I was hit! We were bombing and a fragment from somewhere hit my thumb knuckle. I coaxed out 1 drop of blood, Alas! no more!!' He was also delighted to have been ordered to join the 2nd Manchesters, a Regular Regiment reputedly of 'well-trained troops and genuine "real-old" Officers'. His spiritual barometer began to fall, however, on the train to Étaples.★ He most likely had to travel in a cattle-truck like that in which Private Sam Hardie made 'a most miserable journey'

★ Until 1914, a sleepy fishing-port of 5,800 inhabitants, visited mainly by painters in search of the picturesque, Étaples and its surrounding hills housed 100,000 soldiers by 1917. Its British cemetery, the largest in France, reached to the horizon.

three weeks before. That night, Owen lay awake in a windy tent in the middle of a vast encampment.[4]

When the order came for him to proceed, he found himself entering more open country, an expanse of frozen downland across which were strung, on taut roads lined with leafless trees, villages often no more than a cluster of farm buildings and a few one-storey houses. Those nearer the Front, he was to discover, had usually been shelled by both sides until steep roofs showed blackened ribs, shutters drooped from twisted hinges, and the only shelter to be had was in the cellar. He joined the 2nd Manchesters at Halloy, a hillside village four miles from Doullens, where they were resting and licking their wounds after being badly mauled in severe fighting around Beaumont Hamel on 18 November. The tattered remnants of the Battalion had held their section of the line all the next day, before being relieved by the 1st Dorsetshire Regiment on 20 November. The following day they came back into the line in support and there remained until, on the 23rd, they went into billets at Mailly-Maillet and, on the 24th, moved back into the training area about Halloy. On the march they were met by the new divisional general, who complained to their commanding officer, as his six officers and one hundred and fifty men and transport went by, that they 'had no intervals'. Lieutenant-Colonel Luxmoore informed him that what he was looking at was the Battalion.

Owen was one of 527 officers and men who joined the 2nd Manchesters during the following weeks. On 4 January he wrote to his mother:

Since I set foot on Calais quays I have not had dry feet. . . .

At the base . . . it was not so bad. We were in the camp of Sir Percy Cunynghame,* who had bagged for his Mess the Duke of Connaught's chef.

After those two days, we were let down, gently, into the real thing, Mud.

It has penetrated now into that Sanctuary my sleeping bag, and that holy of holies my pyjamas. For I sleep on a stone floor and the servant squashed mud on all my belongings; I suppose by way of baptism. We are 3 officers in this 'Room', the rest of the house is occupied by servants and the band;

---

* Lieutenant-Colonel Sir Percy Cunynghame (1867–1941).

the roughest set of knaves I have ever been herded with. Even now their vile language is shaking the flimsy door between the rooms.

I chose a servant for myself yesterday, not for his profile, nor yet his clean hands, but for his excellence in bayonet work. For the servant is always at the side of his officer in the charge and is therefore worth a dozen nurses. Alas, he of the Bayonet is in the Bombing Section, and it is against Regulations to employ such as a servant. I makeshift with another.

Everything is makeshift. The English seem to have fallen into the French unhappy-go-lucky non-system. There are scarcely any houses here. The men lie in Barns.

Our Mess Room is also an Ante and Orderly Room. We eat & drink out of old tins, some of which show traces of ancient enamel. We are never dry, and never 'off duty'.

On all the officers' faces there is a harassed look that I have never seen before, and which in England, never will be seen – out of jails. The men are just as Bairnsfather* has them – expressionless lumps.

We feel the weight of them hanging on us. I have found not a few of the old Fleetwood Musketry party here. They seemed glad to see me, as far as the set doggedness of their features would admit.

I censored hundreds of letters yesterday, and the hope of peace was in every one.[5]

On 6 January the Battalion left Halloy and marched seven miles southwest, down through woods to the River Authie, up the other side of the valley, and on over chalk downland to Beauval. 'The awful state of the roads and the enormous weight carried, was too much for scores of men.' The officers also carried full packs, but Owen was fortunate in having a horse for part of the way. They arrived in freezing rain and, as he was making his damp bed in his tent he heard 'the Guns for the first time. It was a sound not without a certain sublimity'. So it seemed to the hero of Richard Aldington's autobiographical novel:

Suddenly, far away in front and to the left, a quick flash of light pierced the blackness and Winterbourne heard a faint boom. The guns! He waited, straining eyes and ears, in the freezing darkness. Silence. Then again – flash. Boom. Flash. Boom. Very distant, very faint, but unmistakable. The guns. They must be getting near the line.[6]

---

* Bruce Bairnsfather (1888–1959), artist and journalist, whose war cartoons were famous. They were published in *Fragments from France, The Better 'Ole, Bullets and Billets, From Mud to Mufti,* etc.

At four o'clock in the morning of 8 January, the guns woke Owen from his sleep in the tent he was sharing with the Lewis Gun Officer. They had 'begged stretchers from the doctor to sleep on', in a vain attempt to keep 'the intense damp cold' out of their bones. Later that day the Battalion moved forward again, in buses, to Bertrancourt, a deserted village on top of a hill. Owing to a misunderstanding, no billets had been prepared for them but, by the time Owen wrote home again, he had discovered,

or rather my new chosen and faithful Servant discovered a fine little hut, with a chair in it! A four-legged chair! The Roof is waterproof, and there is a Stove. There is only one slight disadvantage: there is a Howitzer just 70 or 80 yards away, firing over the top every minute or so. I can't tell you how glad I am you got me the ear-defenders. I have to wear them at night. Everytime No. 2 (the nearest gun) fires, all my pharmacopæia, all my boots, candle, and nerves take a smart jump upwards. This phenomena is immediately followed by a fine rain of particles from the roof. I keep blowing them off the page.

From time to time the Village is shelled but just now nothing is coming over. Anyhow there is a good cellar close to.

I am Orderly Officer today and stamp all the Battalion's letters. This has taken an age, and I have only a minute or two before I must despatch the Post.

I chose to spend an hour today behind the guns (to get used to them). The Major commanding the Battery was very pleasant indeed. He took me to his H.Q. and gave me a book of Poems to read as if it were the natural thing to do!!

But all night I shall be hearing the fellow's voice:

Number Two – FIRE!

Please send the compass: 2 Manchester Regt. B.E.F. I also need 50 Players Cigarettes & some plain chocolate. There is nothing in all this inferno but mud and thunder.[7]

He and his brother occupants of this inferno were now dressed, like Cromwellian troopers, in steel helmets, buff jerkins of leather, gauntlets, and rubber waders reaching to their hips. The last were indispensable. 'In $2\frac{1}{2}$ miles of trench which I waded yesterday there was not one inch of dry ground. There is a mean depth of 2 feet of water.' He had been on a tour of the line that the 2nd Manchesters were to occupy. The little party had been shelled going up across the open country, but 'only one 4.7 got anywhere near, falling plump in the road, but quite a minute after we had passed the spot'. At Bertrancourt, Owen told his mother, his days were pretty busy,

tho' there is only a short 'parade'. The men do practically nothing all day but write letters; but officers have frequent meetings over schemes, maps, instructions, and a thousand cares. . . .

Now I am not so uncomfortable as last week, for my new servant who has been a chemist's assistant, has turned out not only clean & smart, but enterprising and inventive. He keeps a jolly fire going; and thieves me wood with much cunning.

My Company Commander (A Company) has been out here since the beginning: 'tis a gentleman *and an original* (!)★

Next in command is Heydon,† whom I greatly like, and once revered as the assistant Adjutant at Witley & Oswestry.

Then come I, for the remaining subalterns are junior. I chose no. 3 Platoon. I was posted to 2, but one day I took No. 3 in tow when its officer left, because I liked the look of the men.

Even as they prophesied in the Artists, I have to take a close interest in feet, and this very day I knelt down with a candle and watched each man perform his anointment with Whale Oil; praising the clean feet, but not reviling the unclean.‡

As a matter of fact, my servant and one other, are the only non-verminous bodies in the platoon; not to say Lice-ntious.

Today's letters were rather interesting. The Daddys' letters are specially touching, and the number of x x x to sisters and mothers weigh more in heaven than Victoria Crosses.[8]

Thinking of his own home, he speculates on his chances of getting leave: two or three times, 'assuming the war lasts another year'. His mother is urged to have no Chloride of Lime in the house. 'Our water is overdosed with it enough to poison us. But in the Mess we can get Perrier fortunately.' Some miles away, in another sector of the Somme, a Coldstream Guards subaltern wrote in his diary: 'Last night at Mess the ginger-ale was frozen. We thawed some but when

---

★ Captain (later Major) H. R. Crichton Green (1892–1963), the Manchester Regiment. In 1939 he rejoined, and was Camp Commandant at Le Mans until the Dunkirk evacuation. Later he commanded the Regimental Depot of the Manchester Regiment.

† Second-Lieutenant A. Heydon. Died of wounds April 1917.

‡ Compare this with the more extended allusion to the New Testament quoted on p. 185 below.

we poured it out it froze in the glasses. The Perrier water froze as soon as we opened a bottle.'[9]

On 12 January Owen led his platoon up to the Front, and in front of it, to hold a dugout in the middle of No Man's Land, probably near – if not among – the shell-torn gullies and ridges of Beaumont Hamel.

We had a march of 3 miles over shelled road then nearly 3 along a flooded trench. After that we came to where the trenches had been blown flat out and had to go over the top. It was of course dark, too dark, and the ground was not mud, not sloppy mud, but an octopus of sucking clay, 3, 4, and 5 feet deep, relieved only by craters full of water. Men have been known to drown in them. Many stuck in the mud & only got on by leaving their waders, equipment, and in some cases their clothes.★

High explosives were dropping all around [us], and machine guns spluttered every few minutes. But it was so dark that even the German flares did not reveal us.

Three quarters dead, I mean each of us $\frac{3}{4}$ dead, we reached the dug-out, and relieved the wretches therein. I then had to go forth and find another dug-out for a still more advanced post where I left 18 bombers. I was responsible for other posts on the left but there was a junior officer in charge.

My dug-out held 25 men tight packed. Water filled it to a depth of 1 or 2 feet, leaving say 4 feet of air.

One entrance had been blown in & blocked.

So far, the other remained.

The Germans knew we were staying there and decided we shouldn't.

Those fifty hours were the agony of my happy life.

Every ten minutes on Sunday afternoon seemed an hour.

I nearly broke down and let myself drown in the water that was now slowly rising over my knees.

Towards 6 o'clock, when, I suppose, you would be going to church, the shelling grew less intense and less accurate: so that I was mercifully helped to do my duty and crawl, wade, climb and flounder over No Man's Land to visit my other post. It took me half an hour to move about 150 yards.

I was chiefly annoyed by our own machine guns from behind. The seeng-seeng-seeng of the bullets reminded me of Mary's canary. On the whole I can support the canary better.

In the Platoon on my left the sentries over the dug-out were blown to nothing. One of these poor fellows was my first servant whom I rejected.

★ See 'Dulce et Decorum Est', line 5, quoted on p. 228 below.

If I had kept him he would have lived, for servants don't do Sentry Duty. I kept my own sentries half way down the stairs during the more terrific bombardment. In spite of this one lad was blown down and, I am afraid, blinded.★

This was my only casualty.

The officer of the left Platoon has come out completely prostrated and is in hospital.

I am now as well, I suppose, as ever.

I allow myself to tell you all these things because *I am never going back to this awful post*. It is the worst the Manchesters have ever held, and we are going back for a rest.

I hear that the officer who relieved me left his 3 Lewis Guns behind when he came out. (He had only 24 hours in). He will be court-martialled.[10]

Later that week, from a ruined farm in a ruined village, Owen wrote again to his mother:

We all sleep in the same room where we eat and try to live. My bed is a hammock of rabbit-wire stuck up beside a great shell hole in the wall. Snow is deep about, and melts through the gaping roof, on to my blanket. We are wretched beyond my previous imagination – but safe.

Last night indeed I had to 'go up' with a party. We got lost in the snow. I went on ahead to scout – foolishly alone – and when, half a mile away from the party, got overtaken by

GAS

It was only tear-gas from a shell, and I got safely back (to the party) in my helmet, with nothing worse than a severe fright! And a few tears. Some natural, some unnatural.

Here is an Addition to my List of Wants:

Safety Razor (in my drawer) & Blades
Socks (2 pairs)
6 Handkerchiefs
Celluloid Soap Box (Boots)
Cigarette Holder (Bone, 3d. or 6d.)
Paraffin for Hair.

(I can't wash hair and have taken to washing my face with snow.)

Coal, water, candles, accommodation, everything is scarce. We have not always air! When I took my helmet off last night – O Air it was a heavenly thing!. . . .

★ See 'The Sentry', discussed on p. 274 below.

They want to call No Man's Land 'England' because we keep supremacy there.

With a reference to *The Pilgrim's Progress*, read beside his parents' sitting-room fire, he continues his description of the battlefield:

It is like the eternal place of gnashing of teeth; the Slough of Despond could be contained in one of its crater-holes; the fires of Sodom and Gomorrah could not light a candle to it – to find the way to Babylon the fallen.

It is pock-marked like a body of foulest disease and its odour is the breath of cancer.★

I have not seen any dead. I have done worse. In the dank air I have *perceived* it, and in the darkness, *felt*. Those 'Somme Pictures' are the laughing stock of the army – like the trenches on exhibition in Kensington.

No Man's Land under snow is like the face of the moon chaotic, crater-ridden, uninhabitable, awful, the abode of madness.

To call it 'England'!

I would as soon call my House (!) Krupp Villa, or my child Chlorina-Phosgena.

Now I have let myself tell you more facts than I should, in the exuberance of having already done '*a Bit.*' *It is done*, and we are all going and farther back for a long time. A long time. The people of England needn't hope. They must agitate. But they are not yet agitated even. Let them imagine 50 strong men trembling as with ague for 50 hours![11]

The 2nd Manchesters were not withdrawn, and for the rest of January lived – or died – through fire and ice. In one place, Owen's platoon had no dugouts,

but had to lie in the snow under the deadly wind. By day it was impossible to stand up or even crawl about because we were behind only a little ridge screening us from the Bosches' periscope.

We had 5 Tommy's cookers between the Platoon, but they did not suffice to melt the ice in the water-cans. So we suffered cruelly from thirst.

The marvel is that we did not all die of cold. As a matter of fact, only one of my party actually froze to death before he could be got back, but I am not able to tell how many have ended in hospital. I had no real casualties from shelling, though for 10 minutes every hour whizz-bangs fell a few yards short of us. Showers of soil rained on us, but no fragments of shell could find us.

★ See 'The Show', discussed on pp. 242–5 below.

I had lost my gloves in a dug-out, but I found 1 mitten on the Field. I had my Trench Coat (without lining but with a Jerkin underneath.) My feet ached until they could ache no more, and so they temporarily died. I was kept warm by the ardour of Life within me. I forgot hunger in the hunger for Life. The intensity of your Love reached me and kept me living. I thought of you and Mary without a break all the time. I cannot say I felt any fear. We were all half-crazed by the buffetting of the High Explosives. I think the most unpleasant reflection that weighed on me was the impossibility of getting back any wounded, a total impossibility all day, and frightfully difficult by night.

We were marooned on a frozen desert.

There is not a sign of life on the horizon and a thousand signs of death.

Not a blade of grass, not an insect; once or twice a day the shadow of big hawk, scenting carrion.[12]

The aesthete, botanist, poet, and Vicar's assistant recoiled not only from the ubiquitous evidence of man's inhumanity to man, but from that of man's violence to nature and the natural order:

Hideous landscapes, vile noises, foul language and nothing but foul, even from one's own mouth (for all are devil ridden), everything unnatural, broken, blasted; the distortion of the dead, whose unburiable bodies sit outside the dug-outs all day, all night, the most execrable sights on earth. In poetry we call them the most glorious. But we sit with them all day, all night . . . and a week later to come back and find them still sitting there, in motionless groups, THAT is what saps the 'soldierly spirit' . . .[13]

He was recollecting the emotions of the past month in the comparative tranquillity of a city out of earshot of the guns, having received a message on 30 January from the Acting Adjutant of the Battalion: 'You will proceed to ABBEVILLE for Course of Instruction in Transport Duties commencing on the 2. 2. 17. You should report yourself to the Advanced Horse Transport Depot not later than the 1. 2. 17.'* Telling his mother of this 'heavenly-dictated order', he wrote:

---

* On the back of the message form, WO pencilled some lines from Rabindranath Tagore's *Gitanjali*, beginning: 'When I go from hence let this be my parting word, that what I have seen is unsurpassable.' He quoted these words to SO in August 1918, the day before his last embarkation leave was over.

Prefix .... Code .... m.	Words	Charge		This message is on a/c of :	Recd. at .... Ω.
Office of Origin and Service Instructions.					Date........................
....	Sent				From......................
....	At................m.		...............Service.	
....	To			By ....
....	By		(Signature of "Franking Officer.")	

TO   Lieut W. E. S. Owen   OR 120

| Sender's Number. | Day of Month. | In reply to Number. | |
| * O.R. 120. | 30-1-17 | | AAA |

You will proceed to ABBEVILLE
for Course of Instruction in
Transport Duties commencing on the
2-2-17. You should report yourself
to the Advanced Horse Transport
Depot not later than the
1-2-17.

     Authority 32nd Division Q 378/2

     W K Witkin

         Lieut A Har...

O. C. 2nd Bn Manchester Regiment

From			
Place			
Time			

The above may be forwarded as now corrected.   (Z)

....
Censor.   Signature of Addressor or person authorised to telegraph in his name.
* This line should be erased if not required.
753,000. W 2126—M500. H. W. & V., Ld. 6.16.

Me in Transports? Aren't *you*? When I departed, the gloom among the rest of the Subs. and even among Captains, was a darkness that could be felt. They can't understand my luck.

It doesn't necessarily mean a job as Transport Officer straight away, but here I am, in a delightful old town billeted in a house with a young Scotch Officer.

True, we can get no fuel and the very milk freezes in the jug in a few minutes. True, I am sorely bruised by riding. True, this kind of Life is expensive. But I have not been so full of content since the middle of November last.

Tell Colin how we have to ride all manner of horseflesh in the School, cantering round & round for hours, without stirrups, and folding arms and doing all kinds of circus tricks.[14]

The dysentery that had afflicted him for some time was soon cured by 'civilized life';[15] but the Scotch officer, with whom he had to share a bed, so disturbed him 'by rolling in every midnight' that a day or two later he moved into a hut. There, he slept with a petrol lamp burning beneath his bed, but in the morning 'the top blanket was stiffish with frost'. He was elected Mess President of the School Mess and in the evening went off in the Mess cart, with a fine clatter of hooves and wheels, to shop for provisions. There was a letter from Bobbie de la Touche,★ and three precious parcels from Mahim bringing him cigarettes, biscuits, the gingerbreads that were Susan Owen's speciality, potted meat, handkerchiefs, boracic powder, and Quassia chips to be dissolved in water as a disinfectant. And, on 12 February, he told his mother:

I am settling down to a little verse once more, and tonight I want to do Leslie's subject 'Golden Hair' and O. A. J.'s 'Happiness'.† Leslie tells me that Miss Joergens considers my Sonnet on 'The End' the finest of the lot.

★ Bobbie and Johnny de la Touche left Downside in July 1916 and transferred to Stonyhurst College, near Blackburn, Lancashire, where Charles and David had already arrived as pupils from Mérignac. Miss de la Touche was now in charge of a hospital for Belgian refugees in Surbiton, Surrey.

† LG, Olwen Joergens, and WO had for some time been writing poems on set subjects. 'The End' (*CP*, p. 89), 'Happiness' (*CP*, p. 93), and 'Purple' (*CP*, p. 135) all started as set subjects. LG's *The Nymph* (see pp. 239–40 below) includes *his* poems 'Happiness', 'Golden Hair', and 'Purple'. For Wilfred's further opinion of his own 'Happiness', see *CL*, p. 482. Olwen Joergens did not include any of these set subjects in her collection, *The Woman and the Sage*.

Naturally, because it is, intentionally, in her style! It is in Leslie's possession now. I think hers on 'Golden Hair' very fine indeed.[16]

His own 'Golden Hair', one manuscript of which is dated 'Abbeville. Feb. 1917', is a high-flown literary exercise of almost no merit whatsoever – a fact he must have recognized, writing the word 'BAD' in the margin against a particularly abysmal couplet. Also written in Abbeville was the sonnet 'Happiness', whose first draft returned to a dominant theme of his 1916 poems:

In a later version, 'we' replaced 'I', the cloying phrases 'Mother's boy' and 'mother-arms' were dropped, and the poem everywhere tightened:

> Ever again to breathe pure happiness,
> The happiness our mother gave us, boys?
> To smile at nothings, needing no caress?
> Have we not laughed too often since with joys?
> Have we not wrought too sick and sorrowful wrongs
> For her hands' pardoning? The sun may cleanse,
> And time, and starlight. Life will sing sweet songs,
> And gods will show us pleasures more than men's.
>
> Yet heaven looks smaller than the old doll's-home,
> No nestling place is left in bluebell bloom,
> And the wide arms of trees have lost their scope.
> The former happiness is unreturning:
> Boys' griefs are not so grievous as youth's yearning,
> Boys have no sadness sadder than our hope.[18]

Owen told his mother:

My 'Happiness' is dedicated to you. It contains perhaps two good *lines*. Between you an' me the sentiment is all bilge. Or nearly all. But I think it makes a creditable Sonnet. You must not conclude I have misbehaved in any way from the tone of the poem (though you might infer it if you knew the tone of this Town.) On the contrary I have been a very good boy.[19]

The Transport Duties Course ended on Sunday 25 February and Owen wrote home that he expected to be '4 or 5 days journeying' back to the Battalion. It had taken him that long to reach Abbeville – thumbing lifts in one lorry and six buses – at the beginning of the month. The long straight roads over the rolling plains of Picardy were cratered with shellfire, and many gaps had been torn in their plane and poplar colonnades. Now, on his way back to the Front, under quickening buds, he wrote a cheerful letter to Harold – who had just survived an aeroplane crash at the Royal Naval Air Station, Chingford – ending: 'It is 10 o'clock; and I must now be turned out of the Café, and will go and doze on my luggage, probably until

Manchester Regiment working party, January 1917

Dawn.'[20] His forecast was accurate. It was 1 March, a fine sunny day, when he reached the Battalion's dugout Headquarters in an open field beside the straggling village of Bouchoir, eighteen miles south-east of Amiens.

Although there was still snow on the ground, there was the promise of spring in the air and a hint of a break not only in the weather but in the frozen pattern of the Front. The earliest intimations of the latter had been received, though hardly then perceived, on one or two bright days towards the end of October 1916, when British aviators had observed that fresh earth had been turned up north of Quéant, twelve miles south-east of Arras and fourteen and a half miles east of the front line at Monchy au Bois.[21] A special reconnaissance was ordered, which resulted in a report, received on 9 November, that the Germans were constructing a trench from Quéant to a point east of Neuville Vitasse. The day before, there had appeared in the General Headquarters' Intelligence Summary a statement from a Russian prisoner of the Germans, who had escaped into the French trenches, that 2,000 of his fellow countrymen were making concrete dugouts, protected by wire, near St. Quentin. It was hardly surprising that at the British G.H.Q. no connection was then made between these two reports.

On the other side of the front line, the German High Command had realized that their troops were exhausted, demoralized, and could not endure another year like 1916, nor could they be replaced.[22] While the British Army was drawing reinforcements from the Empire, and the French Army from the French colonies, the German leaders could only raise new divisions by reducing establishments and drawing on reserves; in short, by redeploying their forces rather than by increasing them. Hopes of forming a Polish Army had already died and, on the Home Front, Germany was feeling the constrictions resulting from British control of the high seas. It was decided, therefore, that on the Western Front, the German Army must stand on the defensive, in the hope that a major submarine offensive would cut off the enemy's supplies and reinforcements and enable the Army

Soldiers in a trench outside Arras, February 1917

to attack again. The German Admiralty estimated that unrestricted submarine warfare would have decisive effects within six months. General Ludendorff, the German Commander-in-Chief, thought this optimistic, but believed that these effects would be visible within a year.

In November 1916, the German High Command decided, initially as a precaution, to construct a strong defensive line from a point just north of Quéant to Cerny en Laonnois. General Ludendorff considered that a withdrawal to this 'Siegfried-Stellung', or Hindenburg Line as it came to be called, would save sufficient troops for an offensive to be mounted elsewhere, perhaps in Italy, in that it shortened his Front by twenty-five miles and disposed of two potentially vulnerable salients. His High Command, however, at that time disapproved of a voluntary withdrawal on so large a scale. Later, it considered a smaller withdrawal on one northern sector of the Front, but eventually was persuaded, by Crown Prince Rupprecht and others, of the strategic advantages of retiring to the Siegfried-Stellung in one move. Accordingly, a detailed scheme of withdrawal was drawn up and given the code name 'Alberich', after the malicious dwarf of the *Niebelung Saga*, because a principal feature of the plan was that the land between the present Front and the new position was to be made a wasteland. All civilians were to be removed, all roads blown up, all wells filled in or polluted. Not so much as a stable or a fruit tree was to be left standing. In the event, half a dozen villages were spared and their occupants allowed to await the Allied advance, but ten times as many civilians were moved back behind the Hindenburg Line.

'Line' is not an adequate translation of 'Stellung', and its use by the British betrays a certain misconception. The Siegfried-Stellung was, in fact, not a line but a defensive zone on the whole British front, except, curiously enough, on that northern section between Quéant and Neuville Vitasse which was attacked in April. From Quéant southward it had been observed that there existed a second system about a mile and a half in rear of the foremost and like it consisting of fire and support trenches some 200 yards apart. This was actually the original 'Hindenburg Line', the advanced position having been begun in early February to remedy defects in the original siting. The chief advantages of the new position were, first, that it was sited, as far as possible, on a reverse instead of on a forward slope, and, secondly, the provision of artillery observation posts at least 500 yards behind the front trench, overlooking it and its approaches, and at the same time clear of the smoke and dust of hostile bombardments.

The re-siting afforded an opportunity to lay out on virgin ground, far from the enemy, a position in accordance with the new system of defence in depth introduced by General Ludendorff.

The original first system now became the support position and artillery-protection line. It marked the rear of what was known as the 'battle zone' and the front of a 'rear zone'. When labour became available this rear zone was completed by yet another system, which gave the whole 'Siegfried Position' a depth of from six to eight thousand yards. In front of the 'battle zone' – that is, in front of the new first-line system – there was an outpost zone some 600 yards deep, to deny to the attacker observation over it. In some cases this zone was covered by another strong entrenchment, but its normal defence was a line of piquets supported by squads, each with a light machine gun, in shallow dug-outs. In the battle zone itself there were disposed chequerwise fortified localities containing concrete machine-gun emplacements. The trenches thus became, in theory at least, merely an element in a system of defence which was not linear but zonal.

These defences, though they varied somewhat in different sections, represented the application of mass production to fortification. All the woodwork was uniform in design, the dug-out doors, for example, being turned out to a pattern from the sawmills literally by the thousand. Comparatively shallow dug-outs of ferro-concrete, also to a fixed pattern, were constructed beneath the parapet for each squad, and there were also mined dug-outs. The barbed-wire obstacle was particularly formidable, stretched on corkscrew pickets, generally in three belts, each ten to fifteen yards in depth and five yards or more apart, and, in front of the fire trench, in a zig-zag pattern, so that machine guns firing from the re-entrant angle could sweep the sides. No troops who saw it before rust had touched it will forget the sinister impression made by its blue sheen in the light of afternoon. Observation posts were protected, cable was buried, and a network of light railways was laid to serve the new position.

The demands made by its construction upon labour, material and transport were immense.* Russian prisoners were employed to a large

* In addition to great numbers of barges on the canals, 1,250 train-loads of engineer stores were sent up, and an average of 65,000 workmen were employed daily. However, as the train movement extended from mid-October to mid-March, it represented only about eight extra trains a day, hardly sufficient to excite the curiosity of the British Intelligence Service.

extent, though, according to the British Intelligence, for the most part in the early stages and for the rough work. The troops themselves and con- scribed Belgian civilians carried out the main portion of the task, though in many cases the ferro-concrete dug-outs and emplacements were made by German firms, who brought out their own skilled workmen.[23]

Virtually nothing of this was known to the Allied Intelligence until February. Acting on the reports of escaped prisoners, the Royal Flying Corps made a number of gallant attempts to reconnoitre and photograph the area between Quéant and St. Quentin, but these were largely frustrated by mist, rain, snow, low-lying cloud, and German aircraft, which at that time were greatly superior to the British models. The legendary Baron Manfred von Richthofen with six machines, operating from Douai aerodrome, shot down thirteen British planes in one day.

Although the Hindenburg Line was neither reconnoitred nor photographed until the Germans were retreating to it in mid-March, the British had increasing evidence of a local withdrawal. On 20 and 21 February their wireless operators intercepted German messages ordering German operators to dismantle their stations to the north of Bapaume and prepare to move back. At 9.30 on the 24th, the 53rd Brigade of the 18th Division reported that its patrols had passed through South Miraumont Trench and were pushing on, unresisted, into Petit Miraumont. Similar reports were soon coming in from other units as, to their astonishment, they penetrated the enemy lines often without seeing a living German or hearing a shot fired.

On Sunday 25 February, as Owen left Abbeville, the 2nd Man- chesters were moved forward with the rest of the 14th Brigade and took over a section of the line from the French near the village of Fresnoy. When he joined them on 1 March, he found himself posted to B Company. This was commanded by a Lieutenant (acting Captain) Sorrel, whom Owen referred to in a letter to his mother that day as 'poet Sorrel'.* He went on to say:

---

* Lieutenant S. Sorrel, M.C., Manchester Regiment, was invalided home a few weeks later with shell-shock. In March 1918 he was a Staff Captain (Assistant Military Landing Officer), and was listed on the Army Reserve in August 1918. I have been unable to identify him as a poet.

There is small chance of doing Transport for a long time if ever. Howsoever, this is a glorious part of the Line, new to us, and indeed, to the English (sh!) Most comfortable dug-outs, grass fields, woods, sunshine, quiet. True we are in reserve today, but I hear the very front line is a line, and a quiet one.

My letter to Harold left yesterday by the Army Post. It was in an astonishing way I had your parcel. A man rose up from a hole in a field holding it above his head. It was a fine moment. I soon rushed down & tore it open. Socks most specially valuable, as my servant forgot to put any spare in my Trench Kit. Likewise, I took no Cigarettes, hoping to find 50 in the Parcel. Lo! here are thousands! How good of you all. I smoke Harold's with reverence.

I shall not touch the goodies until the very front line is reached.

The Post is waiting to go.

Yours as ever, but slightly happier than usual.   W.E.O.[24]

After a night spent in a dugout, on lousy straw left (together with 'postcards, picturing embraces, medals, roses and mistletoe') by the French *poilus*, his pastoral illusions were violently dispelled. He began a letter to his brother Colin 'with a gas-alarm on'. This was followed by a tremendous artillery barrage and the sudden order 'Stand to Arms' that caused the letter to be abruptly abandoned.

While finding it hard to imagine that only two days ago he had been 'living civilly', he was clearly well-satisfied with his trench companions. Captain Sorrel, who on one occasion gave him 'the choice of writing a Sonnet before 7.30 or going with the next Fatigue Party', he both liked and respected.

He chokes filthiness as summarily as I ever heard a Captain do, or try to do. He is himself an aesthete, and not virtuous according to English standards, perhaps, but no man swears in his presence, nor broaches those pleasantries which so amuse the English officer's mind.

He seems to be one of the few young men who live up to my principle: that Amusement is never an excuse for 'immorality', but that Passion may be so.

I find this Company in a far better state than A, partly, of course, because of good sergeants, but Sorrel has a fine control.[25]

A number of the soldiers he had met before. And when a sniper fired at him as he stood a moment on the parapet of a trench, directing a Fatigue Party digging in the front line, the first voice to hiss 'Get down, Sir!' was that of a private who had been in his Fleetwood musketry party the year before. 'One of those to whom I swore I would never tolerate near me at the Front. I remember his total score was 5!!'

He now seldom refers to the dangers and deprivations of life in a frozen dugout, and when he does, the tone is cheerful or wry. No trace remains of the self-pitying hypochondria sometimes discernible in his boyhood letters, though he is as solicitous as ever of the health of those at Mahim. He tells his mother: 'I sleep well; I eat well; I am well. Surely better than any of you at home. . . . Did I not warn Colin about his dirty hands? Has the new servant had any effect on your strength?' Susan's self-pitying hypochondria had in no way diminished. It would seem that, because her son did not complain, she assumed he had less to complain about than she with her weakness, her sore throat. He replies tenderly:

How I hope that by now the pain at least and the Malady of it are gone; and that there is a fair sun healing you!
We have gone back to severe cold and snow. This village is half destroyed and our billets are not half so cozy as dug-outs.[26]

However, like many another soldier who at the time made little of his own suffering in the trenches, Owen resented 'the illusory War Films' currently showing in England such a bowdlerized version of the truth.
On 9 March he was again sent up nearer the line

in charge of a party of Dug-Out Diggers. It is a soft job. I take the men up sometimes by day, sometimes by night, so that (as today) I lie snug in my blankets until lunchtime. We are 4 officers living in this cellar; our servants cook for us. It is a relief to be away from the Battalion for a while. How I hope it will last. It *may* spin out 3 weeks.

It did not last three days. On the night of 13/14 March he was groping his way through pitch darkness 'to see a man in a dangerous state of exhaustion' when he fell into 'a kind of well'.[27] It was only about fifteen foot deep, but he caught the back of his head on the way down. 'The doctors (not in consultation!) say I have a slight con-

cussion, but I dont feel at all fuddled.'* Four days later, forgetting
it was his twenty-fourth birthday, he wrote:

My dearest Mother,
    I am in a hospital bed, (for the first time in life.)
    After falling into that hole (which I believe was a shell-hole in a floor,
laying open a deep cellar) I felt nothing more than a headache, for 3 days;
and went up to the front in the usual way – or nearly the usual way, for I
felt too weak to wrestle with the mud, and sneaked along the top, snapping
my fingers at a clumsy sniper. When I got back I developed a high fever,
vomited strenuously, and long, and was seized with muscular pains. The
night before last I was sent to a shanty† a bit farther back, & yesterday
motored on to this Field Hospital, called Casualty Clearing Station 13.‡
It is nowhere in particular that I know, but I may be evacuated to Amiens,
if my case lasts long enough. For I began to get right again immediately
after getting into these sheets 'that soon smooth away trouble.'§ The
physician handed me over to the surgeon. But my head is not broken or
even cut in any way. My temperature etc. *may not* have had any relation
to the knock, and the first doctor said he only hoped it *had*. Anyhow it was
normal yesterday, and below today, and the only abnormal thing about
me now is that I don't want a cigarette. That, then, should not worry you.
I have now told you everything, and I hope, dear Mother, that you are duly
grateful – to me, and concerning the whole circumstance.[28]

The cheerful tone of this and his letters over the next few days was
principally the result of a natural relief at being in a warm bed – alive
and well – rather than in a waterlogged dugout. An additional
element was elation at the good news from the Front. On 19 March

---

    * It is not clear where this accident happened. Edmund Blunden understood (from SO,
who presumably had it from her son) that it was at Le-Quesnoy-en-Santerre, a cluster of
farms one and a half miles – of land level as a lawn – southeast of Bouchoir. This is probably
correct, although another report states that 'he fell down a well at Bouchoir, and was
momentarily stunned'. However, in that the Battalion was at that time occupying dugouts
at Bouchoir, and Wilfred wrote on 11 March that he was 'nearer the Line'. Le-Quesnoy-en-
Santerre seems the more likely. On 21 March he wrote to his mother: 'One of the villages
mentioned in the Daily Mail, thus: "we captured a farm so many miles North East of
Q . . ." was the one to which I have been going every day or night last week.' [*CL*, p. 444]
    † The Military Hospital at Nesle, 'a town hospital where I paused 3 days'. [*CL*, p. 544]
    ‡ This was at Gailly. See below, pp. 183–4.
    § Rupert Brooke, 'The Great Lover', lines 35–6.

he wrote to Colin: 'I know something of the Advances',[29] and two days later told his mother: 'I am getting up today, and perhaps by the time you receive this I shall be starting back to overtake my Battalion, if it is not chasing along too fast.' He was too optimistic on both counts.

The German High Command's 'Alberich' programme – for which the Emperor signed the order on 4 February – had been scheduled to begin on 9 February with the removal of material and artillery behind the new Front.[30] This stage, which included the demolitions, was due to be completed on 15 March and to be followed by two to four 'marching days': two days on the flanks, three between Nauroy and Courcy le Château, and four on a small section between St. Quentin and La Fère. Intense British pressure, however, forced Prince Rupprecht to order a preliminary with-drawal on 18 February to his R 1 Line,* and again on 11 March to his R 2 Line. Between 17 and 20 March the Fourth Army was pressing forward comparatively rapidly along its whole Front, as the Germans withdrew to the shelter of the Hindenburg Line. Despite its enforced modifications, the 'Alberich' programme was 'a masterly piece of organization on the part of Crown Prince Rupprecht and his Chief of Staff, General von Kuhl'.[31] The Germans fell back in good order, fighting a number of successful minor rear-guard actions.

Back in his bed in the 13th Casualty Clearing Station at Gailly on the Somme Canal, Owen knew only that the British were advancing and chafed to know more: 'the Battalion . . . for all I know may be openly warfaring, or perhaps is now clean wiped out'. He was also growing desperate for books and wrote to his mother: 'One of the sisters brought me some novels, about as palatable as warm water to a starving jaguar. Your remarks on Crocketts' last,† remind me that I once said his books were like sawdust – on which an ox has just been slaughtered.' Outside, snow was falling, but there was a stove in the ward and beside this Owen sat in a padded kimono reading

---

* See endpaper map.
† Samuel Rutherford Crockett (d. 1914), whose romantic novels included *Princess Penniless* (1908) and *Old Nick and Young Nick* (1910).

his battered copy of *The Poems of E. B. Browning*, vol. 2, inscribed
'Bouchoir/Somme/March: 1917'.[32] His pencil (he had lost his pen
on the way to the 13th C.C.S.) marked two passages in *Aurora Leigh*:

> See the earth,
> The body of our body, the green earth
> Indubitably human, like this flesh
> And these articulated veins through which
> Our heart drives blood! there's not a flower of spring,
> That dies ere June, but vaunts itself allied
> By issue and symbol, by significance
> And correspondence, to that spirit-world
> Outside the limits of our space and time,
> Whereto we are bound. Let poets give it voice
> With human meanings; else they miss the thought,
> And henceforth step down lower, stand confessed
> Instructed poorly for interpreters, –
> Thrown out by an easy cowslip in the text. (p. 140)

and

> Earth's crammed with heaven,
> And every common bush afire with God:
> But only he who sees, takes off his shoes;
> The rest sit round it, and pluck blackberries,
> And daub their natural faces unaware
> More and more, from the first similitude. (p. 228)

Another passage, he wrote to his sister Mary, 'rather winded me,
yea wounded me', and he transcribed it for her:

> Many fervent souls
> Strike rhyme on rhyme, who would strike steel on steel
> If steel had offered, in a restless heat
> Of doing something. Many tender souls*
> Have strung their losses on a rhyming thread,
> As children, cowslips: – the more pains they take,
> The work more withers, – Young men, ay, and maids,
> Too often sow their wild oats in tame verse,
> Before they sit down under their own vine,

---

* WO wrote 'hearts' instead of 'souls' and mistranscribed Mrs. Browning's punctuation
in a number of places where I have silently corrected it.

And live for use. Alas, near all the birds
Will sing at dawn, and yet we do not take
The chaffering swallow for the holy lark.　(p. 30)

This passage had struck him, he told Mary, because

I amuse myself with drawing plans for Country Houses and Bungalows, especially Bungalows. I worked my wits all day on one,★ and, within the prescribed limits, it is about perfect, for the intended occupant – solitary me.

You see I am thinking of sitting down under my own vine and living for use, some day, and a concrete presentment of the Vine should be incentive.[33]

He elaborated his day-dreams in more practical detail for his brother Colin, who was then working on a farm.

In my walk this afternoon, considering at leisure the sunshine and the appearance of peace (I don't mean from the news) I determined what I should do after the war.

I determined to keep pigs.

It occurred to me that after five years development of one pig-stye in a careful & sanitary manner, a very considerable farm would establish itself.

I should like to take a cottage and orchard in Kent Surrey or Sussex, and give my afternoons to the care of pigs. The hired labour would be very cheap, 2 boys could tend 50 pigs. And it would be the abruptest possible change from my morning's work.[34]

His letter to his favourite and not altogether unliterary brother ended with evidence of other daydreams and another occupation beside the simmering stove.

Perhaps you will think me clean mad and translated by my knock on the head. How shall I prove that my old form of madness has in no way changed? I will send you my last Sonnet, which I started yesterday. I think I will address it to you.

Adieu, mon petit. Je t'embrasse.　　　　　　　　　　　W.E.O.

★ HO saw this after the War and remembers it as a detailed and loving piece of work.

SONNET with an Identity Disc.

If ever I had dreamed of my dead name
High in the Heart of London; unsurpassed
By Time forever; and the fugitive, Fame,
There taking a long sanctuary at last,

— I'll better that! Yea, now, I think with shame
How once I wished it hidd'n from its defeat
Under those holy cypresses, the same
That mourn around the quiet place of Keats.

Now rather let's be thankful there's no risk
Of gravers ~~matching~~ scoring it with hideous screed.
For let my gravestone be this body-disc
Which was my yoke. Inscribe no date, nor deed.

But let thy heart-beat kiss it night + day.....
Until the name grow vague and w an away

Although this sonnet[35] openly acknowledges its debt to Keats's beginning 'When I have fears that I may cease to be', Owen shows a new self-confidence in his master's presence. His final quatrain and couplet became, after considerable revision,

Now, rather, thank I God there is no risk
Of gravers scoring it with florid screed . . .
But let my death be memoried on this disk.
Wear it, sweet friend. Inscribe no date nor deed.
But may thy heartbeat kiss it night and day
Until the name grow blurred and wear away.*

Keats's 'fair creature' is recognizably the original of Owen's 'sweet friend' – whom few readers would guess to be his brother – but the use of the identity disc gives this sonnet a distinct and poignant identity of its own.

Writing to Mary on 25 March, he shows that he has lost nothing of his old fondness for children:

I went a joy ride on a Motor Ambulance, a Daimler (as pictured in the *Sketch* last week) and so passed a vivid afternoon. The car was going in the direction of the Front, and I stopped at a certain village where refugees from the regained area were just arriving: all hags & children. I had a long talk with a boy of 14, who if he had been 15 would not have been liberated. He could not spell his name, since he has worked on the fields since he was 11. He did not look by any means starving, but had known nothing but scanty food for $2\frac{1}{2}$ years. I plied him with chocolate, and drew the following information. That the Germans carried off all men over 15; left 5 days bread rations for the remainder, set fire to almost every building, choked up the wells with farmyard refuse and disappeared.[36]

To his mother he writes, with irony eloquent of his altered attitude to religion, of a visit to a 'great Gothic Church',† where he had

listened under the nave, as Belloc says, for the voice of the Middle Ages. All I could hear was a voice very much beyond the middle age. However I stayed to vespers; and after leaning my hat and stick up against a piece of the true Cross, I sat and regarded the plants (with their paper flowers wired on them), and St. John in bathing costume looking ruefully at another saint in a gold dressing-gown; and the scarlet urchins holding candles and chewing, – probably the grease.

---

* I cannot accept the EB/CDL readings of lines 11 and 14. The word 'fade', incidentally, in the second of these, does not appear in any draft, and is patently less effective than the pun on 'Wear' in line 12.
† Probably at Corbie.

Very different is the passionate compassion of his description of an injured pilot whom he was helping the ward sister to nurse at night.

At the end of March he was discharged from hospital and spent four days in pursuit of his advancing Battalion. On the night of 3 April he

bedded down with a family of refugees,★ 3 boys, 2 tiny girls: a good class socially, and of great charm personally. I was treated as a god, and indeed began to suspect I have a heart as comprehensive as Victor Hugo's, Shakspere's, or your own. In 24 hours I never took so many hugs & kisses in my life, no, not in the first chapter even. They took reliefs at it.[37]

Next day he reported to his Battalion Headquarters on the outskirts of St. Quentin to find that, while he had been on the road, the 2nd Manchesters had been engaged in a fierce action.

On the morning of Sunday 1 April, the Battalion had been ordered to move to a village about five miles distant on their right flank called Germaine.[38] They found it in a sheltered hollow and billets were allotted in the expectation that they were to spend the night there. However, at about one o'clock, they were ordered to move again, along a valley and over a river, and to rendezvous with the rest of the Brigade at Château Pommery. Lance-Corporal Sam Hardie afterwards wrote in his diary:

about 4 p.m. we were 'fell in' and marched off without any tea scarsely, and rested in a large field near the line, oh, it was terrible to see the poor fellows simply dead beaten as we hadn't had any sleep for 4 or 5 nights.

We landed after dodgeing the shells all the way, and our Company Officer showed us N.C.O.s the map and our objective and asked us to try to influence the men and keep them going as 'these two villages had to be taken at all costs' he said.

In the darkness they had missed the Château, as that – or what remained of it – was hidden by a dense screen of trees. For a few hours the Brigade rested in that large field and made ready for 'the coming fury'. On the morning of 1 April the village of Savy had been captured by the 97th Brigade, and that afternoon the 96th Brigade

★ Probably the Lemaire family. See *CL*, p. 452.

had taken Savy Wood. There, however, they had been pinned down by accurate machine-gun fire from a quarry about 500 yards up a glacis slope rising from the forward edge of the wood. Rectangular in shape, the quarry was about 250 yards long by 150 yards wide, and the enemy machine-guns were sited in dugouts set in its steep yellow sand cliffs. At midnight, the 14th Brigade was moved up over green fields, along the west edge of Savy Wood, and halted behind the railway embankment. The railway ran through the wood, and beyond it, to the north-east, open grassland rose gently for about 1,000 yards to Francilly-Selency. From there the ground sloped down into a shallow valley and then rose again, this time more steeply, to Selency, which was to be the Brigade's final objective.

In the words of Sam Hardie's diary:

At 5 minutes to 5 in the morning our Artillery opened out and let them have it for a good five minutes, then we walked slowly under the fire until we spotted a few Germans, a few rounds from our rifles set them going, and off we went after them as fast as we could go, we soon 'dispersed of them' alright. We went a little further, and spotted a crowd of them and they put a machine-gun on us, there was a Lewis-gunner alongside me, and he put it into action at once, they didn't stay to see the effect, they flew. Next we shifted a crowd about six or seven and half a dozen field guns, I can't really say what became of these men, but the guns were captured, this seemed to give our Coys. encouragement and on we went until a strange sensation came over me, I suddenly felt weak and down I went.

That day, nine officers and sixty-two other ranks of the 2nd Manchester Regiment fell – two officers and ten other ranks killed – as they drove the enemy out of the quarry and advanced to capture, first, Francilly-Selency and, then, Selency.

There, on high ground overlooking St. Quentin – a city dominated by the majestic, battered, bulk of its gothic church – Owen rejoined them and was transferred to A Company. Under the spirited leadership of 2nd Lieutenant Taylor,★ they had borne the brunt of the assault on the quarry, and had captured six machine-guns. Writing to his mother on 8 April, Easter Sunday, Owen told her:

★ He was awarded the Military Cross for his part in this action.

Distant view of St. Quentin from the British front line trench, April 1917

We stuck to our line 4 days (and 4 nights) without relief, in the open, and in the snow. Not an hour passed without a shell amongst us. I never went off to sleep for those days, because the others were far more fagged after several days of fighting than I fresh from bed. We lay in wet snow. I kept alive on brandy, the fear of death, and the glorious prospect of the cathedral Town* just below us, glittering with the morning. With glasses I could easily make out the general architecture of the cathedral: so I have told you how near we have got.[39]

Thirty miles to the north-west, another 2nd Lieutenant, Edward Thomas, was gazing at another cathedral town through his field-glasses. That night he wrote in the Walker's Back-Loop pocket book (bound in pigskin, price two shillings), which he used as a diary:

---

* St. Quentin.

8.   A bright warm Easter day but Achicourt shelled at 12.30 and then at 2.15 so that we all retired to cellar. I had to go over to battery at 3 for a practice barrage, skirting the danger zone, but we were twice interrupted. A 5.9 fell 2 yards from me as I stood by the f/C post. One burst down the back of the office and a piece of dust scratched my neck. No firing from 2—4. Rubin left for a course.[40]

Early next morning, while directing the fire of 244 Siege Battery during the opening barrage of the Battle of Arras, Edward Thomas was killed in his Observation Post. That Easter weekend, another countryman poet was hit on the Western Front, but Private Ivor Gurney of the Gloucesters was more fortunate. He survived to be gassed at Passchendaele and linger on for twenty years in a lunatic asylum.

Owen continued his 'diary' to his mother:

It was unknown where exactly the Bosche was lying in front of us. The job of finding out fell upon me. I started out at midnight with 2 corporals & 6 picked men; warning other Regiments on our flanks not to make any mistake about us. It was not very long before the Hun sent up his verilights, but the ground was favourable to us, and I and my Corporal prowled on until we clearly heard voices and the noises of carrying & digging. When I had seen them quite clearly moving about, and marked the line of their entrenchment it might seem my job was done; but my orders were to discover the force of the enemy. So then I took an inch or two of cover and made a noise like a platoon. Instantly we had at least two machine guns turned on us, and a few odd rifles. Then we made a scramble for 'home'.

Another night I was putting out an Advanced Post when we were seen or heard and greeted with Shrapnel. The man crouching shoulder to shoulder to me gets a beautiful round hole★ deep in his biceps. I am nothing so fortunate, being only buffeted in the eyes by the shock, and whacked on the calf by a spent fragment, which scarcely tore the puttee.

On 8 April the Battalion was withdrawn five miles to Beauvois for a rest, and that afternoon, as Owen was finishing tea in a cellar 'with something like Sunday peace serenity', he heard the unexpected rattle of machine-guns. He rushed up to see a German Albatross

---

★ See the unfinished poem 'Beauty', *CP*, 140.

scout plane 'come shuddering down the sky'. With a new automatic pistol he had bought bumping in his pocket, he ran across the fields to the tangled wreckage of the plane. The pilot was dead, and Owen took his bloodstained handkerchief as a souvenir. The letter recounting this episode, and alluding obliquely to a visit by Field-Marshal Haig, ends in mid-sentence and so was posted, for orders had been received recalling the Battalion to the Front.

They marched back to Savy and on 12 April received instructions that the French intended to attack St. Quentin and, in the event of their being successful, the 2nd Manchesters and the 15th Highland Light Infantry were to protect their left flank. These orders were modified and their execution postponed until 14 April, when the Battalion moved forward to Savy Wood. To reach this, some open ground had to be crossed and no sooner had the first wave of infantry passed over the crest of the hill than the enemy placed a hurricane barrage of 10.5 cm. and 15 cm. high explosive shells in the path of the second wave. The Battalion advanced into and through it as steadily as if on parade, each line keeping its distance and dressing, and every carrier retaining his load.★ Owen later described those moments and what followed:

The sensations of going over the top are about as exhilarating as those dreams of falling over a precipice, when you see the rocks at the bottom surging up to you. I woke up without being squashed. Some didn't. There was an extraordinary exultation in the act of slowly walking forward, showing ourselves openly.

There was no bugle and no drum for which I was very sorry. I kept up a kind of chanting sing-song: Keep the Line straight!

Not so fast on the left!

Steady on the Left!

Not so fast!

★ The editors of the *Collected Letters* follow WO in calling this the action at Feyet (pp. 452 n. and 458 n.), but contemporary maps of the district show no place of that name. There is, however, a village of Fayet, half a mile north-east of Selency, and it may well have been there that WO experienced the bombardment described in the letter quoted on p. 179 above. I believe that when, four months later at Craiglockhart, he mentioned 'the Barrage at Feyet' in a letter to his mother (see below, p. 199), either his memory was at fault or he was referring to those '4 days (and 4 nights) without relief, in the open'.

Then we were caught in a Tornado of Shells. The various 'waves' were all broken up and we carried on like a crowd moving off a cricket field. When I looked back and saw the ground all crawling and wormy with wounded bodies,★ I felt no horror at all but only an immense exultation at having got through the Barrage. We were more than an hour moving over the open and by the time we came to the German Trench every Bosche had fled. But a party of them had remained lying low in a wood close behind us, and they gave us a very bad time for the next four hours. . . .[41]
[the] trench which we had just taken was only a foot deep in places, & I was obliged to keep passing up & down it. As a matter of fact I rather enjoyed the evening after the Stunt, being only a few hundred yds. from the Town, as you knew, and having come through the fire so miraculously: and being, moreover, well fed on the Bosche's untouched repast!! It was curious and troubling to pick up his letters where he had left off writing in the middle of a word!. . . .[42]

The Colonel sent round this message the next day: 'I was filled with admiration at the conduct of the Battalion under the heavy shell-fire . . . The leadership of officers was excellent, and the conduct of the men beyond praise.' The reward we got for all this was to remain in the Line 12 days. For twelve days I did not wash my face, nor take off my boots, nor sleep a deep sleep. For twelve days we lay in holes, where at any moment a shell might put us out. I think the worst incident was one wet night when we lay up against a railway embankment. A big shell lit on the top of the bank, just 2 yards from my head. Before I awoke, I was blown in the air right away from the bank!† I passed most of the following days in a railway Cutting, in a hole just big enough to lie in, and covered with corrugated iron. My brother officer of B Coy, 2/Lt Gaukroger lay opposite in a similar hole.‡ But he was covered with earth, and no relief will ever relieve him, nor will his Rest be a 9 days-Rest.[43]

On 21 April the 14th Brigade was relieved by the 182nd Brigade of the 61st (2/South Midland) Division and moved back to the little, tree-surrounded village of Quivières, where it was quartered in

---

★ See the discussion of the poem 'The Show', pp. 242–5 below.

† It was probably this experience that resulted in WO's subsequent shell-shock.

‡ This single-track railway cutting, in the middle of Savy Wood, is nowhere more than 15 ft. deep. Something of a mystery surrounds the death of 2nd Lieut. H. Gaukroger, since the official records state that he was killed on 2 April.

cellars. This was called a rest period, although, wrote Owen to his mother,

we rise at 6.15 and work without break until about 10 p.m. for there is always a Pow-Wow for officers after dinner. And if I have not written yesterday, it is because I must have kept hundreds of Letters uncensored, and enquiries about Missing Men unanswered. . . .[44]

The censor's pen, however, had time to write in the cellar where he and his companions lay serried:

Le Christianisme.

So the church Christ was hit and burned
Under its rubbish and its rubble.
In cellars, safe packed huddled saints lie serried,
Well out of hearing of our trouble.

One Virgin still immaculate
Smiles on for war to flatter her.
She's halo'd with an old tin hat,
But a piece of hell will batter her.

* Quivières.

On 1 May Owen was observed by his Commanding Officer, Lieutenant-Colonel Luxmoore, to be behaving strangely. He was told to report to the Battalion Medical Officer, who found him to be shaky and tremulous and his memory confused. Clearly, he was in no condition to command troops; and so, on 2 May, he wrote to his mother from the 13th Casualty Clearing Station:

* Quivières itself has no church.

Here again! The Doctor suddenly was moved to forbid me to go into action next time the Battalion go, which will be in a day or two. I did not go sick or anything, but he is nervous about my nerves, and sent me down yesterday – labelled Neurasthenia. I still of course suffer from the headaches traceable to my concussion. This will mean that I shall stay here and miss the next Action Tour of Front Line; or even it may mean that I go further down & be employed for a more considerable time on Base Duty or something of the sort. I shall now try and make my French of some avail . . . having satisfied myself that, though in Action I bear a charmed life, and none of woman born can hurt me, as regards flesh and bone, yet my nerves have not come out without a scratch. Do not for a moment suppose I have had a 'breakdown'. I am simply *avoiding* one.

Though he was later to regret the manner of his departure from the Battalion, and particularly that it was the Colonel who had first noticed he was not himself, he writes cheerfully of an encounter with an old school friend, 'Hartop of the Technical', now a Pack Store Corporal in the R.A.M.C. For a fortnight his hopes of being moved 'further down' appeared to be coming to nothing, but he did not care. He was in congenial company, well looked-after, and the weather was hot. Writing to reassure his sister, he offered an interesting self-diagnosis: 'You know it was not the Bosche that worked me up, nor the explosives, but it was living so long by poor old Cock Robin (as we used to call 2/Lt. Gaukroger), who lay not only near by, but in various places around and about, if you understand. I hope you don't!'[45]

The 13th Casualty Clearing Station was situated at Gailly, a diminutive village astride the Somme Canal, which, Wilfred wrote to Mary, was 'much used by the Army'.[46] Perhaps remembering his brother's water-colour of 'The Canal, Uffington Village',[47] he had added: 'A pleasant life for khaki. Why doesn't Harold try it? *The Inland Water Transport Service*'. Now, one hot May afternoon, he and a fellow patient were taken six miles down the beautiful, tree-lined canal on a steam-tug, an experience later to pass into a poem, 'Hospital Barge at Cérisy'.★ Another poem, 'Sunrise',[48] he enclosed in the letter to his mother describing his river trip. It is so bad that

★ See below, p. 249. Cérisy is one and a half miles down the Somme Canal from Gailly.

one suspects his critical judgement was temporarily affected by his neurasthenia. Some evidence of his mental state is afforded by 'a fantasy in the language of the 'Auth: Ver: of 1611' included in a letter to Colin. A light-hearted *jeu d'esprit*, its free associations are not without some significance:

And he knowing that the time of harvest was near at hand, and of the creeping things that creep upon the earth, went down into that water and washed seven times.
And he was covered with boils from head to foot.[49]

The language of the Bible rises like water in the well of his subconscious mind, polluted by war, like those in the ravaged countryside he had so recently crossed. Writing of this unimportant exercise to his mother, he adds an important commentary:

I think the big number of texts which jogged up in my mind in half-an-hour bears witness to a goodly store of them in my being. It is indeed so; and I am more and more Christian as I walk the unchristian ways of Christendom. Already I have comprehended a light which never will filter into the dogma of any national church: namely that one of Christ's essential commands was: Passivity at any price! suffer dishonour and disgrace; but never resort to arms. Be bullied, be outraged, be killed; but do not kill. It may be a chimerical and an ignominious principle, but there it is. It can only be ignored: and I think pulpit professionals are ignoring it very skilfully and successfully indeed.

Have you seen what ridiculous figures Frederick & Arthur Wood★ are cutting? If they made the Great Objection, I should admire them. They have not the courage.

To begin with I think it was puny of Fritz to deny his name. They are now getting up a petition, mentioning their 'unique powers' 'invaluable work' and so on, and wish to carry on their work from *82 Mortimer St. W.* as usual. I do not recollect Christ's office address in Jerusalem, but in any case I don't think He spent much time there.

St. Paul's business premises, if I remember, were somewhat cramped, not to say confined.

But I must not malign these Brethren because I do not know their exact Apologia.

★ Frederick ('Fritz') and Arthur Wood were travelling brother evangelists. See *CL*, p. 105.

And am I not myself a conscientious objector with a very seared conscience?

The evangelicals have fled from a few Candles, discreet incense, serene altars, mysterious music, harmonious ritual to powerful electric-lighting, overheated atmosphere, palm-tree platforms, grand pianos, loud and animated music, extempore ritual; but I cannot see that they are any nearer to the Kingdom.

Christ is literally in no man's land. There men often hear His voice: Greater love hath no man than this, that a man lay down his life – for a friend.

Is it spoken in English only and French?

I do not believe so.

Thus you see how pure Christianity will not fit in with pure patriotism. . . .

(This practice of *selective ignorance* is, as I have pointed out, one cause of the War. Christians have deliberately *cut* some of the main teachings of their code.)[50]

A week later he went down with Trench Fever and was further discomforted by a sudden complete change of hospital staff. In a day or two, however, he was well again and able to write a cheerful twenty-first-birthday letter to Mary, who was now a nurse. Thoughts of evacuation were now uppermost in his mind. He was due to go on 28 May, but at the last moment his name and another were struck off the list. On 6 June, with his name once again on the list, he wrote lightheartedly to his mother:

I go down today. Where to? – Nobody knows. May be in the Hosp. Train for days.

Health: quite restored.

Mood: highest variety of jinks.

Weather: sub-tropical.

Time: 11 a.m.

Appearance: sun-boiled lobster.

Hair: 8% Grey.

Cash in hand: 5 francs.

Size of Socks: same as previous consignment.

Sole Complaints: Nostalgia
                 Mosquito Bites

Last Book Read: *A picked Company* by Belloc.

Clothing: sparse, almost *faun.*

Religion: Primitive Christian.
Aim in War: Extinction of Militarism *beginning* with Prussian.
Aim in Life: Pearls *before* Swine.★[51]

Again his hopes of evacuation were disappointed, this time at the Railhead.

The Train was there, but no accommodation for Officers. The O.C. Train a mi*nute* doctor, with many papers and much pince-nez, refused to let us board: especially as a Major who was with us expressed himself thus: 'Aw I decline. I *eb*solutely decline, to travel in a coach where there are – haw – *Men*!'

This Major is an unconscionable snob,† and consequently suffers something from my humour.

It was slightly too hot that afternoon: they put some twenty Germans into this sumptuous train, and left us stamping on the platform: some indeed lying on stretchers in blankets under the staring sun. When we got back to the Hospital we were the objects of some very ungratifying applause from the unlucky ones left behind.

Finally, at the third attempt, he was lucky himself, and on 11 June reached No. 1 General Hospital at Etretat on the Channel coast, five miles north of Le Havre. He was given a bed in a marquee on the front lawn, overlooking the sea, and was ministered to by American doctors and nurses. Then on 12 or 13 June he crossed from Le Havre to Southampton 'in a luxurious West Indian Liner' with a cabin to himself. From the docks he was taken to the Royal Victoria Hospital (known then as the Welsh Hospital, Netley) which, with its imposing façade on Southampton Water, had been the largest military hospital in the world when it was built in 1863.‡

Early in the morning of 25 June, Owen appeared before a Medical Board at Netley, which reported: 'There is little abnormality to be observed but he seems to be of a highly-strung temperament. He has

---

★ A reference to his pig-farming plans.

† Probably Major Dempster. See below, p. 188.

‡ A quarter of a mile long, it was severely criticized for its design by Florence Nightingale on her return from the Crimea. The wards were dark and poorly ventilated; and the upkeep a continuous drain on Government finances until the hospital was at last demolished in 1966.

slept well while here.' He was described as unfit for General Service for six months, and posted immediately to Craiglockhart War Hospital, Edinburgh, for special observation and treatment. He left Southampton at eleven a.m. with a brother officer with whom he travelled up to London. There he bought a new hat at Peter Robinsons and changed into a new collar, tie, and tie-pin. Thus transformed, he made for Burlington House, where he was disappointed by the 1917 exhibition. After tea in the Shamrock Tea Rooms, 'perhaps the most eminently respectable exclusive and secluded in Town', he was strolling down New Bond Street when he ran into

the last person on earth or under the earth that I wished to meet: Major, now Colonel, Dempster, of the 2nd Battalion. We stopped, of course, and he pretended to be very affable and cordial. Yet I know a more thorough-bred Snob does not exist – even in the imagination of Thackeray. To meet him in my first hour in town. Alas![52]

He was measured for a pair of new trousers at Pope and Bradley's; then ate a cheap dinner, and went to King's Cross an hour before his train was due to leave so as to be sure to get a corner seat. He read some Israel Zangwill* as far as the Midlands where, wondering how many miles he was from Mahim, he fell asleep.

---

* Jewish novelist, playwright, and lecturer (1864–1926). *Children of the Ghetto* was his best-known work.

8

CRAIG-LOCKHART

He woke as the train rounded the coast by Dunbar,[1] his spirits rising with the sun over the Pentland hills and, at last, the high roofs of Edinburgh. The city's noble profile, coming clear of the mist, must have reminded him of that other bright day, five summers before, when he first set foot on Waverley Station. Now, his appetite sharpened by his journey and the seventy steps to the North British Hotel, he there ate a huge breakfast before walking 'the lovely length of Princes Street'. A taxi then drove him through the city's southern suburbs to the gates of the Craiglockhart Hydropathic Establishment and up the long avenue of lime trees to his first view of the building in which he was to spend four of the most formative months of his life.

His first impressions, however, were far from encouraging. Built between 1877 and 1880 in a heavy Italianate style, intended no doubt to promote expectations of Latin luxury, the façade of Craiglockhart Hydro would be daunting enough in a Tuscan setting. The dark flank of Wester Craiglockhart Hill, 'the Craig', upreared like a breaking wave only a hundred yards behind the building, gives it an even more forbidding aspect. The new arrival's first impression of its exterior is reinforced by the echoing gloom of the corridors beyond the black and white marble flags of the entrance hall. These corridors received no natural light, as the patients' rooms opened off them to left and right. Owen's faced north[2] and was probably on the third floor where the corridor narrowed to the width of a ship's companionway. He found Craiglockhart 'too full of officers', and must have seen it in much the same light as a fellow inmate who arrived a month later and subsequently wrote:

Outwardly, [Craiglockhart] War Hospital was . . . elaborately cheerful. Brisk amusements were encouraged, entertainments were got up, and serious cases were seldom seen downstairs. . . .[3]

The doctors did everything possible to counteract gloom, and the wrecked faces were outnumbered by those who were emerging from their nervous disorders. But the War Office had wasted no money on interior decoration; consequently the place had the melancholy atmosphere of a decayed hydro, redeemed only by its healthy situation and pleasant view of the Pentland Hills. By daylight the doctors dealt successfully with these disadvantages, and Slateford,* so to speak, 'made cheerful conversation'.

But by night they lost control and the hospital became sepulchral and oppressive with saturations of war experience. One lay awake and listened to feet padding along passages which smelt of stale cigarette-smoke; for the nurses couldn't prevent insomnia-ridden officers from smoking half the night in their bedrooms, though the locks had been removed from all doors. One became conscious that the place was full of men whose slumbers were morbid and terrifying – men muttering uneasily or suddenly crying out in their sleep. Around me was that underworld of dreams haunted by sub-merged memories of warfare and its intolerable shocks and self-lacerating failures to achieve the impossible. By daylight each mind was a sort of aquarium for the psychopath to study. In the day-time, sitting in a sunny room, a man could discuss his psycho-neurotic symptoms with his doctor, who could diagnose phobias and conflicts and formulate them in scientific terminology. Significant dreams could be noted down, and Rivers† could try to remove repressions. But by night each man was back in his doomed

---

* Craiglockhart is situated in the Slateford district of Edinburgh. Hence SS's use of the name Slateford War Hospital in *Sherston's Progress*.

† Dr. W. H. R. Rivers (1864–1922) had charge of about 100 shell-shocked patients at Craiglockhart. He had come there as a Major in the R.A.M.C., from Magull War Hospital near Liverpool, and his service in these two hospitals marks the final phase of a rich and varied experience in the fields of psychology, ethnology, and neurology. When he joined the staff of Magull War Hospital, the treatment of the mental disorders later known as shell-shock or neurasthenia was regarded with suspicion. In the eyes of those in the War Office, a man was either wounded or well. Dr. Rivers's pioneering work in the treatment and rehabilitation of nerve-shattered soldiers played a significant part in changing official attitudes to such patients. An account of his work is to be found in his posthumous book, *Conflict and Dream*. In this, SS features as 'patient B'; a compliment he returned in *Siegfried's Journey* with his sympathetic portrait of the generous and good doctor.

sector of a horror-stricken front line where the panic and stampede of some ghastly experience was re-enacted among the livid faces of the dead. No doctor could save him then, when he became the lonely victim of his dream disasters and delusions.[4]

There was, however, a brighter side to life at Craiglockhart. Though the building itself was gloomy, its situation had its advantages. These are described in a lavishly illustrated brochure about the Hydro, dated 1903:

This Popular and Extensive Establishment is situated in the western outskirts of Edinburgh, in a charming position, sheltered from easterly winds by the adjoining richly wooded hill of Craiglockhart. The Building, from its elevated site, commands a magnificent panoramic view of the valley of the Forth and adjacent counties, with the Ochils and Grampians in the distance. The prospect, as presented to the eye of the Visitor, from the Establishment, has been graphically described by Sir Walter Scott in the well-known passage of 'Marmion'

> 'Still on the spot Lord Marmion stayed,
> For fairer scene he ne'er surveyed.
>
> . . . .
>
> Such dusky grandeur clothed the height,
> Where the huge Castle holds its state,
>   And all the steep slope down,
> Whose ridgy back heaves to the sky,
> Piled deep and massy, close and high,
>   MINE OWN ROMANTIC TOWN!
>
> . . . .
>
> Yonder the shores of Fife you saw;
> Here Preston-Bay and Berwick-Law;
>   And, broad between them rolled,
> The gallant Firth the eye might note,
> Whose islands on its bosom float,
>   Like emeralds chased in gold.'

An artist's impression of that 'magnificent panoramic view' gives due prominence to the romantic ruins of Craiglockhart Castle, a thirteenth-century keep connected with the Lockhart of Lee family. Since Owen's first literary production at the hospital was to be a historical ballad, it is likely that he learnt what he could (which would not have been much) about the history of the Castle and its purlieus.[5]

The keep was probably built as one of the chain of signal towers designed to give early warning of enemy approach from the south into medieval Scotland. More would no doubt be known of its history in those violent times if Edward I had not carried off with the Stone of Scone three chests of Scottish national records. In the middle of the fifteenth century, the Castle re-emerges in the possession of the Kincaid family, whose persistent blood-feuds with their neighbours led to their lands being forfeited at the beginning of the seventeenth century. In 1609, the estate was purchased by George Foulis, a wealthy goldsmith, who had bought his way into favour at the court of James VI; and when Cromwell marched north, his troopers fired everything that would burn on the Craiglockhart lands. Subsequently, they were owned and sold by the Gilmour, Lockhart, Porteous, and Monro families; and, in 1865, part of the estate was purchased by the City of Edinburgh Parochial Board. On it they erected a poorhouse for 132 males of 'good' character, 84 of 'doubtful' character, and 60 'known to be of bad' character, and three corresponding categories of females. Then in 1877 another section of the property, comprising some thirteen acres, was bought by the newly-formed Craiglockhart Hydropathic Company, who undertook to erect within three years buildings worth not less than £10,000 to be used as a Hydropathic. And so it came about, when the new Craiglockhart Hydro opened its doors in 1880, that the rich and poor of Edinburgh resided on the same hill overlooking 'the Valley of the Forth and adjacent counties'. The venture never fulfilled its shareholders' hopes. Perhaps it was too dark, or its terms too expensive; too far from the city, or too close to the poorhouse. At all events, an air of genteel melancholy as pervasive as rising damp had entered the bones of the building long before it was opened as a Military Hospital, under the Red Cross, in the summer of 1916.

Owen sensed this at once. However, he cannot but have been heartened by his introduction to the Medical Officer to whom he had been assigned. Captain Brock had nothing of the academic reputation of his colleague Captain Rivers, but he would seem to have been a man of energy and charm. And, like his new patient, he was an enthusiastic amateur naturalist. We find him in the first issue

(28 April 1917) of *The Hydra/Journal of the Craiglockhart War Hospital*, under the heading 'Poultry Keeping':

At the instigation of Captain Brock, and owing to the generous gift of a certain lady, a small poultry farm had been successfully started. Led by Lieut. Lees and Lieut. Ritchie, a small body of enthusiasts sallied out one morning and erected a hen-house and pen on the most up to date lines. The hens have been obtained for the Hospital. An incubator was started, but it has proved an incubus. Two officers undertook to pay it the necessary attention, and, no doubt, they did their duty. In fact, we know one of them felt the weight of his responsibility very keenly, and one morning, at about 2 o'clock, paid a visit to the baths to see how his embryotic charges were faring. The Sister caught him coming back up the stairs and woke him up. But that had nothing to do with the fate which ultimately befell the experiment. Some unsuspecting person knocked the top off the thermo-meter, with the consequence that the poor wee things were next roasted in their shells and then frozen. To the abashed enthusiasts we would say: '*Nil desperandum*,' or why not try day-old chicks?

In the second issue of *The Hydra* (12 May), we learn that the poultry-keepers have suffered a further loss – that of their chairman – but, 'due largely to the interest taken in the association by the C.O. and Captain Brock', membership has increased and much has been achieved.

With the advent of finer and more spring-like weather considerable progress has been made in the garden. All the available ground has been dug, and some of it is already planted. . . . efforts are being made to secure a further piece of ground, so that, if the war continues, we may yet see the Association the proud possessor of at least 'three acres and a cow'. Mean-while, lest inaction should damp the enthusiasm of the members who yearn to get back to the land, the Association proposes to undertake the care and upkeep of the tennis lawn and bowling-greens.

This was the prevailing tone of Craiglockhart, by day at any rate: an energetic optimism, everyone throwing himself into some – usually physical – activity. If it was not gardening or poultry-keeping, it might be badminton, billiards, bowls, croquet, cricket, golf, tennis, swimming or water-polo in the heated pool in the basement.

Owen had only been at Craiglockhart a day or two when his honorary aunt, Nellie Bulman, with characteristic kindness sent 'an ambassadress with strawberries and cream'.[6] His first intimation of this was the surprising announcement by 'a fool of a butler-orderly': 'Young lady to see you, Sir!' He replied 'I dont think, but what's it like?' only to discover that 'it' was standing a yard away from him, round the corner: 'a Miss Henderson, a pleasant young lady, from what I could make out of her Scotch; a trifle nervous of me at first; but I did my best: and was sorry I called her Miss Ferguson so often.'

Afterwards he wrote to Mrs. Bulman:

How exceedingly kind of you to send Miss Henderson to see me, and with such a goodly present! A good friend might have sent me strawberries, but only a very special friend could have remembered the cream!

I have also to thank you for the encouragement of your Letter received in France when encouragement was most needed; but when to answer letters was a physical impossibility. Unfortunately, if I delay an answer for a month, it becomes a moral impossibility! Even this I might have written two days ago; but you will forgive me, my Auntie Nelly, and charitably put it down to my distraught state of mind? (For you are all Charity, and I am beginning to discover the sources of my own Mother's sweetness.)

I am not able to settle down here without seeing Mother. I feel a sort of reserve and suspense about everything I do. Otherwise I am quite well – far better than, say, in the good days at Kelso.

I have endured unnameable tortures in France; but I know that I have not suffered by this war as you have and are suffering.* I felt your sympathy with me out there; but now, my dear Auntie Nelly, it is all on my part.

Believe me, very sincerely, and, may I not say affectionately, yours,

Wilfred Owen[7]

Writing the same day to Leslie Gunston, Wilfred sends him the '2nd Draught' of a sonnet 'The Fates'† written late the night before. Unable to sleep, he had read *The Usurper* by W. J. Locke until three a.m. and 'noticed it never grew quite dark all night'. If the sonnet is somewhat stilted, the 'Ballad of Lady Yolande' on which, so he tells his cousin, he is at work, is hardly more promising. It begins in the manner of Sir Walter Scott, with an Owenite description of the heroine's page:

---

* Her son Bill and her daughter's fiancé, Walter Forrest, had been killed in action.
† See *CP*, p. 122.

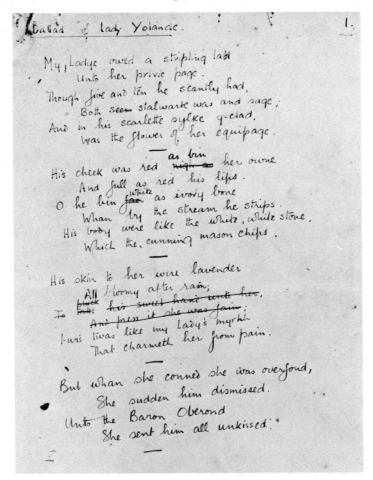

Owen's description of the recognition and rejection of a guilty love for a beautiful boy is of some psychological interest, but his ballad has little literary merit. This he must have recognized himself as, in the calm of Craiglockhart, his judgement like a jolted compass rediscovered its true north. He never finished the 'Ballad of Lady Yolande'.

Instead, he began another long poem, this time in blank verse on a subject of Dr. Brock's suggesting: the mythic encounter of Hercules and Antaeas, the giant who derived invincible strength from contact with the earth.★ The moral for the lapsed botanist in the shell-shock hospital is clear enough. Owen warmed to his subject, and the resulting fragment has a marked physical power:

The Wrestlers

So neck to neck and obstinate knee to knee
Wrestled those two; and peerless Heracles
Could not prevail nor catch at any vantage;
But those huge hands which small had strangled snakes
& Let slip the writhing of Antaeas' wrists;
Those clubs of hands that wrenched the necks of bulls
Now fumbled round the slim Antaeas' limbs
Baffled. Then anger swelled in Heracles,
And terribly he grappled broader arms,
And yet more firmly fixed his grasping feet,
And up his back the muscles bulged and shone
Like climbing banks and domes of towering cloud.
Many who watched that wrestling say he laughed,—
But not so loud as on Eurystheus of old,
But that his pantings, seldom loosed, long pent,
Were like the sighs of lions at their meat.
Men say their fettered fury tightened hour by hour,
Until the veins rose tubrous on their brows
And froth flew thickly shivered from both beards.
As pythons shudder, bridling-in their spite
So trembled that Antaeas with held strength,
While Heracles,— the thews and cordage of his thighs
Straitened and strained beyond the utmost stretch
From quivering heel to haunch like sweating
hawsers—
But only staggered backward. Then his throat

★ See *CP*, p. 120.

Growled, like a great beast when his meat is touched,
As if he smelt some guile behind Antæas,
And knew the buttressed bulking of his shoulders
Bore not the mass weight to move it one thumbs' length.

But what it was so helped the man none guessed,
Save Hylas, whom the fauns had once made wise
How earth herself empowered him by her touch,
Gave him the grip and strengency of winter,
And all the ardour of the invincible spring;
How all the blood of June glutted his heart;
And the wild glow of huge autumnal storms
Stirred on his face, and flickered from his eyes;
How, too, Poseidon blessed him fatherly
With wafts of vigour from the keen sea waves,
And with the subtle coil of currents —
Strange underflows, that maddened Heracles.
And towards the night they sundered, neither thrown.
Whereat came Hylas running to his friend

The violent verbs from which the poem derives much of its power
are a clear legacy of the battlefield, as is such a phrase as 'the wild
glow of huge autumnal storms'.

On the evening of 13 July, the lapsed botanist made a move to
renew his own contact with the earth. He attended an enthusiastic
preliminary meeting of a Field Club

at which Mr. Chase gave a paper on 'Mosses of the Craiglockhart District,' illustrated by specimens, diagrams, and microscopic slides. At the close it was resolved that a field club should be definitely constituted, that there should be a meeting every Monday evening for a paper and discussion, and that, if possible, excursions should be arranged. The following office-bearers were elected: – President, Capt. Brock; secretary, Mr. Chase. Recruits are wanted. Don't wait to be pushed. 'The wind's on the heath.' . . . One who apparently came to last Friday's meeting in order to do penance for his sins, writes: – 'To most of us, the subject of moss smelt mouldy with fusty suggestiveness. . . . Moss! – the unkempt beard of senile ruins; the pall of dead paths that lead nowhere; the praying-stool of hermits. What attachment has it for the rolling stones that the war has made us all? Mr. Chase, with a microscope, drawings, and lively description, showed it to be one of the most beautifully interesting of living things. And just as the whole plant world sprang from mosses, and much humbler growths than mosses, so we hope that from this beginning will develop an important and varied system of natural work. One gentleman objected to our calling our club a Natural History Society, because natural history reminded him of school-marms and spectacles. We do not want all our excursions to be through the jungle of a *hortus siccus*.

'Our broodings over the face of the earth, and the firmament, and the waters under the earth, will be quite primitive – without form, but, we hope, not void.'

The style – studded with puns, quotations from Borrow and the Bible – is unmistakable. Between that meeting and the publication of the anonymous correspondent's account of it, a long-standing ambition had been fulfilled. Wilfred Owen found himself enthroned in an editorial chair. *The Hydra* was his.

Much else was happening to him. He had been visited by 'Dr. Brock's ladies', a group of Edinburgh women who took a kindly interest in the rehabilitation of Craiglockhart patients; he had been shown over munitions works and brass foundries; he had spent a morning 'beating out a plate of copper into a bowl'; and was planning expeditions to be made with his mother, who had come up to stay with Mrs. Bulman.[8] A few days later, he writes to Leslie Gunston:

On Mond. next I lecture the 'Field Club' – a Nat. Hist. association, on the lines of our old Society★ – Geological, (you & me) & Botanical (Vera). Do you remember: you old Black Moth? Well, the days have come when I am one of the founders of a real learned society. My subject has the rather journalese Title of 'Do Plants Think?' – a study of the Response to Stimuli & Devices for Fertilisation, etc. I have no books yet, but I remember a number of useful points from your big Cassell's (I think it was Cassell's) studied in 1911. Meanwhile I'm beastly bothered with our Mag. (herewith) *and* I'm [to] take German Lessons at the Berlitz, Edin.[9]

The lecture that Owen delivered on the evening of Monday 30 July offers a revealing exposition of his ideas about Nature. He set out, as he said,

to demonstrate by a number of instances, that Plants have all the elements of perception, and if not consciousness, at least *senscience*: that they have the glimmerings of sight; that vaguely and sleepily, they feel; they feel heat and cold, dryness and damp, and the contact of bodies, that they are even able to smell, and are as well aware of the force of gravity as any of the animals. And further, taken as a whole, the Plant Kingdom exhibits what I can only call Forethought. The same motives which make us wear tin-helmets in certain environments, and carry bayonets, much the same motives which prompt us in youth to wear gorgeous socks & neckties, and persons over-age to dress soberly, and to hoard food: also actuate a plant, when it produces special protective coverings, sharpens its spines, wastes its young substance in riotous colours, allows those colours to fade immediately fertilization is accomplished.

At eleven o'clock that night Owen wrote triumphantly to his mother:

The Lecture was a huge success, & went on till 10.20!! At least I was answering cross-questions until that time. My swotting & pottering of the good old Matric. days, and my laborious escapes from Dunsden Vicarage to Reading College have been well crowned tonight. I have *only once* since getting through the Barrage at Feyet felt such exultation as when winding up to my peroration tonight!. . . .
The 'only once' was when I saw you gliding up to me, veiled in azure, at the Caledonian.† I thought you looked very very beautiful and well,

★ The AGBS. See above, p. 44. LG was known as Black Moth, WO as Carnation.
† Hotel.

The HYDRA

Journal of the Craiglockhart War Hospital

No. 7   JULY 21st, 1917   Price 6d

CONTENTS

	PAGE		PAGE
Editorial	7	The Chronicles of a V.O.S.	12
Notes and News	7	Photographic Notes	15
Be Still, my Soul	9	Correspondence	15
The Counter Attack	10	Arrivals	16
Concerts	11	Departures	16
Short Stories	11	Transfers	16

H. & J. Pillans & Wilson, Printers, Edinburgh.

through the veil, and especially on the night of the concert. But without the veil I saw better the supremer beauty of the ashes of all your sacrifices: for Father, for me, and for all of us. . . .

I must have the Magazine ready by tomorrow morning.

This, the eighth issue of *The Hydra*, opened with a punning editorial and ended with the usual lists of ARRIVALS and DEPARTURES. The first of these included the name of 2nd Lieut. Siegfried Sassoon, R.W.F.,★ which probably meant nothing to the editor of *The Hydra* as he read his proofs.

A week later, he describes himself to his mother as

a sick man in hospital, by night; a poet, for quarter of an hour after breakfast; I am whatever and whoever I see while going down to Edinburgh on the tram: greengrocer, policeman, shopping lady, errand boy, paper-boy, blind man, crippled Tommy, bank-clerk, carter, all of these in half an hour; next a German student in earnest; then I either peer over bookstalls in back-streets, or do a bit of a dash down Princes Street, – according as I have taken weak tea or strong coffee for breakfast.[10]

He had just spent the afternoon with 2nd Lieut. J. B. Salmond of the Black Watch who, as a former *Daily Mail* sub-editor, was going to take *The Hydra*'s printer in hand. Salmond had written for the *Boys Own Paper* and no doubt impressed Owen with the financial opportunities of that form of journalism, for he subsequently jotted down an idea for a short story on a sheet of paper headed 'B.O.P. Stories for Magazines'.

After talking to Salmond, Owen went upstairs with him to the hospital cinema, and that evening an ambition as old as his desire to be a journalist came within sight of fulfilment. As he told his mother,

Pockett† enrôled me as Mr. Wallcomb, in *Lucky Durham*:‡ a fashionable

---

★ Royal Welch Fusiliers.

† Lieutenant J. W. G. Pockett and 2nd Lieutenant J. C. Isaacson, R.F.C., and their wives, who were at this time living nearby, were all professional actors.

‡ A comedy by the actor-manager Wilson Barrett (1847–1904), first performed at the King's Theatre, Hammersmith, 28 August 1905. Wilfred's interest in the theatre was

young fellow, whose chief business in the play is introducing people. . . .

Pockett, and Mrs. Pockett, Isaacson and Mrs. Isaacson (Portia) are all in it, so I shall know what it really feels like to be 'on the stage'. Only the first 2 Acts are being done next Sat., finishing the following week.

He had recently bought Tennyson's poem *The Lover's Tale*,[11] and went on to say:

The other day I read a Biography of Tennyson, which says he was unhappy, even in the midst of his fame, wealth, and domestic serenity. Divine discontent! I can quite believe he never knew happiness for one moment such as I have – for one or two moments. But as for misery, was he ever frozen alive, with dead men for comforters. Did he hear the moaning at the bar, not at twilight and the evening bell only, but at dawn, noon, and night, eating and sleeping, walking and working, always the close moaning of the Bar; the thunder, the hissing and the whining of the Bar?

Tennyson, it seems, was always a great child.
So should I have been, but for Beaumont Hamel.[12]

Two days later, Owen, Captain Brock, five other members of the Field Club, and the nineteen-year-old son of one Captain Mackenzie took the mid-day train from Slateford to Balerno

whence they struck out for the hills. The route lay by Threipmuir Reservoir and Bavelaw Castle (at which point there were two desertions), then *via* the Green Cleuch, and round the flank of the Black Hill to Loganlee Waterfall:

---

considerable, and it was known in the family that he drafted a full-length play at Craiglockhart. The MS was never seen, but the following note survives, on headed Craiglockhart paper:

Two Thousand

Act I Scene I	The Lord of Europe's Dining Room, London
Scene II	Schoolroom
Act II	(2 days later)
Act III	Secret Meeting House under The Atlantic: reached by private submarine

---

Purpose:	To expose war to the criticism of reason.
Plot:	The federation of America with Europe by personal violence to the American Emperor.
Interest:	Dress: Manners, Machines, References to men of this century.
	e.g. who *was* Lloyd George?

this little cascade comes down very prettily in a small amphitheatre formed by horizontal layers of old red sandstone and conglomerate. Then round we swung into 'Habbie's Howe', and soon were 'discussing' scones and jam and fresh eggs in the shepherd's cottage at the head of the reservoir. The homeward stretch by Glencorse Reservoir, and then over the hill to Bonaly and Colinton, was done at a good pace, as we had no late passes and couldn't face the C.O.'s wrath. Botanically, of course, heather was the feature of the excursion. Two wanderers from Shropshire saw no small resemblance between the Pentlands and the Longmynd range, on the Welsh border.[13]

The party arrived back a quarter of an hour late for dinner. That evening, after the last rehearsal for *Lucky Durham*, Owen sat down to write to his mother. Perhaps the cries of soldiers tossing in their tortured sleep reminded him of what was happening in trenches across the Channel. At all events, his old bitterness, unmuffled by the comforts of Craiglockhart, broke from him again:

I'm overjoyed that you think of making bandages for the wounded. Leave Black Sambo ignorant of Heaven. White men are in Hell. Aye, leave him ignorant of the civilization that sends us there, and the religious men that say it is good to be in that Hell. (Continued, because important) Send an English Testament to his Grace of Canterbury, and let it consist of that one sentence, at which he winks his eyes:

'Ye have heard that it *hath* been said: An eye for an eye, and a tooth for a tooth:

But I say that ye resist not evil, but whosoever shall smite thee on thy right cheek, turn to him the other also.'

And if his reply be 'Most unsuitable for the present distressing moment, my dear lady! But I trust that in God's good time . . . etc.' – *then there is only one possible conclusion*, that there are no more Christians at the present moment than there were at the end of the first century.

While I wear my star and eat my rations, I continue to take care of my Other Cheek; and, thinking of the eyes I have seen made sightless, and the bleeding lad's cheeks I have wiped, I say: Vengeance is mine, I, Owen, will repay.

Let my lords turn to the people when they say 'I believe in . . . Jesus Christ', and we shall see as dishonest a face as ever turned to the East, bowing, over the Block at Tyburn.[14]

The following evening, the Hospital's Saturday concert ended with the first act of *Lucky Durham* which (if *The Hydra* of 18 August is to be believed) was a considerable success. Owen, proud of his make-up (applied by Isaacson★ 'with a real Bensonian touch'), felt at ease and evidently enjoyed himself. On 15 August, giving his mother an account of that evening, he for the first time mentions the newcomer to Craiglockhart.

I have just been reading Siegfried Sassoon, and am feeling at a very high pitch of emotion. Nothing like his trench life sketches has ever been written or ever will be written. Shakespere reads vapid after these. Not of course because Sassoon is a greater artist, but because of the subjects, I mean. I think if I had the choice of making friends with Tennyson or with Sassoon I should go to Sassoon.

That is why I have not yet dared to go up to him and parley in a casual way.

A day or so later he plucked up courage and knocked, gently, on Sassoon's door. A voice answered, the door opened, and Owen advanced into blazing sunlight and the most important meeting of his life. Though it was to prove hardly less important for Sassoon, Siegfried had no inkling of this at the time.

Short, dark-haired, and shyly hesitant, he stood for a moment before coming across to the window, where I was sitting on my bed cleaning my golf clubs. A favourable first impression was made by the fact that he had under his arm several copies of *The Old Huntsman*. He had come, he said, hoping that I would be so gracious as to inscribe them for himself and some of his friends. He spoke with a slight stammer, which was no unusual thing in that neurosis-pervaded hospital. My leisurely, commentative method of inscribing the books enabled him to feel more at home with me. He had a charming honest smile, and his manners – he stood at my elbow rather as though conferring with a superior officer – were modest and ingratiating. He gave me the names of his friends first. When it came to his own I found myself writing one that has since gained a notable place in the roll of English poets – Wilfred Owen. I had taken an instinctive liking to him, and felt that I could talk freely. During the next half-hour or more I must have spoken mainly about my book and its interpretations of the War. He listened

★ At one time a member of Benson's company.

eagerly, questioning me with reticent intelligence. It was only when he was departing that he confessed to being a writer of poetry himself, though none of it had yet appeared in print.

It amuses me to remember that, when I had resumed my ruminative club-polishing, I wondered whether his poems were any good! He had seemed an interesting little chap but had not struck me as remarkable. In fact my first view of him was as a rather ordinary young man, perceptibly provincial, though unobtrusively ardent in his responses to my lordly dictums about poetry. Owing to my habit of avoiding people's faces while talking, I had not observed him closely. Anyhow, it was pleasant to have discovered that there was another poet in the hospital and that he happened to be an admirer of my work.[15]

To all outward appearances, there could hardly be two men less alike than Wilfred Owen and Siegfried Sassoon. At 5 ft. 5½ ins, Owen was almost a foot shorter than the stately Sassoon, whose long face and lean athletic figure gave him something of the look of one of those thoroughbred horses that, before the War, he had hunted three days a week. Not for him the sixpenny ride on the sands of Scarborough or New Brighton. Descended from those 'jewelled merchant Ancestors',[16] the banker Sassoons, Siegfried was born (six and a half years before Wilfred) with a silver spoon in his mouth more expensive than any in Plas Wilmot. He was brought up by his mother, his father having left his wife when his son was five. As with Owen, the dominant domestic presences of his childhood and youth were female: his nanny, his grandmother, the elegant socialite Mrs. Sassoon, her friends Ellen Batty and Wirgie (Helen Wirgman), and a regiment of devoted domestics. When he was old enough to go to Marlborough, he shuttled between all-male and all-female worlds, and grew up with the shrivelled emotions, the well-bred reserve of his class. Cambridge and the History Tripos did not appeal to him, so he left without taking a degree – nine years before Owen recognized it as one of his 'most terrible regrets' that he never had the chance of going to Oxford.[17]

There being no pressure on him to choose a career or earn a living, Sassoon spent his days in the saddle or on the golf-links; his evenings at the ballet, the opera, or his London club. From 1906, when he published his first, privately-printed *Poems*, he began to move in

literary circles and by August 1914 was acquainted with the likes of
Edmund Gosse and Edward Marsh, Rupert Brooke and W. H.
Davies. As if in acknowledgement of some subconscious need for
more demanding employment, he had himself medically examined
for the Army on 1 August 1914 and was wearing his ill-fitting khaki
on the first morning of the Great War. Since then he had fought – at
Mametz Wood and in the Somme Offensive of July 1916 – with such
conspicuous gallantry that he had acquired the Military Cross and a
nickname, Mad Jack. However, invalided back to England at the
beginning of April 1917, with a sniper's bullet through his chest, he
had begun to take a different view of the War. On the lawns of
Garsington Manor he met and mingled with such of Lady Ottoline
Morrell's pacifist intellectual friends as Bertrand Russell and Henry
Massingham, editor of *The Nation*. Influenced by them, and with
courage equal to any he had shown in action, he made public a statement sent to his commanding officer:

I am making this statement as an act of wilful defiance of military
authority, because I believe that the war is being deliberately prolonged
by those who have the power to end it.

I am a soldier, convinced that I am acting on behalf of soldiers. I believe
that this war, upon which I entered as a war of defence and liberation, has
now become a war of aggression and conquest. I believe that the purposes
for which I and my fellow-soldiers entered upon this war should have been
so clearly stated as to have made it impossible to change them, and that,
had this been done, the objects which actuated us would now be attainable
by negotiation.

I have seen and endured the sufferings of the troops, and I can no longer
be a party to prolong these sufferings for ends which I believe to be evil
and unjust.

I am not protesting against the conduct of the war, but against the
political errors and insincerities for which the fighting men are being
sacrificed.

On behalf of those who are suffering now I make this protest against the
deception which is being practised on them; also I believe that I may help
to destroy the callous complacence with which the majority of those at
home regard the continuance of agonies which they do not share, and
which they have not sufficient imagination to realize.

July, 1917.   S. Sassoon.

Siegfried Sassoon in 1916

Although, to a certain extent, this 'act of wilful defiance' was successful, in that it formed the subject of a question asked in the House of Commons and received an airing – a hot airing – in the press, Sassoon's protest was eventually smothered by his friend Robert Graves. Graves, who subsequently wrote:

I entirely agreed with Siegfried about the 'political errors and insincerities' and thought his action magnificently courageous. But more things had to be considered than the strength of our case against the politicians. In the first place, he was in no proper physical condition to suffer the penalty which the letter invited: namely to be court-martialled, cashiered, and imprisoned. I found myself most bitter with the pacifists who had encouraged him to make this gesture. I felt that, not being soldiers, they could not understand what it cost Siegfried emotionally. It was wicked that he should have to face the consequences of his letter on top of those Quadrangle and Fontaine-les-Croiselles experiences. I also realized the inadequacy of such a gesture. Nobody would follow his example, either in England or in Germany. The war would inevitably go on and on until one side or the other cracked.[18]

Graves made urgent representations to the military authorities, as well as certain influential civilians, that Sassoon 'should not be allowed to become a martyr to a hopeless cause in his present physical condition'. The War Office was only too glad of an opportunity to hush matters up. A Medical Board was hastily convened and rigged: 2nd Lieutenant Graves testified that his friend – who by now had thrown his Military Cross into the Mersey – suffered from hallucinations of a corpse-strewn Piccadilly and other such symptoms of shell-shock. Three times while giving his statement Graves burst into tears. The Board duly found 2nd Lieutenant Sassoon in need of medical attention and he was despatched to Craiglockhart War Hospital, supposedly under the escort of 2nd Lieutenant Graves. He, however, missed the 'patient's' train and arrived several hours after him.

Little of this would have been known to the young officer who knocked on Sassoon's door and stammered out his request that he might sign the copies of *The Old Huntsman* he had brought with him. He knew him, in so far as he knew him at all, through his book, and there he must have sensed a being more like himself than this elegant sportsman with an expression of boredom on his face.[19] The war poems of *The Old Huntsman* represent the heart of the book, following the long title poem, themselves followed by a number of generally earlier and feebler poems on more literary subjects in more literary language. Owen told Sassoon that he thought 'The Death-Bed' the finest poem in the book. It begins:

He drowsed and was aware of silence heaped
Round him, unshaken as the steadfast walls;
Aqueous like floating rays of amber light,
Soaring and quivering in the wings of sleep, –
Silence and safety; and his mortal shore
Lipped by the inward, moonless waves of death.

This was an interesting choice, in that it was one of *The Old Huntsman*'s more conventional war poems, its language not unlike that of some of Owen's work, a poem with none of the realism, none of the savagery of some others in the book, for example,

'THEY'

The Bishop tells us: 'When the boys come back
'They will not be the same; for they'll have fought
'In a just cause; they lead the last attack
'On Anti-Christ; their comrades' blood has bought
'New right to breed an honourable race.
'They have challenged Death and dared him face to face.'

'We're none of us the same!' the boys reply.
'For George lost both his legs; and Bill's stone blind;
'Poor Jim's shot through the lungs and like to die;
'And Bert's gone syphilitic: you'll not find
'A chap who's served that hasn't found *some* change.'
And the Bishop said: 'The ways of God are strange!'

The treatment of the religious theme in this poem and such others as 'The Redeemer',★ 'Stand-to: Good Friday Morning', and 'The Choral Union' must have won Owen's assent. This chord and others were to be heard again in the poems, the greater poems, that Owen was himself to write in the coming months.

Encouraged by his reception the first time he visited Sassoon, Owen knocked on his door again a few evenings later:

★ '"The Redeemer", I have been trying to write every week for the last three years.' *CL*, p. 489.

when I went in he was struggling to read a letter from Wells; whose hand-writing is not only a slurred *suggestion* of words, but in a dim pink ink! Wells talks of coming up here to see him and his doctor; not about Sassoon's state of health, but about *God the Invisible King*.★

Shyly, Owen produced a sheaf of manuscript poems, which prob-ably included '1914', 'The One Remains', 'Sonnet Autumnal', 'Perversity', 'The Peril of Love', 'To –', 'Maundy Thursday', and 'On my Songs'.

Some of my old Sonnets didn't please him at all. But the 'Antæus' he applauded fervently; and a short lyric which I don't think you know 'Sing me at morn but only with thy Laugh'† he pronounced perfect work, absolutely charming, etc. etc. and begged that I would copy it out for him, to show to the powers that be.

So the last thing he said was 'Sweat your guts out writing poetry!' 'Eh?' says I. 'Sweat your guts out, I say!' He also warned me against early publishing: but recommended Martin Secker for a small volume of 10 or 20 poems.

From this point until Owen left Craiglockhart in November, he and Sassoon would see something of each other most evenings. By day, while one played golf, the other went picnicking with friends, visited Edinburgh Zoo with the Field Club, watched a Model Yacht Regatta and thought how much his father would have liked to compete.[20] And after supper he would go along to Sassoon's room and talk of poetry. Remembering those meetings many years later, Sassoon was to write:

My encouragement was opportune, and I can claim to have given him a lively incentive during his rapid advance to self-revelation. Meanwhile I seem to hear him laughingly implore me to chuck these expository generalizations and recover some of the luminous animation of our intimacy. How about my indirect influence on him? he inquires in his calm velvety voice. Have I forgotten our eager discussions of contemporary poets and the technical dodges which we were ourselves devising? Have I

★ London, 1917.
† 'Song of Songs', *CP*, p. 126.

forgotten the simplifying suggestions which emanated from my unsophisticated poetic method? (For my technique was almost elementary
compared with his innovating experiments.) Wasn't it after he got to know
me that he first began to risk using the colloquialisms which were at that
time to frequent in my verses? . . . Turning the pages of Wilfred's *Poems*,
I am glad to think that there may have been occasions when some freely
improvised remark of mine sent him away with a fruitful idea. And my
humanized reportings of front-line episodes may have contributed something to his controlled vision of what he had seen for himself.[21]

Few readers of 'Songs of Songs' would go so far as Sassoon in
calling it 'perfect work', but interesting it certainly is. Its rhetoric and
archaic diction cannot disguise an element of strenuous experimenta-
tion. Like a painter practising effects of brushwork, the poet appears
more interested in exploring the possibilities of pararhyme★ and
internal assonance than in his avowed subject:

> Sing me at morn but only with your laugh;
> Even as Spring that laugheth into leaf;
> Even as Love that laugheth after Life.

It seems likely that Sassoon's praise of this poem prompted Owen to
apply his technical innovations to something more ambitious. On a
sheet of the same paper as that used for a number of other poems
composed or completed at Craiglockhart he wrote 'From my Diary,
July 1914'. Probably his first extended use of consonantal rhyming,
this has much in common with 'Song of Songs': the 'leaf'/'Life',
'Leaves'/'Lives' rhyme, 'Love that laugheth'/'the love-laugh',
'sigh'/'sighing', 'throbbing', 'leaflets', and the 'midnight'/'gloom'
of the closing lines.

★ For a discussion of the possible origins of WO's para- or consonantal-rhymes, see
Welland, pp. 104–24; but he had been interested in half-rhymes at least since 1912 when he
marked his copy of Symonds, *Shelley* (see above, pp. 69–70). This interest may have been
stimulated in August 1917 by a poem of which he wrote to LG: 'Now, O.A.J's FATE is
a very beautiful poem, very lovely. I do *not* find that the riming of the same word [is] at
all upsetting: and, believe me, a wrong rime is often the right thing to do.' This letter is
mis-dated as '? late May 1914' in *CL*, p. 250. Unfortunately, I have been unable to trace
Miss Joergens's 'Fate'. It does not appear in her only published collection, *The Woman
and the Sage* (see below, p.314).

Another, more easily identifiable relic of the two poets' association remains: an unpublished manuscript poem in Owen's handwriting, but signed S.S.

VISION

~~POETS~~

Men with enchanted faces, who are these,
Following the birds and voices of the breeze?
Men who desire no longer to be wise,
And bear eternal forests in their eyes.

They are all singing of beauty; yet their dreams
Are mute amid that silence hung with green;
Silence of drifting clouds with towering beams
Dazzling the gloom, silence on earth serene.

No song beyond that archway of the hours,
But beauty breaking in a heaven of flowers,
And everywhere the whispering of trees . . .
Men with triumphant faces, who are these?

Sassoon wrote these rather trivial stanzas and showed them to Owen who copied them out. Realizing later that it was not a good poem, Sassoon never published it, but one phrase from it did find its way into print – in line 4 of a poem Owen wrote on 29–30 August:[22]

My Shy Hand.

My shy hand shades a hermitage apart,—
O large enough for thee, and thy brief hours.
Life there is sweeter held than in God's heart,
Stiller than in the heavens of hollow flowers.

> The wine is gladder there than in gold bowls.
> And Time shall not ~~drain thence~~ drain thence, nor trouble spill.
> Sources between my fingers feed all souls,
> Where ~~And~~ thou mayest cool thy lips, and draw thy fill.
>
> Five cushions hath my hand, for reveries;
> And one deep pillow for thy brow's fatigues;
> Languor of June all winterlong, and ease
> For ever from the vain untravelled leagues.
>
> Thither your years may gather in from storm,
> And Love, that sleepeth there, will keep thee warm.

I believe there is detectable in this the first echo of a new music to which Owen was then – perhaps at Sassoon's recommendation – being exposed. Sassoon had given him an inscribed copy of his poem *The Daffodil Murderer* and, writing to his mother on 12 September, Owen quotes from the 'spoof' Preface allegedly by 'William Butler', but in fact by Sassoon himself. It may conceivably have been that this introduced the name of Yeats into their conversation. At all events, it would appear that in August 1917 Owen was introduced to the poems of Yeats, or at any rate tuned in to them for the first time.[24] 'My Shy Hand's' escapist vision of a Romantic Bower of Bliss perhaps owes something to that dominant theme of Yeats's early love poetry, as expressed in 'The Lake Isle of Innisfree' and 'To an Isle in the Water'. The first stanza of the latter poem shares the unusual adjective 'shy' and the rhyme-words 'heart' and 'apart' with the first stanza of 'My Shy Hand'. Yeats's poem opens:

Shy one, shy one,
Shy one of my heart,
She moves in the firelight
Pensively apart.

If the first echo was a faint one, there can be no mistaking the
second. A few weeks later he wrote:

SIX O'CLOCK IN PRINCES STREET

In twos and threes, they have not far to roam,
  Crowds that thread eastward, gay of eyes;
Those seek no further than their quiet home,
  Wives, walking westward, slow and wise.

Neither should I go fooling over clouds,
  Following gleams unsafe, untrue,
And tiring after beauty through star-crowds,
  Dared I go side by side with you;

Or be you in the gutter where you stand,
  Pale rain-flawed phantom of the place,
With news of all the nations in your hand,
  And all their sorrows in your face.[25]

Can one doubt that running through his head were those lines from
Yeats's free translation of Ronsard's sonnet:

. . . one man loved the pilgrim soul in you,
And loved the sorrows of your changing face;

And bending down beside the glowing bars,
Murmur, a little sadly, how Love fled
And paced upon the mountains overhead
And hid his face amid a crowd of stars.

The Hydra continued to take up a good deal of its editor's time. Its
layout had been improved, but by number 10 (1 September) Owen
was having to write a substantial part himself: his editorial, a long
'Field Club' article, and the first of his poems to appear in print,

'Song of Songs'.[26] Sassoon gave the hard-pressed editor a poem of his own, 'Dreamers', which was printed in the same issue.

Like many other occupants of Craiglockhart, Owen suffered at times from 'disastrous dreams',[27] but otherwise his health seems to have been good and Sassoon was later to recall

his consistent cheerfulness. . . . Always the modest disciple, he never struck me as being subject to fits of depression. He seemed to be contented & occupied; his only lapses from cheerfulness were when he was being a bit emotional – about life in general, &, possibly the war, – & his feeling for my poetry – (His emotional moods used to make me feel slightly uncomfortable.) As we got to know one another well, his admiring attitude towards me relaxed – affectionately & diffidently – into occasional signs of being amused by my idiosyncracies – my incoherent way of expressing myself & my voluble outbursts of intolerance & enthusiasm.

W. was the *quiet* one; he spoke slowly – in that rather velvety voice of his – which somehow suggested the Keatsian richness of his poetry; it wasn't a vibrating voice – it had the texture of soft consonants, & suggested crimsons & sumptuous browns.[28]

On Saturday 9 September, Owen lunched with his friend at the Golf Club, and afterwards 'put him to the trial of writing a poem in 3 minutes in the manner of those in the *Graphic*, etc. He produced 12 lines in 4 minutes. Absolutely undistinguishable from the style of thing in the Magazines.'[29] Sassoon, however, produced something better for the 15 September issue of *The Hydra* – 'The Rear-Guard' – a poem, which, like 'Enemies' in *The Old Huntsman*, may be a milestone on the road to Owen's 'Strange Meeting'. The editor himself contributed to this issue another long Field Club notice and a mildly facetious account of life at Craiglockhart, 'in mediaeval jargon', entitled 'Extract from ye Chronicles of Wilfred de Salope, Knight'.

As a change from the hospital and the roundabout of Edinburgh society on which he was now merrily riding, Owen agreed to give lessons on English literature to the boys of the Tynecastle Secondary School. Built in 1912, this was a couple of miles from Craiglockhart, and on the morning of 25 September he gave his first lesson, to 39 boys.[30] Writing to his mother that afternoon, he enclosed his 'two best war Poems'. One was to appear (like 'Song of Songs', anonymously) in *The Hydra* of 29 September:

THE NEXT WAR

War's a joke for me and you,
While we know such dreams are true.
                        SIEGFRIED SASSOON

Out there, we've walked quite friendly up to Death;
   Sat down and eaten with him, cool and bland, –
   Pardoned his spilling mess-tins in our hand.
We've sniffed the green thick odour of his breath, –
Our eyes wept, but our courage didn't writhe.
   He's spat at us with bullets and he's coughed
   Shrapnel. We chorussed when he sang aloft;
We whistled while he shaved us with his scythe.

Oh, Death was never enemy of ours!
   We laughed at him, we leagued with him, old chum.
No soldier's paid to kick against his powers.
   We laughed, knowing that better men would come,
And greater wars; when each proud fighter brags
He wars on Death – for lives; not men – for flags.[31]

Sassoon's influence is clear, and he made no less a contribution to the second poem, which sprang from an unlikely source: the anonymous Prefatory Note to *Poems of Today*, 1916 (Owen possessed the December 1916 reprint), which began:

   This book has been compiled in order that boys and girls, already perhaps familiar with the great classics of the English speech, may also know something of the newer poetry of their own day. Most of the writers are living, and the rest are still vivid memories among us, while one of the youngest, almost as these words are written, has gone singing to lay down his life for his country's cause . . . . there is no arbitrary isolation of one theme from another; they mingle and interpenetrate throughout, to the music of Pan's flute, and of Love's viol, and the bugle-call of Endeavour, and the passing-bell of Death.

It is not difficult to imagine him, stung by those sentiments, sitting down to work on a poem whose approach had been heralded by the bells, 'Bugles that sadden all the evening air', the wailing shells, 'The monstrous anger of our taciturn guns', of two earlier fragments, 'All sounds have been as music' and 'Bugles sang':*

* CP, pp. 127 and 128.

This largely unrhymed first draft he showed to Sassoon as they sat in a corner of one of Craiglockhart's cavernous lounges.[33] The Master suggested 'Anthem for Dead Youth' as a title. His disciple, delighted, added it to the manuscript. Sassoon then proposed a number of other alterations and himself wrote them in in pencil. It would seem that Owen then went away and produced a considerably revised – and rhymed – version:

> Anthem to Dead Youth.
>
> What passing bells for you who die in herds?
>   — Only the monstrous anger of more guns.
> Only the stuttering rifles' rattled words
>   Can patter out your hasty orisons.
> No chants for you, nor balms, nor wreaths, nor bells,
>   Nor any voice of mourning, save the choirs,
> The shrill demented choirs of wailing shells;
>   And bugles calling for you from sad shires.
>
> What candles may we hold to speed you all?
>   Not in the hands of boys, but in their eyes
>   Shall shine the holy lights of long goodbyes.
> The pallor of girls' brows shall be your pall;
>   Your flowers the tenderness of mortal minds;
> And each slow dusk, a drawing-down of blinds.

The octave was tightened in a third – and then a modified fourth – version:

Anthem for Dead Youth.

What passing-bells for you who die in herds?
  – Only the monstrous anger of the guns!
  – Only the stuttering rifles' rattled words
Can patter out your hasty orisons.
No chants for you, nor balms, nor wreaths, nor bells,
  Nor any voice of mourning, save the choirs,
the And shrill demented choirs of wailing shells;
  And bugles calling for you from sad shires.

What candles may we hold to speed you all?
  Not in the hands of boys, but in their eyes
Shall shine the holy lights of long goodbyes.
The pallor of girls' brows shall be your pall;
Your flowers, the tenderness of minds,
And each slow dusk, a drawing-down of blinds.

Wilfred Owen.

Dissatisfaction with the first and third lines led him into a fifth version in which the dead are no longer addressed as 'you' but 'these' and 'them'.

What passing-bells for these po dumb-dying cattle?
— Only the monstrous anger of more guns!
Only the stuttering rifles' rapid rattle
Can patter out their hasty orisons.
No chants for them, nor wreaths, nor asphodels.
Nor any voice of mourning save the choirs
The shrill demented choirs of wailing shells;
And bugles calling for them from sad shires.

What candles may we hold to speed them all?
Not in the hands of boys, but in their eyes
Shall shine the holy gleams of their goodbyes.
The pallor of girls' cheeks shall be their pall.
Their flowers the tenderness of silent minds
And each slow dusk a drawing-down of blinds.

Striking a line through this, he advanced to what was to prove the
final draft.

Anthem for ~~Dead~~ Youth   *Nation*

What passing-bells for these who die as cattle?
   – Only the monstrous anger of the guns.
   Only the stuttering rifles' rapid rattle
Can patter out their hasty orisons.
No ~~music for all them~~ {mockeries} for them; ~~nor~~ from {prayers ~~or~~ nor bells,
Nor any voice of mourning save the choirs,
The shrill ~~demented~~ ~~disconsolate~~ choirs of wailing shells;
And bugles calling ~~sad across the~~ for them from sad shires.

What candles may be held to speed them all?
Not in the hands of boys, but in their eyes
Shall shine the holy glimmers of goodbyes.
~~And~~ The pallor of girls' brows shall be their pall;
Their flowers the tenderness of {silent ~~patient~~ ~~sweet white~~ minds,
And each slow dusk a drawing-down of blinds.

This, too, was shown to Sassoon who, altering 'Dead Youth' to
'Doomed Youth', gave Owen his final title. He also proposed im-
provements to lines 5 and 13. The last of these had caused particular
difficulty: Owen had already cancelled 'sweet white minds' in favour
of 'silent minds' before Sassoon suggested 'patient minds'. Now,
reading over the finished poem, Sassoon recognized that it was a
masterpiece and it dawned on him

that my little friend was much more than the promising minor poet I had
hitherto adjudged him to be. I now realized that his verse, with its sumptuous epithets and large-scale imagery, its noble naturalness and the depth
of meaning, had impressive affinities with Keats, whom he took as his

supreme exemplar. This new sonnet was a revelation. . . . It confronted me with classic and imaginative serenity.[34]

On 25 September Owen appeared before a Medical Board convened to decide whether or not he should stay on at Craiglockhart. Dr. Brock, he knew, was of the opinion that he should have an extension. Telling his mother two days later that the Board had not yet made known its decision, he went on to say:

> I think one of the most humanly useful things I am doing now is the teaching at Tynecastle School. Did I tell you what a great time I had on Tuesday with the 39 boys. Their 'Teacher'* is a charming girl, – wife (of course) of an Army Doctor. She had the exquisite tact to offer to leave me alone, but I requested her company for the lesson.[35]

He was himself taking lessons – in German – at the Berlitz School. When that course was finished, he was given some private tuition by the Librarian of Edinburgh University, Mr. Frank Nicholson. There were three or four of these lessons and after the last of them, talking in a café of the Germans and their language, Owen spoke as he rarely did of the horrors of the Front. He told Nicholson of photographs of the dead and mutilated that he carried in his wallet and his hand moved towards his breast-pocket, only to stop short as he realized, with characteristic delicacy, that his friend had no need of that particular lesson in reality.[36]

On 1 October he read a paper 'on the classification of soils, soil air, soil water, root absorption and fertility'[37] to the Field Club. A fortnight later, two of 'Dr. Brock's Ladies' took him to meet a Mr. Walter Biggar Blaikie, Chairman of T. and A. Constable Ltd., the Edinburgh printers, whom he discovered

> was a friend of Stevenson's from boyhood. Stevenson's famous old nurse was Blaikie's first. So it was an interesting afternoon; tho' old Blaikie affects a contempt for R.L.S. It is a beautiful thing that children of Tynecastle School, – or of the Birkenhead Institute are able to get nearer to the romantic heart of Stevenson, and really know him in a better way, than this person who played with him before even *Treasure Island* was dreamed of.[38]

* Mrs. Edward Fullerton. HO met her after the War.

Robert Graves, seated centre, September 1917

A more important 'literary' meeting that weekend was with Robert Graves, who arrived at Craiglockhart on the Saturday and was promptly taken off by Siegfried to the golf course. Afterwards, as the three of them talked of poetry, Owen produced a draft of a new poem:[39]

Disabled.

He sat in a wheeled chair, waiting for dark,
And shivered in his ghastly suit of grey,
   Legless, ~~sewn short at elbow.~~
~~Sewn short at one knee, armless~~.   Through the park
Voices of boys rang saddening like a hymn,
Voices of play and pleasure after day,
Till gathering sleep had mothered them from him.

      x   x   x

About this time Town used to swing so gay
When glow-lamps budded in the light blue trees,
And girls glanced lovelier as the air grew dim,
— In the old times, before he threw away his knees.
Now he will never feel again how slim
Girls' waists are, or how warm their subtle hands.
All of them touch him like some queer disease.

      x   x   v

Ah! he was looked at when he used to stand
In parks ~~Each~~ evenings ~~outside the cinemas~~ and please
~~Himself~~ Who ~~mated with him~~ . . . . ~~oh the dear~~!
Ount ; Even ~~great ladies~~ Wealthy old ladies said quite loud, and
~~Unpleasantly~~ the rose behind his ear, . .
And eyed all up and down his reckless gear.

There was an artist silly for his face,
For it was younger than his youth, last year.
Now, he is old; his back will never brace;
He's lost his colour very far from here,
Poured it down shell-holes till the veins ran dry,
And half his lifetime lapsed in the hot race
And leap of purple spirted from his thigh.

     *   *   *

One time he liked a bloodsmear down his leg,
After the matches, carried shoulder-high.
~~After a game it was~~ It was after football, when he'd drunk a peg,
He thought he'd better join. — He wonders why.
Someone had said he'd look a god in kilts.
That's why; and maybe, too, to please his Meg,
Aye, that was it, to please to giddy jilts
He asked to join. He didn't have to beg;
Smiling they wrote his lie; aged nineteen years.
Germans he scarcely thought of; all their guilt
And Austria's, did not move him. And no fears
Of Fear came yet. He thought of jewelled hilts
For daggers in plaid socks; of smart salutes;
And care of arms; and leave; and pay arrears;

Esprit de corps; and hints for young recruits.
And soon, he was drafted out with drums and cheers.

       x   x   x

Some cheered him home, but not as crowds cheer
                                              Goal.

Only a solemn man who brought him fruits
<u>Thanked</u> him; and then enquired about his soul.

        x   x

Now, he will spend a few sick years in institutes,
And do what things the rules consider wise,
And take whatever pity they may dole.
Tonight he noticed how the women's eyes
Passed from him to the strong men that were whole.
How cold and late it is! Why don't they come
And put him into bed? Why don't they come?

Graves was 'mightily impressed'; more, evidently, than Owen was
with him: 'He is a big, rather plain fellow, the last man on earth
apparently capable of the extraordinary, delicate fancies of his
books.'[40] He must have been encouraged and stimulated by their
talk, however, and perhaps as a result composed or completed six
poems in the following week. If the first of them was 'Disabled', the
second was 'Dulce et Decorum Est', which in its early drafts carried
a bracketed dedication 'To Jessie Pope etc'/'To a certain Poetess'.[41]

    Her name may have come up in conversation with Sassoon and

Robert Graves. The author of numerous children's books and several volumes of light verse before the War, Miss Pope in 1914 conjured a sterner, more stirring music from her lyre:[42]

THE CALL

Who's for the trench –
   Are you, my laddie?
Who'll follow the French –
   Will you, my laddie?
Who's fretting to begin,
Who's going to win?
And who wants to save his skin –
   Do you, my laddie?

Who's for the khaki suit –
   Are you, my laddie?
Who longs to charge and shoot –
   Do you, my laddie?
Who's keen on getting fit,
Who means to show his grit,
And who'd rather wait a bit –
   Would you, my laddie?

Who'll earn the Empire's thanks –
   Will you, my laddie?
   Who'll swell the victor's ranks –
   Will you, my laddie?
When that procession comes,
Banners and rolling drums –
Who'll stand and bite his thumbs –
   Will you, my laddie?

That disturbing variation of the 'Who's for tennis' formula, published in the *Daily Mail* of 26 November 1914, Owen might have read in Bordeaux;[43] and in the same paper over the months and years following he would have encountered other poems subsequently collected in *Jessie Pope's War Poems* (1915) and *More War Poems* (1915) and *Simple Rhymes for Stirring Times* (1916). As with his 'Anthem for Doomed Youth' and other poems that were to follow, Owen's strong adverse reaction to someone else's poetry or prose would seem to have released his nightmare memories and his poem:

> Bent double, like old beggars under sacks,
> Knock-kneed, coughing like hags, we cursed through sludge,
> Till on the haunting flares we turned our backs
> And towards our distant rest began to trudge.
> Men marched asleep. Many had lost their boots
> But limped on, blood-shod. All went lame; all blind;
> Drunk with fatigue; deaf even to the hoots
> Of tired, outstripped Five-Nines that dropped behind.
>
> Gas! GAS! Quick, boys! – An ecstasy of fumbling,
> Fitting the clumsy helmets just in time;
> But someone still was yelling out and stumbling
> And flound'ring like a man in fire or lime . . .
> Dim, through the misty panes and thick green light,
> As under a green sea, I saw him drowning.
>
> In all my dreams, before my helpless sight,
> He plunges at me, guttering, choking, drowning.

This *exemplum* is followed by a *moralitas* of passionate indignation, as the poet who loved children addresses himself – with superb rhetorical suspension – to the children's poet who exhorted them to 'play the Game':

> If in some smothering dreams you too could pace
> Behind the wagon that we flung him in,
> And watch the white eyes writhing in his face,
> His hanging face, like a devil's sick of sin;
> If you could hear, at every jolt, the blood
> Come gargling from the froth-corrupted lungs,
> Obscene as cancer, bitter as the cud
> Of vile, incurable sores on innocent tongues, –
> My friend, you would not tell with such high zest
> To children ardent for some desperate glory,
> The old Lie: Dulce et decorum est
> Pro patria mori.★

★ 'The famous Latin tag means of course *It is sweet and meet* to die for one's country. Sweet! and *decorous*!' (WO to SO, *CL*, p. 500).

In mid-week came a letter from Graves which confirmed what Sassoon had said of him: 'he is a man one likes better *after* he has been with one.'

Do you know, Owen, that's a damn fine poem of yours, that 'Disabled.' Really damn fine!

So good the general sound and weight of the words that the occasional metrical outrages are most surprising. It's like seeing a golfer drive onto the green in one and then use a cleek instead of a putter, & hole out in twelve.

For instance you have a foot too much in
     In the old days before he gave away his knees
& in He wasn't bothered much by Huns or crimes or guilts
&   They cheered him home but not as they would cheer a goal
&   Now he will spend a few sick years in institutes
   There is an occasional jingle
              Voices of boys
       & Voices of play and pleasure after day
   And an occasional cliché
            Girls glanced lovelier
            Scanty suit of grey
I wouldn't worry to mention all this if it wasn't for my violent pleasure at some of the lines like the one about 'the solemn man who brought him fruits' & the 'jewelled hilts of daggers in plaid socks' & the 'Bloodsmear down his leg after the matches'.

Owen, you have seen things; you are a poet; but you're a very careless one at present. One can't put in too many syllables into a line & say 'Oh, it's all right. That's my way of writing poetry'. One has to follow the rules of the metre one adopts. Make new metres by all means, but one must observe the rules where they are laid down by custom of centuries. A painter or musician has no greater task in mastering his colours or his musical modes & harmonies, than a poet.

It's the devil of a sweat for him to get to know the value of his rhymes, rhythms or sentiments. But I have no doubt at all that if you turned seriously to writing, you could obtain Parnassus in no time while I'm still struggling on the knees of that stubborn peak.

Till then, good luck in the good work. Yours Robert Graves.

Love to Sassoon.[44]

This advice may have been partly responsible for the two more conventional poems that followed, 'Winter Song' and 'Sonnet: to a Child',[45] both of them addressed to Arthur Newboult, the seven-year-old son of Edinburgh friends. One afternoon he took this little boy – known as Chubby Cubby (having just joined the Wolf Cubs) – to Edinburgh Zoo[46] and was moved by his tender innocence to write:

> But soon your heart, hot-beating like a bird's,
> Shall slow down. Youth shall lop your hair,
> And you must learn wry meanings in our words.
> Your smile shall dull, because too keen aware;
> And when for hopes your hand shall be uncurled,
> Your eyes shall close, being opened to the world.

Owen became a great favourite of the Newboults. Sitting in their sundrenched garden, he would read his poems to Mrs. Newboult and her fourteen-year-old daughter Mary, whom he helped with her homework. They read Dickens together, and she was struck by his compassion as he argued with her father about the rights and working conditions of the miners.[47] Perhaps he had in mind those he had known in the 5th Battalion.★

That week he finished his sonnet 'Music', begun in October 1916,[48] and may have written 'Greater Love'.[49] Once again he reacts against a poem by someone else, in this case Swinburne's 'Before the Mirror/(Verses Written under a Picture†)', which begins:

> White rose in red rose-garden
>   Is not so white;
> Snowdrops that plead for pardon
>   And pine for fright
> Because the hard East blows
> Over their maiden rows
>   Grow not as this face grows from pale to bright.

Owen replies to Swinburne with a love poem of his own (one draft of which is entitled 'To any Beautiful Woman'):

> Red lips are not so red
>   As the stained stones kissed by the English dead.
> Kindness of wooed and wooer.

★ See above, p. 136.
† Of a beautiful woman looking into a mirror, by J. A. Whistler.

Seems shame to their love pure.
O Love, your eyes lose lure
　　When I behold eyes blinded in my stead!

By way of a change from the social round in Edinburgh, Owen and Sassoon would sometimes go out for a drink and a meal to 'The Thistle', a grey stone pub in the main street of Milnathort, a village some thirty miles north of the capital.[50] Owen was evidently delighted by the publican's good French name – Dauthieu – and by his wife's good French cooking. One evening they were invited to dinner, together with two or three other officers, and, after their meal, moved into the little parlour where a large Cameron High-lander played the piano and they sang the songs of the Bing Boys, Violet Loraine, George Robey, and Ivor Novello's 'Keep the Home Fires Burning'. While Sassoon spent most of the evening talking to the Colonel, Owen sat in the window seat with Albertina Marie Dauthieu, the landlord's nineteen-year-old daughter, who thought him gay and charming. He did not speak of his experiences in the trenches, but of his good fortune in meeting Sassoon, who 'was helping him with his work'. She took this as a reference to his soldiering, and later, perhaps to correct what he must have realized was a misunderstanding, he asked her if she had an autograph book. She had, he took it away, and brought it back with a gallant adaptation of a song they had sung together from the opera *Merrie England*, ending:

And so I'll have my posy
Of the fairest flower that blows
Embower'd by the Thistle
And accompanied by a Rose.★

★ In *Merrie England* (1902), written by Basil Hood and composed by Edward German, Sir Walter Raleigh sings:

Let others make a garland
　Of every flower that blows;
But I will wait till I may pluck
　My dainty English rose!
In perfume, grace and beauty
　The rose doth stand apart –
God grant that I, before I die,
　May wear one on my heart!

Wilfred Owen with Arthur Newboult in July 1917

On 27 October, Owen heard that he was to go before a Medical Board the following day and would almost certainly be sent away.[51] Sassoon was distressed by this news and said he would try to persuade Dr. Rivers to have him granted an extension. When nothing came of this, it occurred to him that Owen would enjoy a stay with the Morrells at Garsington Manor, but nothing came of that either. The Board reached the decision expected and, to console his friend,

Sassoon gave him a present: his own annotated copy of Bernard Adams's *Nothing of Importance*.[52] One can imagine him savouring the understatement of that title, for the book is 'a record of eight months at the Front with a Welsh Battalion October, 1915, to June, 1916'; the Battalion is the 1st Royal Welch Fusiliers; and its dead and wounded officers are listed in Sassoon's scrupulous hand on the back of the front fly-leaf. Three days later, they had a last supper at a quiet Club in Edinburgh, vividly recollected in *Siegfried's Journey*:

> After a good dinner and a bottle of noble Burgundy had put us in cheerful spirits, I produced a volume of portentously over-elaborated verse, recently sent me by the author.* From this I began to read extracts – a cursory inspection having assured me that he would find them amusing. It now seems incongruous that my most vivid memory of him, on that last occasion when we were alone together, should be of his surrendering to convulsions of mirth in a large leather-covered arm-chair. These convulsions I shared until incapable of continuing my recital.

> > *What cassock'd misanthrope,*
> > *Hawking peace-canticles for glory-gain,*
> > *Hymns from his rostrum'd height th'epopt of Hate?*

> It was, I think, the word 'epopt' (the grandiloquent poet's version of epopee – otherwise 'epic song') which caused the climax of our inextinguishable laughter, though the following couplet, evidently 'written in dejection', had already scored heavily.

> > *O is it true I have become*
> > *This gourd, this gothic vacuum?*

> Except for the presence of a dignified gentleman – possibly a Writer to the Signet – who was at the far end of the room, we were unobserved. The more we laughed, the more solemnly he eyed us, and this somehow made our hilarity uncontrollable. 'Laughter at its best,' says Max Beerbohm in one of his amaranthine essays, 'goes so far as to lose all touch with its motive, and to exist only, grossly, in itself.' To that pitch we were reduced. And it is conceivable that behind his outward gravity – and the rustling pages of *The Scotsman* – the elderly gentleman may have envied us, or even have been secretly refreshed by our behaviour.

---

* Aylmer Strong, *A Human Voice*, London, 1917. This SS gave to WO. See below, p. 321

When it was time to say goodbye, Sassoon gave Owen a sealed letter. Discovering that it contained a £10 note and Robert Ross's London address, Owen went upstairs to the Club writing-room and loosed off a letter to his friend which he then 'put by'. He caught the midnight train to London, waking in the grey dawn of 4 November with exactly twelve months left to live.

9

SCARBOROUGH AND RIPON

By evening he was back in Shrewsbury, and next day wrote from his attic bedroom to 'My dear Sassoon', thanking him for his sealed letter:

You gave – with what Christ, if he had known Latin & dealt in oxymoron, might have called Sinister Dexterity. I imagined you were entrusting me with some holy secret concerning yourself. A secret, however, it shall be until such time as I shall have climbed to the housetops, and you to the minarets of the world.

Smile the penny! This Fact has not intensified my feelings for you by the least – the least *grame*. Know that since mid-September, when you still regarded me as a tiresome little knocker on your door, I held you as Keats+Christ+Elijah+my Colonel+my father-confessor+Amenophis IV in profile.

What's that mathematically?

In effect it is this: that I love you, dispassionately, so much, so *very* much, dear Fellow, that the blasting little smile you wear on reading this can't hurt me in the least.

If you consider what the above Names have severally done for me, you will know what you are doing. And you have *fixed* my Life – however short. You did not light me: I was always a mad comet; but you have fixed me. I spun round you a satellite for a month, but I shall swing out soon, a dark star in the orbit where you will blaze. It is some consolation to know that Jupiter himself sometimes swims out of Ken!

To come back to our sheep, as the French *never say*, I have had a perfect little note from Robt. Ross, and have arranged a meeting at 12.30 on Nov. 9th. He mentioned staying at Half Moon St., but the house is full.

I have ordered several copies of *Fairies & Fusiliers*,* but shall not buy all, in order to leave the book exposed on the Shrewsbury counters! I'm also getting Colvin's new *Life of Keats*,† no price advertised, but damn it, I'm to enjoy my Leave!

I am spending happy enough days with my Mother, but I can't get sociable with my Father without going back on myself over ten years of thought.[1]

His horizons had expanded since last he was at Mahim. He now found its atmosphere claustrophobic and, three days later, clambered aboard the London train with a sense of liberation and excitement. Arriving at Paddington, he headed for the Regent Palace Hotel at Piccadilly Circus, where he had stayed with the de la Touche boys in September 1915, and having booked himself a room, set off for the Poetry Bookshop.

At 12.30 on 9 November he climbed the steep steps from Pall Mall to the Reform Club where he was greeted by Robbie Ross, Oscar Wilde's friend and editor, then in his late forties one of the most celebrated and popular literary men in London. Of this meeting Owen wrote to Sassoon, who had made it possible:

When he had steered me to a lunch-table I found beside me an upstart rodent of a man, who looked astonished to find himself there. But dear Ross sang out with blessed distinctness 'Mister Arnnoldd Bennnettt'. So I stood up and shook hands. Presently I became aware of a pair of bayonet-coloured eyes, threatening at me from over, as it were, a brown sandbag. 'H. G. Wells!' So I stood up and shook hands. I think these men noticed me because I stood up to them – in two senses. Anyhow I got A.B. into a corner about you, as I will tell you someday. And H.G. talked to me exclusively for an hour. I was only ill at ease with him once, and that was when he tried to make me laugh with him at Bennett's gaudy handkerchief.[2]

The following day, Owen dined with Ross at the Reform Club and stayed there talking until one in the morning. 'I and my work are a success', he told his mother, 'I had already sent something to the

---

* Robert Graves's second book of poems (William Heinemann, London, 1917). See below, p. 313.

† Sir Sidney Colvin, *John Keats, His Life and Poetry* (London, 1917). WO possessed the 1909 impression. See above, pp. 56–7, and below, p. 311.

Nation, which hasn't appeared yet, but it seems the Editor★ has started talking of me'.

Elated with this first taste of fame, he set off for Winchester on 11 November to see Leslie Gunston. They lunched together next day

Robert Ross

and spent the afternoon in the Cathedral. A few days later, Owen wrote to his cousin:

Good of you to send me the Lyric of Nov. 14th. I can only send my own of the same date, which came from Winchester Downs, as I crossed the long backs of the downs after leaving you. It is written *as from* the trenches. I could almost see the dead lying about in the hollows of the downs.[3]

★ Henry William Massingham (1860–1924) was Editor from 1907 to 1923.

He enclosed a poem 'on a soldier whom shrapnel killed asleep',
which may owe something to Rimbaud's 'Le dormeur du val':

Asleep

Under his helmet, up against his pack,
After the so many days of work and waking
Sleep took him by the brow and laid him back.

There, in the happy no-time of his sleeping,
Death took him by the heart. There heaved a quaking
Of life, like child within him leaping,
Then chest and sleepy arms once more fell slack.

And soon the slow, stray blood came creeping
From the intruding lead, like ants on track.

Whether his deeper sleep lie shaded by the shaking
Of great wings, and the thoughts that hung the stars,
High-pillowed on calm pillows of God's making,
Above these clouds, these rains, these sleets of lead,
And these winds' scimitars,
—Or whether yet his thin and sodden head
Confuses more and more with the low mould,
His hair being one with the grey grass
Of finished fields, and wire-scraggs rusty-old,
Who knows?
      Who knows? Who hopes? Who troubles? Let it pass!
He sleeps. He sleeps less tremulous, less cold,
Than we who wake, and waking say Alas!

Nov. 14. 1917.

At the end of the third week in November, his leave being up,
Owen went north to join his Regiment in Scarborough. As in 1905,
his train climbed through a gap in the hills to the high ground from
which the once-fashionable Regency watering-place overlooks the

sea; itself overlooked by the corn-coloured ruins of a twelfth-century castle.

The 3rd/5th, 3rd/6th, and 3rd/7th Manchesters had been amalgamated earlier that year into the 5th (Reserve) Battalion. They had moved to Scarborough a few months before and the men were now quartered in the large red-brick cavalry barracks at Burniston, outside the town. The officers were accommodated more comfortably in the Clarence Gardens Hotel on the edge of the North Cliff. Twelve years before, Owen had played cricket with his family on the beach below. He now found himself Major Domo or Camp Commandant of the Hotel and described his duties to his mother:

I have to control the Household, which consists of some dozen Batmen, 4 Mess Orderlies, 2 Buglers, the Cook, (a fat woman of great skill,) two female kitcheners, and various charwomen!

They need driving. You should see me scooting the buglers round our dining-room on their knees with dustpan and brush! You should hear me rate the Charwoman for leaving the Lavatory-Basins unclean.

I am responsible for finding rooms for newcomers, which is a great worry, as we are full up. This means however that I have a good room to myself, as well as my Office![5]

A few days after he had arrived, he received an inscribed copy of *The Nymph and Other Poems* by Leslie Gunston.[6] This was dedicated to him, in token of the long friendship which had produced so many of the set-piece poems it contained, but Owen's sharpened critical faculties caused him some embarrassment when he came to thank his cousin:

I congratulate you on the Binding & Type. The Dedication Page & the Prefatory Note are set perfectly. Yes, it is rather disappointing to have no Black Lettering. I still think many of the Pieces might have enriched themselves with time. I like best

(1) *The Caradoc*. How much better than a photograph does it souvenir that day! I remember talking about the Croziers,* and plucking them & uncurling them. What was the date of this June?

---

* A description of bracken:
            Like carven croziers are the curled shoots growing
            To bless me as I pass.

(2) *Golden Hair*. This is your very best.
(3) *Sestet of Attar of Roses*
    'red as the dawn of doubtful days' is the best thought in the book.
(4) Ode for A.C.S.
(5) Chopin.
(6) The Colloseum!!

I don't like 'Hymn of Love to England', naturally, at this period while I am composing 'Hymns of Hate'.

I wonder you did not include the Bluebottle thing. I liked that ever so well.

And why omit certain Rose Poems which I remember?

It struck me that there was a little too much osculation throughout the book. People will not know that poetry is your only manner of satisfaction, and may draw wrong conclusions.

I think every poem, and every figure of speech should be a *matter of experience*. That is why I like the first verse of 'Song', and should have omitted the second![7]

He was continuing to write poems himself, and probably from this period dates a curious and disturbing address to Eros, seen as the deity presiding over Canongate in Edinburgh and Covent Garden in London, two districts notorious for their prostitutes:

> Who is the god of Canongate?
> — I, for I trifle with men and fate.
>
> Art thou high in the heart of London?
> — Yea, for I do what is done and undone.
>
> What is thy throne then barefoot god?
> — All pavements where my feet have trod.

Where is thy shrine, then, little god?
— Up secret stairs men mount unshod.

Say what libation ~~may we~~ such men fill?
— Their lift their lusts and let them spill.

Why! do you smell of the moss in Arden?
— If I told you, Sir, your look would harden.

What are you called, I ask your pardon?
— I am called the Flower of Covent Garden.

What shall I pay for you, lily-lad?
— Not all the gold King Solomon had.

How can I buy you, London Flower?
Buy me for ever, but not for an hour.

When shall I pay you, Violet Eyes?
With laughter first, and after with sighs.

But you will fade, my delicate bud?
No, there is too much sap in my blood.

Will you not shrink in my shut room?
No, there I'll break into fullest bloom.

Prominent in a list of 'Books read at Scarborough' in December 1917 appears 'H. Barbusse, *Under Fire*'.★ One of the most moving and terrible of all accounts of life and death on the Western Front, the English translation of Barbusse's original, *Le Feu*, made a deep impact on Owen. The first sign of this appears to be his remark in a letter of 27 November to Sassoon: 'My "Vision" is the result of two hours' leisure yesterday, – and getting up early this morning!'[8] The editors of the *Collected Letters* believe this to be a reference to an unpublished fragment, 'A Vision of Whitechapel', that bears a certain resemblance to 'Who is the god of Canongate?' That Owen had another 'Vision' in mind is indicated by a question in a subsequent letter to Sassoon: 'What do you think of my Vowel-rime stunt in this, and "Vision"?'[9] The existing drafts of 'A Vision of White-chapel' are unfinished, but show its rhymes to be conventional, unlike the vowel-rhymes of the poem we know as 'The Show'.[10] An immediate source of this would seem to be Chapter I of *Under Fire*, which is entitled 'The Vision':

The man at the end of the rank cries, 'I can see crawling things down there' – 'Yes, as though they were alive' – 'Some sort of plant perhaps' – 'Some kind of men' –

And there amid the baleful glimmers of the storm, below the dark disorder of the clouds that extend and unfurl over the earth like evil spirits, they seem to see a great livid plain unrolled, which to their seeing is made of mud and water, while figures appear and fast fix themselves to the surface of it, all blinded and borne down with filth, like the dreadful castaways of shipwreck. And it seems to them that these are soldiers.

Also, perhaps, a passage from Chapter XX, 'Under Fire':

We watch the shadows of the passers-by and of those who are seated, outlined in inky blots, bowed and bent in diverse attitudes under the grey sky, all along the ruined parapet. Dwarfed to the size of insects and worms,

---

★ The others are Robert Nichols, *Ardours and Endurances*, Robert Graves, *Fairies and Fusiliers*, H. G. Wells, *The Stolen Bacillus* and *Wife of Sir Isaac Harman*, Wilfrid Gibson, *Battle*, John Masefield, *Lollingdon Donns* and *The Daffodil Fields*, R. E. Vernède, *War Poems and Other Verses*, R. L. Stevenson, *Dr. Jekyll and Mr. Hyde*, Hilaire Belloc, *Esto Perpetua*, Theocritus, Bion, Moschus [probably in a single volume], Robert Sherard, *The Real Oscar Wilde*, Arnold Bennett, *The Regent* and *Literary Taste*, R. W. Service, Stopford Brooke, *Studies in Poetry*.

they make a queer dark stirring among these shadow-hidden and Death-pacified lands . . . .

Once again, it would appear, a printed source primed Owen's imagination, causing it to produce a vision (and I think that must have been the title of the draft sent to Sassoon) of hell-on-earth described in terms of the human body diseased and mutilated:

THE SHOW.

~~as seen from heaven.~~

My soul looked down from a vague height, with Death,
As unremembring how I rose or why,
And saw a sad land, weak with sweats of dearth,
Gray, cratered like the moon with hollow woe,
And pitted with great pocks and scabs of plagues.

~~its~~ its beard, that a horror of harsh wire
Across ~~the horror of its beard of wire~~
~~I watche~~ There moved thin caterpillars, slowly uncoiled.
It seemed they pushed themselves to be as plugs
Of ditches, where they writhed and shrivelled, killed.

By them had slimy paths been trailed and scraped
Round myriad warts that might be little hills.

From gloom's last dregs these long-strung creatures crept,
And vanished out of dawn down hidden holes.

(And smell came up from those foul openings
As out of mouths, or deep wounds deepening.)

On dithering feet up-gathered, more and more,
Brown strings, ~~and~~ towards strings of gray, with bristling spines,
All migrants from green fields, intent on mire.

Those that were gray, of more abundant spawns,
Ramped on the rest and ate them and were eaten.

I saw their bitten backs curve, loop, and straighten.
I watched those agonies curl, lift, and flatten.

Where^{at}~~fore~~, in terror what that sight might mean,
I reeled and shivered earthward like a feather.

And Death fell with me, like a deepening moan.

And He, picking a manner of worm, which half had hid
Its bruises in the earth, but crawled no further,
Showed me its feet, the feet of many men,
And the fresh-severed head of it, my head.

On another sheet of paper Owen wrote out, as epigraph to this poem, three lines from Yeats's play, *The Shadowy Waters*:

> We have fallen in the dreams the ever-living
> Breathe on the tarnished mirror of the world,
> And then smooth out with ivory hands and sigh.[11]

The full-stop with which Owen ends this quotation was, in Yeats's text, a comma followed by the lines:

> And find their laughter sweeter to the taste
> For that brief sighing.

The speaker, Forgael, a Sea-King of ancient Ireland, has been promised love of a supernatural intensity by certain human-headed birds. These are the souls of the dead, 'the ever-living', whose rich dreams are drawing him irresistibly to his death. It is hard to see the connection between Yeats's epigraph and this poem, unless Owen is implying that the nightmare 'bird's-eye' vision of the battlefield to which he falls is one breathed by 'the ever-living' on 'the tarnished mirror of the world'. If this was his meaning, 'tarnished mirror' suits his purpose better than 'burnished mirror', which was what Yeats in fact wrote. An ironic equation may well have been intended between Yeats's 'ever-living' and Owen's nightmare companion, Death, whom he deifies with a capital letter: 'He, picking a manner of worm . . .'

A more obvious debt to Barbusse appears in the transmutation of a sentence at the end of Chapter IX of *Under Fire*:

> The soldier held his peace. In the distance he saw the night as *they* would pass it – cramped up, trembling with vigilance in the deep darkness, at the bottom of the listening-hole whose ragged jaws showed in black outline all around whenever a gun hurled its dawn into the sky.

Owen expanded this into a vision of 'one of many mouths of Hell':

> Cramped in that funnelled hole, they watched the dawn
> Open a jagged rim around; a yawn
> Of death's jaws, which had all but swallowed them
> Stuck in the bottom of his throat of phlegm.
>
> They were in one of many mouths of Hell
> Not seen of seers in visions; only felt
> As teeth of traps; when bones and the dead are smelt
> Under the mud where long ago they fell
> Mixed with the sour sharp odour of the shell.[12]

The single, chaotic manuscript of this poem enables us to approach a dating of 'Exposure',[13] since at the top of the page is one corrected line from that poem:

> ive
> success~~ions~~ of bullets streak the silence

Edmund Blunden pointed out that Owen's own date, 'February 1916', at the foot of the final manuscript must be a slip of the pen, since the poem describes Owen's experience of February *1917*.* He assumed that 1917 was what Owen meant to write, but the links between his reading of Barbusse and the manuscripts of 'Cramped in that funnelled hole' and 'Exposure' suggest that 'February 1916' was a slip for 'February 1918'. A year's gestation period is, moreover, more likely than that the poet of 1917 should have produced so astonishing and mature a poem from his initial exposure to the reality of the trenches.

The first draft opens:

                              ~~1~~   2

> dark
> Watchful we hear the ~~mad~~ wind tugging on the wire,
>
> ~~human~~
> ~~half-dead~~ ~~human prisoners~~
>   hung up
> Twitching like ~~living~~ agonies among its brambles.
> ~~feeble~~
>
> Northward, eternally, remote artillery rumbles:
>
>   Like the ~~insomnolent~~ unheeded
> ~~Insomnolent rumours~~
>   a   groans & rumours of some other war.
> Like ~~a dull unnatural~~
>   ~~untroubling~~   a dull
>
> What are we doing here?

---

* See above, pp. 158–9.

2   I

Our brains ache in the merciless iced east winds that knive us.

Wearied we keep awake because the night is silent.

    Strange   ~~A few wan droops star shells haunt the ghastly~~
~~A few pale lights~~
         drooping stars confuse our memory of the salient
  ~~And Bla~~
   ~~Wan,~~

                 whisper
Worried by silence sentries ~~listen~~, curious, nervous,

    But nothing happens.

When, in the second draft, these two stanzas are transposed, the reader is led in more logically across the salient to the whispering sentries and the wind in the wire. Nature is felt and seen as a malign presence:[14]

    . . . the merciless iced east winds . . . knive us . . .

Watching, we hear the mad gusts tugging on the wire,
Like twitching agonies of men among its brambles.

Cowering from the murderous wind, the soldiers escape briefly into a vision of benevolent Nature:

We cringe in holes, back on forgotten dreams, and stare, snow-dazed,
Deep into grassier ditches. So we drowse, sun-dozed,
Littered with blossoms trickling where the blackbird fusses,
      – Is it that we are dying?

Slowly our ghosts drag home: glimpsing the sunk fires, glozed
With crusted dark-red jewels; crickets jingle there;
For hours the innocent mice rejoice: the house is theirs;
Shutters and doors, all closed: on us the doors are closed, –
      We turn back to our dying.

The snowflakes that were momentarily transformed into falling blossom become snowflakes again, and the poet's imagination gropes forward numbly from the past to the future:

> To-night, this frost will fasten on this mud and us,
> Shrivelling many hands, puckering foreheads crisp.
> The burying-party, picks and shovels in shaking grasp,
> Pause over half-known faces. All their eyes are ice,
> > But nothing happens.

The reader must pause, too, shocked by the daring brilliance of that semi-pun (a legacy from Keats), 'All their eyes are ice'; their *eyes* have hardened into *ice*.*

On 3 December, he finished 'Wild with All Regrets'[15] – at one gasp, he told Sassoon. Tennyson's *The Princess* had given him his title –

> Deep as first love, and wild with all regret
> O Death in Life, the days that are no more.

And Tennyson it was who triggered off his next poem. In the copy of *The Holy Grail and Other Poems* that he had bought in Edinburgh the previous July,[16] he read 'The Passing of Arthur':

> Then saw they how there hove a dusky barge,
> Dark as a funeral scarf from stem to stern,
> Beneath them; and descending they were ware
> That all the decks were dense with stately forms,
> Black-stoled, black-hooded, like a dream – by these
> Three Queens with crowns of gold: and from them rose
> A cry that shiver'd to the tingling stars,
> And, as it were one voice, an agony
> Of lamentation, like a wind, that shrills
> All night in a waste land, where no one comes,
> Or hath come, since the making of the world.

In his letter of 27 November to Sassoon he had parodied a quotation from Tennyson's 'Merlin and the Dream', which appears as epigraph to 'The Passing of Merlin' in *Songs of England* by the Poet Laureate,

---

* See the 'iced east winds' above. For other of WO's semi-puns, see 'Anthem for Doomed Youth' ('The pallor of girls' brows shall be their pall') and 'Miners' ('Of boys that slept wry sleep and men/Writhing for air').

Alfred Austin. Among the stanzas Owen has marked in his copy is this:[17]

> A wailing cometh from the shores that veil
> Avilion's island valley; on the mere,
> Looms through the mist and wet winds weeping blear
> A dusky barge, which, without oar or sail,
> Fades to the far-off fields where falls nor snow nor hail.

These passages from Tennyson and Austin fused with his memories of a sunny afternoon on the Somme Canal★ to produce

Hospital Barge.

Budging the sluggard ripples of the Somme,
A barge round old Cérisy slowly slewed.
Softly her engines down the current screwed,
And chuckled softly with contented hum;

Till fairy tinklings struck those croonings dumb.
The waters rumpling at the stern subdued.
The lock-gate took her bulging amplitude.
Gently into the gurgling lock she swam.

One reading on the towpath raised his eyes
To watch her lessening westward quietly.
Then, as she neared the bend, her funnel screamed.

And that long lamentation made him wise
How unto Avilon in agony
Kings passed, in the strange barge which Merlin dreamed.

Dec. 8. 1917

★ See above, p. 184. For the final version of this poem, see *CP*, p. 97.

Sometime in the second half of December Robert Graves wrote to Owen: 'For God's sake cheer up and write more optimistically – the war's not ended yet but a poet should have a spirit above wars'.[18] It is tempting to see an answer to this in

Apologia pro Poema Mea.

I, too, saw God through mud, —
  The mud that cracked on cheeks when wretches smiled.
War brought more glory to their eyes than blood,
  And gave their laughs more glee than shakes a child.

Merry it was to laugh there —
  Where death becomes absurd and life absurder.
For power was on us as we slashed bones bare
  Not to feel sickness or remorse of murder.

I, too, have dropped off Fear —
  Behind the barrage, dead as my platoon,
And sailed my spirit surging light and clear
  Past the entanglement where hopes lay strewn;

And witnessed exultation —
  Faces that used to curse me, scowl for scowl,
Shine and lift up with passion of oblation,
  Seraphic for an hour; though they were foul.

I have made fellowships —
Untold of happy lovers in old song.
For love is not the binding of fair lips
With the soft silk of eyes that look and long,

By Joy, whose ribbon slips, —
But wound with war's hard wire whose stakes are
                                  strong;
Bound with the bandage of the arm that drips;
Knit in the webbing of the rifle-thong.

I have perceived much beauty
In the hoarse oaths that kept our courage straight;
Heard music in the silentness of duty;
Found peace where shell-storms spouted reddest
                                      spate.

Nevertheless, except you share
With them in hell the sorrowful dark of hell,
Whose world is but the trembling of a flare
And heaven but as the highway for a shell,

You shall not hear their mirth:
You shall not come to think them well content
By any jest of mine. These men are worth
Your tears. You are not worth their merriment.

The fact that this fair copy[19] is dated 'Nov. 1917.' could mean that some elements of the poem were in Owen's head before Graves's letter brought them together. But whether or not it was the catalyst, one ingredient is unquestionably Graves's poem

TWO FUSILIERS

And have we done with War at last?
Well, we've been lucky devils both,
And there's no need of pledge or oath
To bind our lovely friendship fast,
By firmer stuff
Close bound enough.

By wire and wood and stake we're bound,
By Fricourt and by Festubert,
By whipping rain, by the sun's glare,
By all the misery and loud sound,
By a Spring day,
By Picard clay.

Show me the two so closely bound
As we, by the wet bond of blood,
By friendship, blossoming from mud,
By Death: we faced him, and we found
Beauty in Death,
In dead men breath.[20]

Owen was enjoying Scarborough. 'Life here,' he told his mother, 'is a mixture of wind, sand, crumbs on carpets, telephones, signa-tures, clean sheets, shortage of meat, and too many money-sums. But I like it.'[21] He was beginning to haunt furniture shops and auctions in search of pieces for 'the cottage' he spoke of having after the War.[22] On 19 December he went up to Edinburgh for the week-end. Returning to Craiglockhart, he met Dr. Brock,

whose first word was 'Antaeas!' which they want immediately for the next Mag! Shall have to spin it off again while up here. Crowds of the men I knew are still at the Hydro, and thought I had come back relapsed (N.B. I had very little sleep last night.)

Then I went off to Tynecastle. They were in the act of writing Christmas Letters to me! My address was on the Blackboard. And 'original' Christmas Cards were all over the room! I am going to see the Grays this afternoon & may stay with them tomorrow. Am feeling *very* fit, in spite of the wretched weather, & journey.

Christmas in the Clarence Gardens Hotel was 'very mopish', mainly because the Commanding Officer, 'a terrible old misanthrope in the morning', held an orderly room for punishments – forbidden in King's Regulations on Christmas Day – and shouted at everyone in sight. On New Year's Eve, at first in a more cheerful mood, Owen reviewed his life:

I am not dissatisfied with my years. Everything has been done in bouts:

Bouts of awful labour at Shrewsbury & Bordeaux; bouts of amazing pleasure in the Pyrenees, and play at Craiglockhart; bouts of religion at Dunsden; bouts of horrible danger on the Somme; bouts of poetry always; of your affection always; of sympathy for the oppressed always.

I go out of this year a Poet, my dear Mother, as which I did not enter it. I am held peer by the Georgians; I am a poet's poet.

I am started. The tugs have left me; I feel the great swelling of the open sea taking my galleon.

Last year, at this time, (it is just midnight, and now is the intolerable instant of the Change) last year I lay awake in a windy tent in the middle of a vast, dreadful encampment. It seemed neither France nor England, but a kind of paddock where the beasts are kept a few days before the shambles. I heard the revelling of the Scotch troops, who are now dead, and who knew they would be dead. I thought of this present night, and whether I should indeed – whether we should indeed – whether you would indeed – but I thought neither long nor deeply, for I am a master of elision.

But chiefly I thought of the very strange look on all faces in that camp; an incomprehensible look, which a man will never see in England, though wars should be in England; nor can it be seen in any battle. But only in Étaples.

It was not despair, or terror, it was more terrible than terror, for it was a blindfold look, and without expression, like a dead rabbit's.

It will never be painted, and no actor will ever seize it. And to describe it, I think I must go back and be with them.

On 12 January there was a pit explosion at the Podmore Hall Colliery, Halmerend, in which 155 men and boy miners were killed;

and shortly afterwards Wilfred told his mother he had written
'a poem on the Colliery Disaster; but I get mixed up with the War
at the end. It is short, but oh! sour!'[23] Before the fire in his grate,
which smoked horribly in the wind,[24] he wrote:[25]

Miners.

There was a whispering in my hearth,
 A sigh of the coal,
Grown wistful of a former earth
 It might recall.

I listened for a tale of leaves
 And smothered ferns;
Frond-forests; and the low, sly lives
 Before the fauns.

My fire might show steam-phantoms simmer
 From Time's old cauldron,
Before the birds made nests in summer,
 Or men had children.

But the coals were murmuring of their mine,
 And moans down there
Of boys that slept wry sleep, and men
 Writhing for air.

And I saw white bones in the cinder-shard,
    Bones without number;
(For many hearts with coal are charred),
Many the muscled bodies charred;
    And few remember.

I (And) thought of some who (at) worked dark pits
    Of war, and died,
Digging the rock where Death reputes
    Peace lies indeed.

Comforted years will sit soft-chaired
    In rooms of amber;
The years will stretch their hands, well-cheered
    By our live's ember.

The centuries will burn rich loads
    With which we groaned,
Whose warmth (will) shall lull their dreaming lids,
    While songs are crooned.
But they will not dream of us poor lads,
    Left in the ground.
    (Lost)

Probably before the same fire Owen drafted his more famous vision of 'The hell where youth and laughter go'.[26] One draft is on the same paper (with a distinctive watermark) as that used in the composition of 'Apologia Pro Poemata Meo', 'Cramped in that funnelled hole', 'Hospital Barge at Cérisy', 'Wild with all Regrets', 'Conscious', 'The Show', etc.

The title and the theme of 'Strange Meeting' are taken from Shelley's poem *The Revolt of Islam* (Canto V, lines 1828–36):

> And one whose spear had pierced me, leaned beside,
> With quivering lips and humid eyes; – and all
> Seemed like some brothers on a journey wide
> Gone forth, whom now strange meeting did befall
> In a strange land, round one whom they might call
> Their friend, their chief, their father, for assay
> Of peril, which had saved them from the thrall
> Of death, now suffering. Thus the vast array
> Of those fraternal bands were reconciled that day.

As editor of *The Hydra*, Owen had published Sassoon's poem 'The Rear Guard' in which the speaker,

> Groping along the tunnel, step by step,
> . . . saw some one lie
> Humped at his feet, half-hidden by a rug,
> And stooped to give the sleeper's arm a tug.

The sleeper proves to be dead, and the narrator

> climbed through darkness to the twilight air,
> Unloading hell behind him step by step.[27]

This poem and a soldier's terrible cry from *Under Fire* – 'When I'm sleeping I dream that I'm killing him over again'[28] – may also have contributed something to Owen's nightmare vision:

> It seemed that out of battle I escaped
> Down some profound dull tunnel, long since scooped
> Through granites which titanic wars had groined.

Yet also there encumbered sleepers groaned,
Too fast in thought or death to be bestirred.
Then, as I probed them, one sprang up, and stared
With piteous recognition in fixed eyes,
Lifting distressful hands as if to bless.
And by his smile, I knew that sullen hall,
By his dead smile I knew we stood in Hell.[29]

The vision of a subterranean Hell, its 'many mouths' agape for the unwary, can be traced back through 'Miners', 'Cramped in that funnelled hole', 'The Kind Ghosts', 'Deep under turfy grass and heavy clay', and even 'Uriconium', to the Calvinist Hell of which Owen must have heard at his mother's knee.

To his great delight, *The Nation* accepted 'Miners', his first poem to appear in a national magazine, by the same post as he received an invitation to Robert Graves's wedding.[30] On 23 January he travelled down to London, had lunch with Ross at the Reform, and then walked up to St. James's Piccadilly for the wedding. This he thought 'nothing extraordinary'. The bridegroom had a different view of it:

Nancy had read the marriage-service for the first time that morning, and had been so horrified that she all but refused to go through with the wedding, though I had arranged for the ceremony to be modified and reduced to the shortest possible form. Another caricature scene to look back on: myself striding up the red carpet, wearing field-boots, spurs, and sword; Nancy meeting me in a blue-check silk wedding-dress, utterly furious; packed benches on either side of the church, full of relatives; aunts using handkerchiefs; the choir boys out of tune; Nancy savagely muttering the responses, myself shouting them in a parade-ground voice.

Then the reception. At this stage of the war, sugar could not be got except in the form of rations. There was a three-tiered wedding-cake and the Nicholsons had been saving up their sugar and butter cards for a month to make it taste like a real one; but when George Mallory lifted off the plaster-case of imitation icing, a sigh of disappointment rose from the guests. However, champagne was another scarce commodity, and the guests made a rush for the dozen bottles on the table. Nancy said: 'Well, I'm going to get something out of this wedding, at any rate,' and grabbed a bottle. After three or four glasses, she went off and changed back into her land-girl's costume of breeches and smock. My mother, who had been thoroughly enjoying the proceedings, caught hold of her neighbour, E. V. Lucas, the essayist, and exclaimed: 'Oh, dear, I wish she had not done that!'[31]

Owen had brought his friend a present of eleven Apostle Spoons. He said the twelfth had been court-martialled for cowardice and was awaiting execution.[32]

Something of the same note is audible in his letter of 18 February to his mother:

If I do not read hymns, and if Harold marks no Bible, or Colin sees no life-guide in his prayer-book, it is no bad sign. I have heard the cadences of harps not audible to Sankey, but which were strung by God; and played by mysteries to Him, and I was permitted to hear them.

There is a point where prayer is indistinguishable from blasphemy. There is also a point where blasphemy is indistinguishable from prayer.[33]

There followed an early version of 'The Last Laugh',[34] beginning:

'O Jesus Christ!' one fellow sighed.
And kneeled, and bowed, tho' not in prayer, and died.

'Things look stupefyingly catastrophic on the Eastern Front', he wrote home, and indeed, they did. An armistice between Russia and Germany had been signed on 15 December, but on 10 February the negotiations at Brest Litovsk broke down. The Germans denounced the armistice and their armies advanced on Petrograd. In a Scarborough oyster-bar a new friend of Owen's, Philip Bainbrigge,[35] 'opined that the whole of civilization is extremely liable to collapse'. A tall, weedy man with glasses and a notable wit, Bainbrigge was a master at Shrewsbury School. Like most of Owen's friendships, this was interrupted when, in the second week of March, he was transferred to the Northern Command Depot at Ripon. He went cheerfully enough, but was disappointed with what he found: 'An awful Camp – huts – dirty blankets – in fact WAR once more. Farewell Books, Sonnets, Letters, friends, fires, oysters, antique-shops. Training again!'[36] Three days after he arrived he was struck down by a fever, but was soon sufficiently recovered to walk across the dales to Fountains Abbey and back. The afternoon of his twenty-

fifth birthday he spent, appropriately, in Ripon Cathedral, the home
of St. Wilfred. With sunshine, exercise, and a supply of apples and
gingerbread from home, his health improved and his spirits rose.
The camp was in fields to the west of Ripon and, walking into town
down Borage Lane, he found a room to let in a narrow cottage and
moved in. A stream, murmuring over its boulders and stones, kept
him company on his way to work and back. There were lesser

The cottage in Borage Lane, with skylight

celandines beside his path and the buds were opening overhead. On Easter Sunday he wrote to his mother:

Outside my cottage-window children play soldiers so piercingly that I've moved up into the attic, with only a skylight. It is a jolly Retreat. There I have tea and contemplate the inwardness of war, and behave in an owlish manner generally.

One poem have I written there; and thought another. I have also realized many defectuosities in older compositions.

The enormity of the present Battle numbs me.[37]

On the Western Front the German Army, reinforced by fifty-two divisions released from the Eastern Front, had launched a massive attack against the British 3rd and 4th Armies. Their trenches were overrun and they were falling back towards the sea. Owen knew all the place-names in the newspaper accounts of the fighting:

Fancy the old 13th C.C.S. being in German hands! Even Nesle, a town hospital where I passed 3 days, is occupied. . . .

All the joy of this good weather is for me haunted by the vision of the lands about St. Quentin crawling with wounded.

Early in April he had a 48-hour leave in Shrewsbury. Harold was there and, when the time came for Tom and Susan to go to bed, Tom said to his sons:

'You two have not seen each other for a long time. I'll leave you to talk. Come up when you like. Good night, boys.'

While the others were settling down for the night Wilfred made up the fire and I went out to the coal-shed and filled both scuttles. We sat quietly until we knew they were all asleep and then stole into the small kitchen and made a pot of coffee. For quite a long time there was an uneasy silence between us. I think we were both loath to say anything which might bring about a return of the hectoring talk which had been so usual with us all our lives. To-night this was dead. Drinking our coffee we both stared into the fire, remote and deep in thought. Much later, we drifted into desultory talk without saying anything of importance until, straightening up, I said to him: 'You have made up your mind to get back to the front line as soon as possible, haven't you?'

'Yes I have, Harold, and I know I shall be killed. But it's the only place that I can make my protest from. What about you?'

It was then I told him that I was expecting to go on a dangerous mission in a very short time and that I too did not have much hope of survival.

They talked on by the sinking fire about the War and about women – whom Wilfred said he liked but could not allow to distract him from his poetry. Nothing must do that when so little time was left to him: months at the most, and perhaps only weeks.[38] At last they fell asleep in their chairs, waking to a gloomy dawn at twenty past six. After lunch, Harold helped his brother pack his valise and carried it to the station for him.

As the train ran in an inspector came up – we knew that Father had left his special instructions – and told us to follow him. When he came to an empty compartment he put Wilfred in and locking the door walked away.

Wilfred and I did not shake hands or wish each other luck; it seemed too futile somehow. Instead, leaning out of the window and putting his hands on my shoulders, he said:

'Do remember, Harold, you can't paint and I can't write poetry unless we both somehow make some money, so start thinking about how you will do it.'

'Let's get this awful war over first, you Old Wolf.'

'Yes, yes . . . but think hard about this. Without *some* money nothing is possible.'[39]

Those were the last words Harold was to hear him speak.

As had happened at Craiglockhart and Scarborough, no sooner was Owen settled in at 7 Borage Lane than poems began stirring in his head: 'Insensibility' first,[40] perhaps a reply to Wordsworth's 'Character of the Happy Warrior' and Harold Monro's 'Youth in Arms'; and then 'A Terre',[41] an expansion of 'Wild with all Regrets'. On 4 May he was able to send his mother the last stanza of 'The Draft'. In its final form, this poem makes its bitter statement with brilliant economy, its calm surface mined with ironies:

THE SEND-OFF

Down the close darkening lanes they sang their way
To the siding-shed,
And lined the train with faces grimly gay.

Their breasts were stuck all white with wreath and spray
As men's are, dead.

Dull porters watched them, and a casual tramp
Stood staring hard,
Sorry to miss them from the upland camp.

Then, unmoved, signals nodded, and a lamp
Winked to the guard.

So secretly, like wrongs hushed-up, they went.
They were not ours:
We never heard to which front these were sent.

Nor there if they yet mock what women meant
Who gave them flowers.

Shall they return to beatings of great bells
In wild train-loads?
A few, a few, too few for drums and yells,

May creep back, silent, to still village wells
Up half-known roads.[42]

In the middle of May, Owen took a short leave in London. He rented a flat in Half-Moon Street above Robbie Ross's 'for 7/6 with breakfast'. One evening he dined with Ross at the Reform Club and, afterwards, his host telephoned Osbert Sitwell and asked him round to meet the new poet. In the comfortable warmth of Ross's sitting-room, Sitwell found

a young officer of about my age – he was three months younger than myself –, of sturdy, medium build, and wearing a khaki uniform. His face was rather broad, and I think its most unusual characteristics were the width of eye and forehead, and the tawny, rather sanguine skin, which proclaimed, as against the message of his eyes – deep in colour and dark in their meaning –, a love of life and a poet's enjoyment of air and light. His features were mobile but determined, and his hair short and of a soft brown. His whole appearance, in spite of what he had been through, gave the impression of being somewhat young for his age, and, though he seemed perfectly sure of himself, it was easy to perceive that by nature he was shy. He had the eager, supple good manners of the sensitive, and was eager and receptive, quick to see a point and smile. His voice – what does his voice sound like across the years? A soft modulation, even-toned, but with a warmth in it (I almost hear it now), a well-proportioned voice that signified a sense of justice and of compassion.[43]

He spent one afternoon at the War Office with another new friend, Captain Charles Scott Moncrieff,[*] who was trying to get him a home posting as lecturer to a cadet battalion. During two days and two nights in London he had only three hours sleep, and returning to Ripon wrote triumphantly to his mother:

My 'reception' in London has been magnificent. The upshot is that I am to have my work typed at once, and send it to Heinemann, who is certain to send it to Ross to read for him!![44]

And four days later:

I've been 'busy' this evening with my terrific poem (at present) called 'The Deranged'.[†] This poem the Editor of the *Burlington Magazine* – (a 2/6 Arts Journal which takes no poetry) – old More Adey,[‡] I say, solemnly prohibited me from sending to the *English Review*, on the grounds that 'the *English Review* should not be encouraged'.!!!!
Five years ago this would, as you suggest, have turned my head – but nowadays my head turns only in shame away from these first flickers of the limelight. For I am old already for a poet, and so little is yet achieved.
And I want no limelight, and celebrity is the last infirmity I desire.
Fame is the recognition of one's peers.

---

   [*] Charles Kenneth Scott-Moncrieff (1889–1930), later to become the translator of Proust. A captain in the KOSB, with an MC, he had been invalided home and now had a staff job.
   [†] This became 'Mental Cases', *CP*, pp. 69–70.
   [‡] William More Adey (1858–1942), Joint Editor of the *Burlington Magazine* 1911–19.

I have already more than their recognition: I have the silent and immortal friendship of Graves and Sassoon and those. Behold are they not already as many Keatses?[45]

In the first week of June he was posted back to Scarborough and billeted not in the Clarence Gardens Hotel but a tent with a cinder

Charles Scott Moncrieff in May 1918

floor in the Cavalry Barracks. This was soon exchanged for one with long grass and buttercups all round. His friend Lieutenant Priestley, who was President of the Officers' Mess Committee, had two apartments in the Barracks which he allowed Owen to use; and there he received 'an urgent request from the Sitwells in London for more of my poems for their 1918 Anthology★ which is coming out immediately. This on the strength of 'The Deranged', which S. Moncrieff showed them the other day.'

Osbert Sitwell sent him an epigram he had composed on the French Premier, M. Clemenceau – of whom, in moments of catastrophe and crisis, it would be reported in the English press: 'On being informed of these happenings, Monsieur Clemenceau announced that he was fully satisfied' –

ILL WINDS

Up on the Cross, in ugly agony,
The Son of Man hung dying – and the roar
Of earthquakes rent the solemn sky
Already thundering its wrath, and tore
The dead from out their tombs . . . then Jesus died –
But Monsieur Clemenceau is fully satisfied![46]

Thanking him for this, Owen elaborated Sitwell's image:

For 14 hours yesterday I was at work – teaching Christ to lift his cross by numbers, and how to adjust his crown; and not to imagine he thirst till after the last halt; I attended his Supper to see that there were no complaints; and inspected his feet to see that they should be worthy of the nails. I see to it that he is dumb and stands to attention before his accusers. With a piece of silver I buy him every day, and with maps I make him familiar with the topography of Golgotha.

At Ross's suggestion, and no doubt with Sitwell's encouragement, in July he began assembling his poems for a book to be entitled *Disabled & Other Poems*. It would seem that he decided on this after rejecting *With Lightning and with Music*† and *English Elegies*. The

---

★ *Wheels*, the annual miscellany of contemporary poetry founded by Edith Sitwell with the assistance of her brother Osbert. In *Wheels*, 1919 (dedicated to WO's memory), were included 'Strange Meeting', 'The Show', 'À Terre', 'The Sentry', 'Disabled', 'The Dead-Beat', and 'The Chances'.

† A quotation from Shelley's 'Adonais', xii. On the same sheet of paper as that listing these titles, WO wrote down the names of those to receive copies of the book: 'S.S., R. Graves, Leslie, P.B. [Poetry Bookshop], Mrs. Gray, Mrs. Fullerton, Dr. Sampson, Dr. Brock, Miss Wyer [?], R. Meiklejohn, Dr. Rayner, Laurent Tailhade, A. Bennett, H. G. Wells, Johnny de la Touche, Bainbrigge, Lady Margaret Sackville, R. Nichols, W. B. Yeats, J. Drinkwater[?]'

second of these alternatives suggests that he had already drafted, or at least was considering, his Preface. This, perhaps the most famous literary manifesto of the twentieth century, he left not as a finished and final statement but as a single rough draft:

This book is not about heroes. English Poetry is not yet fit to speak of them.
   Nor is it about deeds, or lands, nor anything about glory, honour, might, majesty, dominion, or power, except War.
   Above all I am not concerned with Poetry.
   My subject is War, and the pity of War.
   The Poetry is in the pity.
   Yet these elegies are to this generation in no sense consolatory. They may be to the next. All a poet can do today is warn. That is why the true Poets must be truthful.
   If I thought the letter of this book would last, I might have used proper names; but if the spirit of it survives – survives Prussia – my ambition and those names will have achieved themselves fresher fields than Flanders . . .[47]

His draft lists of contents, which include such poems recently written at Scarborough as 'Inspection' and 'Futility',[48] must have been drawn up before 30 July when he wrote 'The Kind Ghosts',[49] which does not appear. He wrote this having just heard that Sassoon, who had returned to the Front in May, was back in London with a bullet wound in his head. Coming in from a dawn patrol on 13 July, he was mistaken for a German and shot by one of his own N.C.O.s. This news would seem to have clarified Owen's thoughts about his own future. 'Now must I throw my little candle on his torch, and go out again', he wrote to his mother.[50] 'I am much gladder to be going out again than afraid. I shall be able to cry my outcry, playing my part.'[51] He ended a new poem, 'The Calls':

> For leaning out last midnight on my sill,
> I heard the sighs of men, that have no skill
> To speak of their distress, no, nor the will!
>   A voice I know. And this time I must go.[52]

To Charles Scott Moncrieff he wrote, on 11 August: 'I was struck off the draft by the M.O. this morning. He wont pass my cardiac valves. . . . Yes, I got myself put on the draft list of 22 officers, but couldn't work it this time.'[53]

Having a few days' leave, he joined his mother in Hastings where Colin, now a cadet in the Royal Flying Corps, was stationed. Returning to Scarborough, on 26 August he was certified 'fit to proceed overseas' and instructed to report to the Embarkation Commandant at Folkestone the following Saturday. His embarkation leave found him again in Hastings. On his last day with his mother, as they stood together looking out across the Channel towards France, he quoted to her a favourite passage from Tagore: 'When I go from hence, let this be my parting word, that what I have seen is unsurpassable.'[54]

In London he, Scott Moncrieff, and Osbert Sitwell passed a golden evening listening to Violet Gordon Woodhouse play the harpsichord, and afterwards, sitting in the Physic Garden opposite Osbert Sitwell's house in Swan Walk,[55] they 'tired the sun with talking and sent him down the sky'. Sassoon was visited in the American Women's hospital at Lancaster Gate and, later, Owen wrote to him:

Goodbye –
   dear Siegfried –
I'm much nearer to you here than in Scarborough, and am by so much happier.
   I have been incoherent ever since I tried to say goodbye on the steps of Lancaster Gate. But everything is clear now; & I'm in hasty retreat towards the Front. Battle is easier here; and therefore you will stay and endure old men & women to the End, and wage the bitterer war and more hopeless.
   When you write, please address to Mahim,
Monkmoor Rd.
Shrewsbury.
What more is there to say that you will not better understand unsaid.
Your W.E.O.[56]

At Folkestone, thinking of Shelley's 'Lines written in Dejection' but himself feeling far from dejected, he went down to the sunlit beach, bathed, and there met 'a Harrow boy, of superb intellect &

refinement; intellect because he hates war more than Germans; refinement because of the way he spoke of my Going, and of the Sun, and of the Sea there; and the way he spoke of Everything'. A few months before, he had found Horace Vachell's novel about Harrow, *The Hill*, 'lovely and melancholy reading';[57] and with that meeting and much else on his mind, he boarded the boat for Boulogne.

10

FRANCE

The great German offensives of March and April had exhausted the attackers, as the French and British troops had earlier been exhausted by their offensives; and the Allied armies had recovered confidence with each assault beaten off, just as the Germans had before. On 15 July, the enemy launched what was to prove their last offensive. East of Rheims the French fell back, but as the attackers pressed forward they found themselves caught between the fire of French machine-guns. Then, on 18 July, the defenders made a counter-thrust at the exposed flank of the German advance. Ludendorff broke off the advance towards Paris and his armies fell back across the River Marne. Their withdrawal from the Château Thierry salient was in its last phase when Wilfred Owen again set foot on French soil.

On 1 September he reached Étaples and found it 'vastly more habitable than in 1917. Impossible to feel depressed. All auguries are of good fortune.'[1] His high spirits were partly the result of meeting two literary men. The first, 'an extraordinary hunch-backed little Irishman of very pleasant manners', was Conal O'Riordan, who had succeeded Synge as Director of the Abbey Theatre in 1909 and was now in charge of the YMCA Rest Hut at the Base Camp, Étaples. The second was a large Scotsman, 2nd Lieutenant Murray McClymont of the 2nd/10th (Scottish) Battalion, The King's Liverpool Regiment, who having been gassed and discharged from hospital, was now awaiting a Medical Board. After some days he received an order at breakfast to appear before this at 12 noon on Friday 6

September. Leaving the mess, he returned to his dormitory hut to nurse his resentment at the thought of being seconded to other than a kilted regiment. He was sitting on his bed when the door opened and two officers entered. One of them said to McClymont: 'This is Wilfred Owen. I thought you'd like to know him. He writes poetry too.' With a smile and a flick of his leather-covered stick, he turned on his heel and left them together.[2]

McClymont had had three poems published in *More Songs by the Fighting Men* (December 1917) and gave Owen a copy of this inscribed:

> A little book and a little song.
> The first all right and the last all wrong:
> Which is but meet, let it be known,
>   Since mine the song and the book's for Owen!

That afternoon, under blue skies and a brazen sun, they talked of poetry and Owen mentioned that he had been asked to contribute to *Wheels* (of which McClymont had never heard). They dined together in the mess that evening and talked almost exclusively of Sassoon and his poems. Owen was amused by McClymont's parody of 'The General':

> 'Good-morning, good morning!' the General said,
> As he passed down the Line with a wound in his head.
> Now, we knew he was wounded by the way that he bled,
> And when he got to the Base the poor bugger was dead –
>   (Chorus) HOORAY!

After supper they wandered about the camp, stumbling over duck-boards as daylight faded and darkness fell. At last they said good-night, little knowing that they would never see each other again.

On Monday 9 September, Owen set off with a party of soldiers towards the Front and he wrote to his mother from Amiens:

I have a good room in a large house, with a young officer, – quite bearable, – bound also for the 2nd. Man. There are no window panes, but the valuable hand-lace-curtains remain. I sleep on a table, for which a kind Kiltie has just found me a mattress.[3]

He struck up a friendship with his 'comrade in billets', 2nd Lieutenant F. Potts, who had been a science student at Manchester, and wrote home blithely:

Plenty of French books, plenty of cigarettes, plenty of magnificent life about me, and – enough to eat. No wounded pass through here; as for the poor battered houses they make me merry at heart, for they were all in bad style. And since probably by now the soldiers whose these houses were or were to have been are Unreturning, no pity whatever for their destruction moves me.

I kick joyfully about the debris, and only feel a twinge of sadness when a little child's copy-book or frock or crumpled little hat is laid bare.

Near the Cathedral I picked up a delightful wee lace-surplice, my only souvenir so far.

He sent O'Riordan a cheerfully adapted Field Service Post Card:[4]

NOTHING is to be written on this side except the date and signature of the sender. Sentences not required may be erased. If anything else is added the post card will be destroyed.

[Postage must be prepaid on any letter or post card addressed to the sender of this card]

I am quite well

~~I have been admitted into hospital~~

{ ~~sick~~ } *and am going on well.*

{ ~~wounded~~ } ~~and hope~~ *to be* ~~dis~~*charged soon.*

I am ~~being sent down to the~~ *base*

~~I have received your~~ { ~~letter dated~~ .... }

{ ~~telegram~~ ,, ... }

{ ~~parcel~~ ,, ... }

Letter follows at first opportunity.

I have received no letter from you

{ ~~lately~~ }

{ ~~for a long time~~ }

Signature only } *Owen*

Date 11/9/18

The 2nd Manchesters had, with the rest of the 96th Brigade, been heavily engaged in the second half of August, driving the Germans back from Vermandovillers, Ablaincourt, and Cizancourt (a hamlet between the villages of St. Christ and Misery). At the end of the month the Battalion was withdrawn to Berny. After a week's rest it was ordered forward again and on 6 September marched to Ennemain, thence to Monchy-Lagache, Villévèque, and Marteville, before being withdrawn once more, this time to the Neuville area east of Corbie. Owen, who had been expecting to join them at the Front, heard on 13 September that they were only four miles from Amiens, and two days later reported to the Adjutant. He was assigned to D Company and appointed Bombing Officer to the Battalion although, as he told the Adjutant, he had no special knowledge of bombs.

After dinner that day eight letters were brought to him. His hopes that one might be from Sassoon were disappointed and some days later he wrote to him:

My dear Siegfried,

Here are a few poems to tempt you to a letter. I begin to think your correspondence must be intercepted somewhere. So I will state merely

I have had no letter from you $\begin{cases} \text{lately} \\ \text{for a long time,} \end{cases}$

and say nothing of my situation, tactical or personal.

You said it would be a good thing for my poetry if I went back.

That is my consolation for feeling a fool. This is what shells scream at me every time: Haven't you got the wits to keep out of this?

———————

Did you see what the Minister of Labour★ said in the *Mail* the other day? 'The first instincts of the men *after the cessation of* hostilities will be to return home.' And again –
'All classes *acknowledge* their indebtedness to the soldiers & sailors . . .

About the same day, Clemenceau is reported by the *Times* as saying: '*All* are worthy . . . yet we should be untrue to ourselves if we forgot that the *greatest* glory will be to the splendid poilus, who, etc.'[5]

———————————————

★ George Henry Roberts (1869–1928), Minister of Labour 1917–19.

Clemenceau's speech to the Senate was quoted in full in *The Times* of 19 September, and one paragraph in particular must have aroused Owen's fury with its insistence on total victory:

'All are worthy of victory, because they will know how to honour it. Yet, however, in the ancient spot where sit the fathers of the Republic we should be untrue to ourselves if we forgot that the greatest glory will be to those splendid *poilus* who will see confirmed by history the titles of nobility which they themselves have earned. At the present moment they ask for nothing more than to be allowed to complete the great work which will assure them of immortality. What do they want and what do you? To keep on fighting victoriously until the moment when the enemy will understand there is no possible negotiation between crime and right.'

On the back of a letter (dated 11 September) from Murray McClymont, Owen drafted a poem that took its title from one of the most popular songs on the Western Front:

SMILE, SMILE, SMILE

Head to limp head, the sunk-eyed wounded scanned
Yesterday's *Mail*; the casualties (typed small)
And (large) Vast Booty from our latest Haul.
Also, they read of Cheap Homes, not yet planned,
'For,' said the paper, 'when this war is done
The men's first instinct will be making homes.
Meanwhile their foremost need is aerodromes,
It being certain war has but begun.
Peace would do wrong to our undying dead, –
The sons we offered might regret they died
If we got nothing lasting in their stead.
We must be solidly indemnified.
Though all be worthy Victory which all bought,
We rulers sitting in this ancient spot
Would wrong our very selves if we forgot
The greatest glory will be theirs who fought,
Who kept this nation in integrity.'
Nation? – The half-limbed readers did not chafe
But smiled at one another curiously
Like secret men who know their secret safe.

(This is the thing they know and never speak,
That England one by one had fled to France,
Not many elsewhere now, save under France.)
Pictures of these broad smiles appear each week,
And people in whose voice real feelings rings
Say: How they smile! They're happy now, poor things.[6]

This was probably not finished in time to be sent to Sassoon, but
'The Sentry' was.[7] It had taken a year and a half for the experience
behind that poem★ to work its way into words, and eleven years for
another experience to undergo its transformation into the third
stanza-paragraph of a second poem sent (incomplete) to Sassoon on
22 September:†[8]

SPRING OFFENSIVE

Halted against the shade of a last hill,
They fed, and lying easy, were at ease
And, finding comfortable chests and knees,
Carelessly slept. But many there stood still
To face the stark blank sky beyond the ridge,
Knowing their feet had come to the end of the world.

Marvelling they stood, and watched the long grass swirled
By the May breeze, murmurous with wasp and midge,
For though the summer oozed into their veins
Like an injected drug for their bodies' pains,
Sharp on their souls hung the imminent line of grass,
Fearfully flashed the sky's mysterious glass.

Hour after hour they ponder the warm field, –
And the far valley behind, where the buttercup
Had blessed with gold their slow boots coming up,
Where even the little brambles would not yield
But clutched and clung to them like sorrowing hands.
They breathe like trees unstirred.‡

★ See above, p. 157
† See above, pp. 44 and 55
‡ In the manuscript, this line reads: '~~All they strange day~~ they breathe like trees unstirred.'

Till like a cold gust thrills the little word
At which each body and its soul begird
And tighten them for battle. No alarms
Of bugles, no high flags, no clamorous haste, –
Only a lift and flare of eyes that faced
The sun, like a friend with whom their love is done.
O larger shone that smile against the sun, –
Mightier than his whose bounty these have spurned.

So, soon they topped the hill, and raced together
Over an open stretch of herb and heather
Exposed. And instantly the whole sky burned
With fury against them; earth set sudden cups
In thousands for their blood; and the green slope
Chasmed and steepened sheer to infinite space.

Of them who running on that last high place
Leapt to swift unseen bullets, or went up
On the hot blast and fury of hell's upsurge,
Or plunged and fell away past this world's verge,
Some say God caught them even before they fell.

But what say such as from existence' brink
Ventured but drave too swift to sink,
The few who rushed in the body to enter hell,
And there out-fiending all its fiends and flames
With superhuman inhumanities,
Long-famous glories, immemorial shames –
And crawling slowly back, have by degrees
Regained cool peaceful air in wonder –
Why speak not they of comrades that went under?

Here, nature is at first presented as beautiful and benevolent; but
the soldiers are ominously 'Halted against the shade of a last hill',
and the image of summer oozing into their veins introduces the
general theme of man's unity with nature, only to puncture its
gentle associations with a dark prophecy of the morphia needle.
While they can, the soldiers turn their backs on 'the imminent line
of grass', thinking of 'the far valley behind' with its buttercups and
the humanized brambles that 'clung to them like sorrowing hands'.

K

The men, breathing 'like trees unstirred', are themselves naturalized, if one may so use the word. Then the attack is launched. The benign buttercups become chalices for sacrificial blood and, as summer had oozed into the soldiers' veins, so now their veins ooze back into summer. In 'Spring Offensive' and 'Smile, smile, smile', the figure of the poet does not appear, and the greater objectivity of his later poems is a measure of his maturity and the distance he had travelled from his egocentric boyhood.

On 28 September the 96th Brigade moved forward to Vendelles, a cluster of battered houses and farms on the crest of a smooth upsurge of downland. It was probably there that he wrote to his mother:

Am still sitting on straw under our Tamboo,★ for it is raining again. These few days have been dry & not really cold. You must not suppose I have been uncomfortable. Though I left the last vestige of civilization, in the Civil sense, behind at ————, there is here all but all that a man wants fundamentally; clean air, enough water to wash once a day; plain food and plentiful; letters from Home of good news, shelter from the rain & cold; an intellectual gentleman for Captain; 3 bright & merry boys for my corporals; & stout grizzled old soldiers in my platoon. My Sergeant is a tiny man. We get on very well together.[9]

He went on to describe the second-in-command of the Battalion, Major J. N. Marshall of the Irish Guards: 'the most arrant utterly soldierly soldier I ever came across. . . . Bold, robust, dashing, unscrupulous, cruel, jovial, immoral, vast-chested, handsome-headed, of free, coarse speech'. A fine all-round sportsman, he had been well-known before the War as a breeder of thoroughbred horses. In 1914 he had disposed of his bloodstock stud and joined the Belgian Army as a 1st Lieutenant in the 1st regiment d'artillerie, 1st division d'armie. Before the year was out, he had been severely wounded in the lungs and leg, the first two of ten wounds – one a bayonet thrust in the face – he had received up to September 1918. For his gallant exploits he had been created an Officier l'ordre de Leopold, Chevalier l'ordre de Leopold, and had received the Croix de Guerre, the Medaille Militaire, and the Military Cross. Owen, whose tendency towards hero-worship had showed in his relation-

★ Bivouac.

ship with Sassoon, was clearly fascinated by the fire-eating Major and in such company it was perhaps not surprising that he was himself called 'The Ghost'.

The following day, the Manchesters marched for the Line. They passed through the village of Le Verguier and, as the column emerged at its eastern end, they saw their road winding ahead of them down into the valley of the River Omignon and its junction with the St. Quentin Canal. The roadside verges were bright with the same flowers and grasses that were thickening the hedgerows of home: poppies and purple clover, Michaelmas daisies and Queen Anne's lace. But like storm clouds blocking their way, the dark hills held by the enemy shook out their thunder and lightning.

The singing column crossed the curve of the St. Quentin Canal at Bellenglise, a strongly fortified village which had fallen that morning to the 46th (North Midland) Division. Three Staffordshire Battalions, rushing foot-bridges the enemy had had no time to destroy, swimming and wading the Canal, had swarmed up the east bank, driving the Germans from their trenches with bayonet and grenade. This one division took 4,000 prisoners and 70 guns.[10]

The Manchesters spent that night in old German trenches two miles east of Bellenglise, and next day moved into position near Magny-la-Fosse, a village in a deep hollow of the downs. They came under fire as they did so, losing two men killed and four officers and eighteen men wounded. During the night of 30 September, preparations were made for the 14th Brigade to attack Sequehart; for the 96th Brigade to advance uphill against Joncourt with the 5th Australian Division, and to gain the Beaurevoir-Fonsomme Line at Chataignies Wood in conjunction with the 97th Brigade. At 4 p.m. the Manchesters moved forward, C and D Companies in front, and reached Joncourt with little resistance, but the Beaurevoir-Fonsomme Line was strongly held. However, after savage hand-to-hand fighting, they drove the Germans back from a trench known as Swiss Cottage to a point 1,400 yards south of it, capturing 210 prisoners. The wire was very thick, and the trench itself, though only one foot deep, contained numerous rifle and machine-gun pits. Four tanks aided the attack, while five more followed behind to clear the trenches to the north of the objective. Three of the first four were hit just before zero hour. In one of these, the whole crew except the officer were wounded; but picking up an officer and a man of the Manchesters to work the machine-guns, the tank went into action again. Repeated counter-attacks were made during the night of 1/2 October against the left flank of the 96th Brigade, but the Manchesters successfully held their ground with the assistance of a company of the 15th Lancashire Fusiliers that had been sent forward to reinforce them. In that day's fighting, four men of the 2nd Battalion were killed; 2nd Lieutenant Gregg died of wounds; Captain Somerville, 2nd Lieutenants Johnson, Heyward, Potts, Bowden, and Morris, and 78 other ranks were wounded; and 7 men were missing.

Of his experiences that night and day, Owen wrote to his mother:

I lost all my earthly faculties, and fought like an angel.

If I started into detail of our engagement I should disturb the censor and my own Rest.

You will guess what has happened when I say I am now Commanding the Company, and in the line had a boy lance-corporal as my Sergeant-Major.

With this corporal who stuck to me and shadowed me like your prayers I captured a German Machine Gun and scores of prisoners.

I'll tell you exactly how another time. I only shot one man with my revolver (at about 30 yards!); The rest I took with a smile. The same thing happened with other parties all along the line we entered.

I have been recommended for the Military Cross; and have recommended every single N.C.O. who was with me!

My nerves are in perfect order.

I came out in order to help these boys – directly by leading them as well as an officer can; indirectly, by watching their sufferings that I may speak of them as well as a pleader can. I have done the first.

Of whose blood lies yet *crimson* on my shoulder where his head was – and where so lately yours was – I must not now write.[11]

He continued his account a few days later:

You will understand I could not write – when you think of us for days all but surrounded by the enemy. All one day (after the battle) we could not move from a small trench, though hour by hour the wounded were groaning just outside. Three stretcher-bearers who got up were hit, one after one. I had to order no one to show himself after that, but remembering my own duty, and remembering also my forefathers the agile Welshmen of the Mountains I scrambled out myself & felt an exhilaration in baffling the Machine Guns by quick bounds from cover to cover. After the shells we had been through, and the gas, bullets were like the gentle rain from heaven.

At one point he held 'a most glorious brief peace talk in a pill box', but on this the Germans concentrated their fire and only at nightfall, when they had been relieved by the Lancashire Fusiliers, was Owen able to lead the weary survivors of Captain Somerville's shattered company back to safety.[12]

Later, writing to Siegfried, who for a similar exploit had won the Military Cross whose ribbon he had thrown into the Mersey, he said: 'I'm glad I've been recommended for M.C., & hope I get it, for the confidence it may give me at home.' He did get it,* and the imputation that he was 'unfit to command troops', which had haunted him since April 1917,† was answered with two words and a white and purple ribbon.

On 3 October, the Battalion was relieved by the 1/8 Sherwood Foresters and moved back into dugouts at Lehaucourt on the wooded bank of the St. Quentin Canal. The German artillery, however, had their range and during the relief another 23 men were killed, 70 wounded, and one officer missing. Two days later they were withdrawn to Hancourt, seven miles southeast of Péronne. It was one of those villages devastated – its farms fired, its orchards mutilated – prior to the German withdrawal to the Hindenburg Line in March 1917. Here the Manchesters bandaged their wounds, tried to cough the gas out of their lungs, rested, and wrote letters. Owen confided to Sassoon:

It is a strange truth: that your *Counter-Attack* frightened me much more than the real one: though the boy by my side, shot through the head, lay on top of me, soaking my shoulder, for half an hour.

---

* The citation runs: 'For conspicuous gallantry and devotion to duty in the attack on the Fonsomme Line on 1st/2nd October 1918. On the Company Commander becoming a casualty, he assumed command and showed fine leadership and resisted a heavy counter-attack. He personally manipulated a captured enemy machine gun in an isolated position and inflicted considerable losses on the enemy. Throughout he behaved most gallantly.'

† See above, p. 183.

Catalogue? Photograph? Can you photograph the crimson-hot iron as it cools from the smelting? That is what Jones's blood looked like, and felt like. My senses are charred.[13]

So he had described to his mother the death of his 'excellent little servant Jones', who had been with him since Scarborough and 'whose blood lies yet crimson on my shoulder'. The repetition of 'crimson', a word found nowhere else in his letters and seldom in his poems, suggests a possible link with a fragment that could have been written in the rest period at Hancourt:

> I saw his round mouth's crimson deepen as it fell,
>   Like a Sun, in his last deep hour;
> Watched the magnificent recession of farewell,
>   Clouding, half gleam, half glower,
> And a last splendour burn the heavens of his cheek.
>   And in his eyes
> The cold stars lighting, very old and bleak,
>   In different skies.[14]

Behind that poem lies another, unfinished poem, 'Spells and Incantation', probably begun in September 1915. This much can be salvaged from a heavily corrected working draft written on note-paper of the Regent Palace Hotel, Piccadilly.*

> But pale skin, your pearl skin
> Show this to me and I shall have surprise
> Of every snow-lit dawn before it break.
>
> But clear eyes, your fresh eyes
> Open: that I may laugh, and lightly take
> All air of early April in one hour.
>
> But brown curls, give me your curls
> Full of September mist, half gleam, half glower,
> Let me pass through them like a field of corn.

---

* See below, p. 126.

Your plum mouth, your rose mouth,
Give me with this the fulness of the sum
Of all my summers that are yet to come.★

Significant elements of this sub-Keatsian fragment – mouth, eyes, and the haunting phrase 'half gleam, half glower' – reappear transformed in the later fragment, one might almost say the later version, written with the disciplined sensuality, the passionate intelligence that distinguish Owen's poetry at its best.

It is now possible to see that his gifts were not only gifts of genius, but other gifts that only the gods bestow. He came to the War with his imagination in large measure conditioned and prepared to receive and record the experience of the trenches. Botany and Broxton, Uriconium, and Keats, his adolescent hypochondria, his religious upbringing and later doubts, all shaped him for his subject, as for no other. He wrote more eloquently than other poets of the tragedy of boys killed in battle, because he felt that tragedy more acutely, and his later elegies spring from his early preoccupations as flowers from their stem.

With Captain Somerville in hospital, Owen was still in command of D Company and, although saddened by news of the deaths first of Robbie Ross and then of Philip Bainbrigge, death now meant less to him than formerly. He no longer took the cigarette from his mouth as he wrote Deceased across the letters to be 'returned to sender'. Censoring the outgoing mail, he read: 'Do you know that little officer called Owen who was at Scarborough; he is commanding my Company, and he is a toff I can tell you. No na-poo. Compree?' This compliment he interpreted for his mother: 'A fine fellow, no nonsense about him!'[15] She must have told him that she had been speaking out in favour of a negotiated peace, for he replied:

I am glad you are finding courage to speak. In a previous letter you said you kept quiet. I was not proud of that. The 4th Army General has had to issue an Order:
'Peace Talk must cease in the Fourth Army.'

★ These stanzas do not appear in the version printed in *CP*, p. 138.

Susan Owen was a wiser, if a sadder, woman than she had been before the War, living in blinkered ignorance of the raw facts of man's inhumanity to man. She was ill again, however, and her son wrote to her tenderly:

How happily I think of you always in bed. About the end of November you will start to move about your room. Your room must be arranged. All my Articles of Vertue which you like are to represent me there. My Jacobean Chest; (why not?) my carpets; my tall candlesticks; my pictures; my tables: have them all in.

About Christmas you will start the hardening processes. You will lengthen your walks and your paces. You will grow keen with the keenness of frost and cold, blue sunlight. So you will be ready, early in February, for my Leave. We will walk to Haughmond, and while you are resting on the top, I will run round the Wrekin and back, to warm my feet.

For even were Prussianism removed from London & Berlin and Peace happened before Christmas, I should not get home before January or February.[16]

Such day-dreams were interrupted on 18 October. Early that morning, Owen left the red tent shielded with corrugated iron that had been his billet and began the long march back towards the guns. The Manchesters passed through Bohain, through Busigny where they were joined by a draft of eighty-five men, and on the 25th he wrote with soldierly bravado to his cousin Leslie:

You must not imagine when you hear we are 'resting' that we lie in bed smoking. We work or are on duty *always*. And last night my dreams were troubled by fairly close shelling. I believe only civilians in the village were killed (Thank God). In this house where I stay five healthy girls died of fright when our guns shelled the place last fortnight. You & I have always been open with each other: and therefore I must say that I feel sorry that you are neither in the flesh with us nor in the spirit against War.

There are two French girls in my billet, daughters of the Mayor, who (I suppose because of my French) single me for their joyful gratitude for *La Délivrance*. Naturally I talk to them a good deal; so much so that the jealousy of other officers resulted in a Subalterns' Court Martial being held on me! The dramatic irony was too killing, considering certain other things, not possible to tell in a letter.

Until last night though I have been reading Swinburne, I had begun to forget what a kiss was.[17]

Four days later, the Battalion reached the hill-top village of St. Souplet and again went into the Line. The Germans were falling back, and a sense that the end was in sight no doubt contributed to Owen's good humour when, on the last evening of October, he wrote to his mother from what he called 'The Smoky Cellar of the Forester's House':

So thick is the smoke in this cellar that I can hardly see by a candle 12 ins. away, and so thick are the inmates that I can hardly write for pokes, nudges & jolts. On my left the Coy. Commander* snores on a bench: other officers repose on wire beds behind me. At my right hand, Kellett, a delightful servant of A Coy. in *The Old Days* radiates joy & contentment from pink cheeks and baby eyes. He laughs with a signaller, to whose left ear is glued the Receiver; but whose eyes rolling with gaiety show that he is listening with his right ear to a merry corporal, who appears at this distance away (some three feet) nothing [but] a gleam of white teeth & a wheeze of jokes.

Splashing my hand, an old soldier with a walrus moustache peels & drops potatoes into the pot. By him, Keyes, my cook, chops wood; another feeds the smoke with the damp wood.

It is a great life. I am more oblivious than alas! yourself, dear Mother, of the ghastly glimmering of the guns outside, & the hollow crashing of the shells.

There is no danger down here, or if any, it will be well over before you read these lines.[18]

The 96th Brigade was holding a line west of the Sambre and Oise Canal, north of Ors, and word had been received that the Battalion would shortly take part in an attack over and beyond the Canal.[19] On the night of 31 October/1 November, patrols reported the enemy west of the Canal but holding 'alarm posts' only. The following night, the west bank was systematically cleared; four Germans and three machine-guns being captured.

The night of 3/4 November had been chosen for the crossing of the Sambre Canal. Rain fell until midnight and, when it stopped, a thick mist settled in the valley. Zero hour for the 32nd Division was set for 5.45 a.m. and, as it ticked closer, the assault troops moved into

---

* I have not been able to identify D Company's new commander.

The Sambre and Oise Canal, November 1918

position in little irregular fields about 300 yards from the Canal. With them were men of the Royal Engineers carrying the bridges that were to cross, first, a 3 ft. deep ditch running parallel with the Canal and then, 15 yards beyond it, the Canal itself. The 96th Brigade was 1,000 yards north of Ors, on the left of the 32nd Division's front, with the 2nd Manchesters, 16th Lancashire Fusiliers, and the 15th Lancashire Fusiliers in line from left to right.

When the minute hands touched 5.45 and the shrilling of many whistles was added to the thunder of the British barrage cratering the east bank of the Canal, Owen led his platoon over the dark wet fields. Five minutes after zero, the barrage lifted and the assault troops in extended line moved down the last sloping field and, on planks and duckboards, scrambled over or through the flooded ditch. As they struggled up the last short slope to the muddy tow-path, the first men began to fall. The far bank bristled with German machine-guns, brought up as the British barrage lifted, and behind that parapet they kept up a scorching fire. This the Manchesters and the Lancashire Fusiliers returned, as the 218th Field Company of the Royal Engineers dragged down to the water's edge their serpentine bridge of wire-linked wooden floats. Almost at once the enemy artillery found the range of the west bank, and the bridge was cut by shell- and machine-gun fire. Undaunted, the Engineers set to work to repair it, while bullets splintered the wood in their hands and struck sparks from the wire binding the floats. One by one they fell, on the bank, in the water, until all but two were killed or wounded.

Seeing there was no hope for the survivors or their bridge without more effective covering fire, a nineteen-year-old 2nd Lieutenant of the Manchesters, James Kirk, snatched up a Lewis gun and four magazines and ran down to the water's edge. He climbed on to a raft, paddled to within ten yards of the German machine-gunners and opened fire, forcing them to take cover behind their parapet. Those few precious minutes enabled the Engineers, Major Waters and Sapper Archibald,★ to finish mending the bridge. Then Kirk's machine-gun stopped firing. The last of his magazines was empty. He was wounded in the arm and in the face, but more magazines were paddled out to him, and again he opened fire from his tilting raft. Behind him the bridge was pushed out and two platoons scrambled across. Almost at once, as a lucky shell severed the pontoons, they were cut off, and James Kirk fell forward over his gun, shot through the head.

To the right of the 2nd Manchesters, the 16th Lancashire Fusiliers were in the same perilous predicament. Commanding them that day was Acting Lieutenant-Colonel Marshall of the ten wounds who, not to be outdone by his former Battalion, called for a party of volunteers to repair the broken bridge in front of his position. They rose to him and wrestled with the wire and the small cork rafts at the water's edge until all were killed or wounded. Standing over them, fully exposed on the bank, Marshall for a moment turned his broad back on the enemy and bellowed for another party of volunteers. Again they came forward and he cursed and encouraged them as

★ Both were awarded the Victoria Cross.

they went to work. Miraculously, enough survived to repair the bridge and push it out over the whipped water. Marshall led his men across, only to fall on the far bank with his eleventh and final wound.

Through this hurricane the small figure of Wilfred Owen walked backwards and forwards between his men, patting them on the shoulder, saying 'Well done' and 'You're doing very well, my boy'. He was at the water's edge, giving a hand with some duckboards, when he was hit and killed.[20]

By midday the remnants of the 2nd Manchesters were on the other side of the Canal, having crossed south of Ors by means of a floating bridge supported on kerosene tins. And seven days later, as the guns fell silent on the Western Front, the survivors piled their rifles, took off their helmets, and went to sleep; the living like the dead.

In Shrewsbury, the Armistice bells were ringing when the Owens' front-door bell sounded its small chime, heralding the telegram that Tom and Susan had dreaded for two years.

AFTERWORDS

Armistice Day found Harold Owen on the African Station in the cruiser *Astræa*, whose launching *The Times* had reported on 18 March 1893, the day Wilfred Owen was born.

We were lying off Victoria. I had gone down to my cabin thinking to write some letters. I drew aside the door curtain and stepped inside and to my amazement I saw Wilfred sitting in my chair. I felt shock run through me with appalling force and with it I could feel the blood draining away from my face. I did not rush towards him but walked jerkily into the cabin – all my limbs stiff and slow to respond. I did not sit down but looking at him I spoke quietly: 'Wilfred, how did you get here?' He did not rise and I saw that he was involuntarily immobile, but his eyes which had never left mine were alive with the familiar look of trying to make me understand; when I spoke his whole face broke into his sweetest and most endearing dark smile. I felt no fear – I had not when I first drew my door curtain and saw him there; only exquisite mental pleasure at thus beholding him. All I was conscious of was a sensation of enormous shock and profound astonishment that he should be here in my cabin. I spoke again. 'Wilfred dear, how can you be here, it's just not possible. . . .' But still he did not speak but only smiled his most gentle smile. This not speaking did not now as it had done at first seem strange or even unnatural; it was not only in some inexplicable way perfectly natural but radiated a quality which made his presence with me undeniably right and in no way out of the ordinary. I loved having him there: I could not, and did not want to try to understand how he had got there. I was content to accept him, that he was here with me was sufficient. I could not question anything, the meeting in itself was complete and strangely perfect. He was in uniform and I remember thinking how out of place the khaki looked amongst the cabin furnishings. With this thought I must have turned my eyes away from him; when I looked back my cabin chair was empty. . . .

I felt the blood run slowly back to my face and looseness into my limbs and with these an overpowering sense of emptiness and absolute loss. . . . I wondered if I had been dreaming but looking down I saw that I was still standing. Suddenly I felt terribly tired and moving to my bunk I lay down; instantly I went into a deep oblivious sleep. When I woke up I knew with absolute certainty that Wilfred was dead.[1]

In a corner of the village cemetery at Ors, 'The burying-party, picks and shovels in shaking grasp', did their work, laying LIEUTENANT W. E. S. OWEN. M.C. between PRIVATE W. E. DUCKWORTH and PRIVATE H. TOPPING. In the same rear rank they laid SECOND LIEUT. JAMES KIRK V.C., and a short distance away LIEUTENANT COLONEL JAMES NEVILLE MARSHALL V.C., M.C., AND BAR. The three ranks of uniform gravestones, each with its regimental crest, rank, name, date of death, age, and the simple cross, make a contrast that Wilfred Owen would have appreciated with the florid scrolls, the marble flowers, the wrought-iron crucifixes of the village cemetery. In due course his personal effects – his wallet, his copy of Swinburne's *Poems and Ballads*, his service revolver[2] – found their way back to Mahim, where his mother chose a quotation for his gravestone:

> "SHALL LIFE RENEW
> THESE BODIES?
> OF A TRUTH
> ALL DEATH WILL HE ANNUL"   W.O.

Taken thus out of context, these lines convey a meaning diametrically opposite to that of their source, 'The End':[3]

> Shall Life renew these bodies? Of a truth,
> All death will he annul, all tears assuage? –
> Or fill these void veins full again with youth,
> And wash, with an immortal water, Age?
>
> When I do ask white Age, he saith not so:
> 'My head hangs weighed with snow.'
> And when I hearken to the Earth, she saith:
> 'My fiery heart shrinks, aching. It is death.
> Mine ancient scars shall not be glorified,
> Nor my titanic tears, the seas, be dried.'[4]

But that was not the end; and as Wilfred Owen lies today under his mother's misquotation, the voice of the living man can be heard more clearly in a sentence written a few hundred yards away, perhaps the last he ever wrote: 'Of this I am certain you could not be visited by a band of friends half so fine as surround me here.'

NOTES

Appendixes
  A   The Owen and Shaw Families
  B   Poems and Fragments not in the *Collected Poems*
  C   Wilfred Owen's Library

Chapter 1.   Oswestry

The principal source for this chapter is *JFO*, 1, pp. 1–16.

1   On 4 November 1797.
2   Held in the Salop County Council Library, Oswestry Branch.
3   The Croeswylan district of Oswestry takes its name from the Croeswylan ('cross of wailing') stone, originally the base of a tall cross to which the sick came to make supplication in 1559 when the sweating sickness raged with such violence that it claimed upwards of 500 victims.
4   Edward Salter died on 10 January 1830, Mary Salter on 22 February 1842.
5   See Isaac Watkin, *Oswestry with an Account of its Old Houses, Shops, Etc., and Some of their Occupants*, London and Oswestry, 1920, p. 211; and *Bye-Gones 1897–98*, Oswestry and Wrexham, 1899, p. 12.
6   *The Oswestry and Border Counties Advertizer*, 20 January 1897, p. 8.
7   *JFO*, I, p. 10 and *CL*, p. 341.
8   Ibid., pp. 2–3.
9   Hannah Owen, née Pace. Details of John Owen and his household are to be found in his 1851 Census return. See Public Record Office microfilm, reference HO. 107/2169 ff 711v. and 712r.
10   Then known as the Church of Saints Mary and Nicholas. The dedication of the 'Chapel of Wich Malbanc' in the thirteenth century was 'The Blessed Virgin Mary'. The dual dedication, for which there appears to be no historical justification, is first recorded in 1786. It continued to be used until about 1856 when it fell into disuse.
11   *JFO*, I, pp. 5–6.
12   Messrs. Williams and Nicholson's catalogue of 'the whole of the household furniture, implements & effects' of Plas Wilmot, near Oswestry, to be sold by auction on Tuesday 16 March 1897.
13   *JFO*, I, p. 2.
14   Edward Shaw's will was proved in London on 11 March 1897.
15   John Milton, *Paradise Lost*, Bk. XII, lines 645–7.

Chapter 2.   Birkenhead

The principal sources for this chapter are *JFO*, I, pp. 17–121, and *CL*, pp. 21–31.

1   *JFO*, I, p. 19.
2   *CL*, p. 21.
3   *JFO*, I, p. 40.
4   Ibid., pp. 53–4.
5   Ibid., pp. 46–8.
6   *CP*, p. 149.

7   [G. W. Harris and W. E. Williams], *Birkenhead Institute/Its Foundation and Growth/1889–1949*, privately printed, Birkenhead, n. d., p. 15. My account of the school owes much to its two chroniclers.

8   The school's accounts ledger, dated 30 April 1900, has written against the name of Owen Wilfred E.S.: 'This boy commenced attendance on June 11th, charged ½ fees/due'. The *CL* dating (1901 on p. 9, 1900 on p. 22 n.) must be wrong.

9   *JFO*, I, p. 34.

10   Ibid., pp. 49–51.

11   Ibid., p. 22.

12   Ibid., pp. 25–7.

13   A. S. Paton, 'Wilfred Owen – His Childhood in Birkenhead', *A Tribute to Wilfred Owen*, compiled by T. J. Walsh, Birkenhead, n. d., pp. 6–7.

14   Ibid.

15   *JFO*, I, p. 92.

16   Letter from Mr. A. S. Paton.

17   *JFO*, I, p. 61.

18   Letter from Mr. A. S. Paton.

19   *CL*, p. 21.

20   On reconsideration, Harold Owen believed 1902 to be more likely than 1901, the date given for this holiday in *CL*, p. 139 n.

21   *JFO*, I, pp. 69–70.

22   Ibid., p. 75.

23   Ibid., pp. 81–3.

24   Ibid., p. 84.

25   Susan Owen told Edmund Blunden that Wilfred 'must have been about ten years old when I took him for a holiday to Broxton' [*CP*, p. 148]. Harold Owen confirmed that the date 1907 given in *CL*, p. 352 n., must be wrong.

26   HO in conversation.

27   Leslie Gunston, 'From the Caradoc in June', *The Nymph and Other Poems*, 1917. See p. 313 below.

28   *JFO*, I, pp. 77–8.

29   *Shirley*, p. 183. See p. 309 below.

30   Ibid., p. 223.

31   Ibid., p. 318.

32   *CP*, p. 148.

33   *JFO*, I, p. 103.

34   Ibid., pp. 104–5.

35   Ibid., pp. 33–5.

36   Ibid., pp. 35–6.

37   Ibid., p. 38.

38   Letter from Mr. Eric Smallpage.

39   *JFO*, I, p. 85.

40   *CL*, p. 22.

41   *JFO*, p. 61. See also p. 113.

42   Ibid., I, p. 97.

43   Ibid., pp. 113–14, and *CL*, p. 31 n.

44   *JFO*, I, p. 107.

45   Ibid., pp. 107–12.

46   *CL*, p. 514.
47   This may have earned him his place on the Abbeville Transport Course. See above, p. 159.
48   A. S. Paton, *op. cit.*, p. 6.
49   This uncle did not own the farm, as stated in *CL*, p. 22 n., nor did Wilfred holiday there in 1903. His Letter 3, *CL*, p. 22, must date from 1905. The farm belonged to Mr. Jones, the farmer.
50   *CL*, p. 25.
51   Letter from Miss M. Paton.
52   *CL*, p. 26.
53   Letter from Mr. A. S. Paton.
54   *CL*, p. 26.
55   Mr. A. S. Paton in conversation.
56   *CL*, p. 27.
57   *JFO*, I, pp. 105–7, and *CL*, p. 30.
58   Letter from Mr. Eric Smallpage.
59   *CL*, p. 30.
60   LG in conversation.
61   *JFO*, I, p. 48.
62   Ibid., pp. 112–13.
63   The LNWR and the GWR.
64   *JFO*, I, p. 114.
65   See below, p. 317.
66   *JFO*, I, pp. 119 and 123.

Chapter 3.   Shrewsbury

The principal sources for this chapter are *JFO*, I, pp. 123–227, and *CL*, pp. 32–88.

1   *JFO*, I, pp. 123–4.
2   Ibid., III, pp. 19–20.
3   The Rev. Frederick Roberts, Vicar of St. Giles, Shrewsbury, 1894–1921.
4   *CL*, p. 33.
5   *JFO*, I, pp. 150–1.
6   Ibid.
7   Ibid., p. 138.
8   See below, p. 319.
9   Mr. Roy Denville Jones in conversation.
10   *JFO*, I, pp. 139–40.
11   HO said that he and Colin discovered Uffington in the summer of 1907 and not later, as *JFO* seems to imply.
12   *JFO*, I, p. 172.
13   Ibid., p. 176.
14   *CP*, p. 52.
15   *CL*, p. 38.
16   *JFO*, III, p. 27.
17   'The Prelude' (1805 edition), Bk I, lines 452–64.
18   *CL*, p. 44.
19   Ibid. Tom and Wilfred had a second holiday together in Brest in July 1909. See *CL*, pp. 50–1.
20   *JFO*, I, p. 156.

21 Ibid., pp. 161–2.
22 Miss Dorothy Iles in correspondence.
23 Mrs. D. J. Denville Jones (née Bickerton) in conversation.
24 *CL*, p. 58.
25 *JFO*, III, p. 21.
26 Wilfred also stayed there in December 1908. See *CL*, pp. 48–9. John Gunston called his houses Alpina and Alpenrose because of a fondness for Switzerland where his daughter Dorothy went to school and where they had a number of happy family holidays.
27 *CL*, p. 57.
28 LG in conversation.
29 Miss N. Knight in conversation.
30 *JFO*, II, p. 217.
31 Ibid., I, p. 188.
32 Ibid., pp. 189–90.
33 *CL*, p. 61.
34 See p. 310 below.
35 *JFO*, I, p. 198.
36 *CP*, p. 147.
37 This opinion supersedes that expressed in my British Academy Chatterton Lecture, *Wilfred Owen*, 1970, p. 10 n.
38 *CP*, p. 127.
39 *CL*, p. 69. See also p. 310 below.
40 Ibid., p. 161.
41 *Keats* [English Men of Letters Series], p. 2.
42 Ibid.
43 Ibid., p. 3.
44 Ibid., p. 6.
45 Ibid., p. 8.
46 21 April.
47 *CL*, p. 69.
48 Five folios of MSS survive, contrary to the assertion in *CL*, p. 9 n.
49 *CL*, p. 254.
50 Ibid., p. 70.
51 Ibid., p. 72.
52 Ibid., pp. 75–6.
53 Ibid., p. 77.
54 Diary of Miss Blanche Bulman.
55 *JFO*, II, p. 46. HO in conversation confirmed that this expedition took place in the summer of 1911.
56 Ibid., pp. 48–9.
57 *CL*, p. 80.
58 Ibid., p. 79.
59 Ibid., p. 80.
60 Ibid., p. 82.
61 Ibid., p. 83.
62 *JFO*, I, pp. 251–2.

Chapter 4.   Dunsden and after

The principal source for this chapter is *CL*, pp. 91–193.

 1   Recollections of his nephew, the Rev. Bernard Wigan, quoted in *CL*, pp. 75–6.
 2   *CL*, pp. 91–2.
 3   Ibid., p. 92.
 4   Ibid., p. 91.
 5   Ibid.
 6   Ibid., p. 93.
 7   Ibid., p. 94.
 8   Ibid., p. 95.
 9   Violet Franklin.
10   *CL*, p. 126.
11   Ibid., p. 229 n.
12   Ibid., p. 118.
13   Ibid., p. 119.
14   Ibid., p. 123.
15   See below, p. 316.
16   *CL*, pp. 94 n. and 98.
17   Ibid., p. 593. The whereabouts of this letter, quoted by EB in the Memoir that prefaced his 1931 edition of the *Poems*, are unknown.
18   Albion House, Old Marlow.
19   *CL*, p. 106.
20   J. A. Symonds, *Shelley*, pocket edition, 1909, p. 113. See below, p. 321.
21   *CL*, p. 108.
22   Ibid., p. 110.
23   'The time was aeon; and the place all earth.'
24   An echo of the line 'Changed from glory into glory' from the hymn 'Love Divine, all loves excelling'.
25   *CL*, p. 128 n.
26   Ibid., p. 97.
27   Ibid., p. 129.
28   Ibid., p. 136.
29   Ibid., p. 141. The quotation is from 'Modern Love', last stanza.
30   All from *A Christmas Carol*.
31   *CL*, p. 131. The verse quotation is from Tennyson, *Idylls of the King: Guinevere*.
32   Letter from Miss Morley to Mr. Roland Duthoy.
33   Diary of Miss Blanche Bulman, from which much of my account of the Owen's Kelso holiday is taken.
34   See below, p. 318.
35   *JFO*, I, pp. 232–3.
36   *CL*, p. 151.
37   Ibid., pp. 153–4.
38   Ibid., p. 159.
39   *The Letters of John Keats*, ed. Maurice Buxton Forman, 3rd edition, 1947, p. 53.
40   *CL*, pp. 74 (Letter 82 must date from autumn 1912, not June 1911) and 161.
41   Dunsden Parish Register of Burials. No other double funeral took place

during WO's time at the Vicarage.
42   *CL*, p. 171.
43   Ibid., p. 173 n.
44   *JFO*, II, pp. 4–5.
45   *CL*, p. 174.
46   Ibid., pp. 174–5.
47   *CP*, p. 100.
48   *CL*, p. 176.
49   Ibid., p. 177.
50   Ibid., p. 181.
51   Letter of 9 April 1818 to John Hamilton Reynolds, *The Letters of John Keats*, ed. Maurice Buxton Forman, 3rd edition, 1947, p. 130.
52   *JFO*, II, p. 263.
53   Ibid., pp. 61–2.
54   *CL*, p. 186.
55   *The Letters of John Keats*, p. 110.
56   'Epistle to John Hamilton Reynolds', lines 90–2.
57   *CL*, pp. 186–7.
58   *JFO*, III, p. 21.
59   'On Wenlock Edge the wood's in trouble'.
60   p. 12.
61   p. 11.
62   Colvin, *Keats*, p. 172.
63   See below, p. 315.
64   *JFO*, II, pp. 118–69.
65   Ibid., pp. 182–3.
66   Ibid., pp. 184–206.
67   Ibid., p. 208.
68   *CL*, p. 191.
69   Ibid., pp. 191–2.
70   *JFO*, II, p. 264.

Chapter 5.   France 1913–15

The principal source for this chapter is *CL*, pp. 197–358.

1   *CL*, p. 198.
2   Ibid., p. 199.
3   Ibid., p. 198.
4   *JFO*, III, p. 53.
5   Ibid., pp. 54–6.
6   *CL*, p. 201.
7   Ibid., p. 207.
8   Ibid., p. 209.
9   Ibid., p. 205.
10   Ibid., p. 219.
11   Ibid., p. 222.
12   Ibid., p. 220.
13   Ibid., p. 221.
14   Ibid., p. 227.

15   Ibid., p. 231.
16   Ibid., p. 232.
17   Ibid., p. 227.
18   Ibid., p. 236.
19   Ibid., pp. 240 and 287.
20   Ibid., p. 243.
21   Ibid., p. 244.
22   Ibid., p. 255.
23   Ibid., pp. 247 and 253.
24   Ibid., p. 259.
25   Ibid., p. 261.
26   Ibid., p. 265.
27   Ibid., pp. 271–2.
28   Philip Larkin, 'MCMXIV', *The Whitsun Weddings*.
29   *CL*, p. 273.
30   Ibid., p. 274.
31   Other, and more probably later, drafts of this poem are entitled 'The Women & the Slain' and 'Ballad of Kings and Christs'.
32   *CP*, p. 129.
33   In *New Numbers*, no. 4.
34   *CL*, pp. 112–3, and pp. 141–2 above.
35   *CP*, p. 117, and p. 211 above.
36   *CL*, p. 275.
37   Ibid., p. 276.
38   *CP*, p. 132.
39   *CL*, p. 276.
40   Ibid., p. 279.
41   Ibid., p. 278.
42   Ibid., p. 234.
43   Ibid., pp. 280–1.
44   Ibid., p. 286.
45   Ibid., p. 281.
46   Ibid., p. 282.
47   See D. S. R. Welland, *Wilfred Owen/A Critical Study*, 1968, for a discussion of Tailhade's influence on WO and his work.
48   *CL*, pp. 284–5.
49   *CP*, p. 134.
50   See below, pp. 312 and 317.
51   Letter from LT to WO of 1 April 1915.
52   *CL*, p. 286.
53   Ibid., p. 290.
54   Ibid., p. 293.
55   Ibid., pp. 295–6.
56   Ibid., p. 298.
57   Ibid., pp. 298–9.
58   Ibid., p. 300.
59   Ibid., p. 305.
60   Ibid., p. 309.
61   Ibid., p. 310.

62 Ibid., p. 318.
63 Ibid., p. 311.
64 Ibid., p. 312.
65 Ibid., p. 313.
66 Ibid., p. 315.
67 Sir Arthur Langford Sholto Rowley (1870–1953), British Consul, Bordeaux, 1912–19, subsequently Consul-General at Barcelona and Antwerp. Knighted 1932, succeeded as 8th Baron Langford in 1952.
68 *CL*, p. 316.
69 Ibid., p. 320.
70 Ibid., p. 322.
71 Ibid., p. 323.
72 Ibid., p. 309.
73 Ibid., p. 317.
74 Ibid., p. 319.
75 Ibid., p. 317 n.
76 Ibid., p. 328.
77 Ibid., p. 333.
78 'That if poetry comes not as naturally as the Leaves to a tree it had better not come at all.' Keats to John Taylor, 27 February 1818. *The Letters of John Keats*, ed. Maurice Buxton Forman, 3rd ed., p. 108.
79 *CL*, p. 333.
80 Ibid., p. 334.
81 *CP*, p. 136.
82 *CL*, p. 338.
83 Ibid., p. 339.
84 Ibid., p. 341.
85 From *Servitude et Grandeur Militaires* (1835).
86 *CL*, p. 342.
87 Ibid., pp. 343–4.
88 Ibid., p. 346.
89 *JFO*, III, pp. 120–1.
90 *CL*, p. 347.
91 Ibid., p. 348.
92 Ibid., p. 349.
93 Ibid., p. 350.
94 Ibid., p. 352.
95 Ibid., p. 351.
96 Ibid., p. 355.

Chapter 6. Training

The principal sources for this chapter are *CL*, pp. 358–418, and *JFO*, III, pp. 132–58.

1 Brigadier-General Sir James E. Edwards, *Military Operations/France and Belgium, 1915*, 1928, p. 391.
2 See below, p. 314.
3 *CL*, p. 359.
4 Ibid., p. 360.

5   Joy Grant, *Harold Monro and the Poetry Bookshop*, 1967, p. 64.
6   *CL*, p. 361.
7   Ibid., p. 362.
8   Ibid., pp. 363–4.
9   Ibid., p. 367.
10 Ibid., p. 370.
11 Ibid., p. 375.
12 See William Cooke, *Edward Thomas/A Critical Biography*, 1970, and R. George Thomas, ed., *Letters from Edward Thomas to Gordon Bottomley*, 1968.
13 For Harold's account of this visit, see *JFO*, III, pp. 141–51.
14 *CL*, p. 382 n.
15 *JFO*, III, pp. 133–5.
16 *CL*, p. 384.
17 Ibid., p. 387.
18 Ibid., p. 388.
19 Ibid., pp. 395–6.
20 Ibid., p. 400.
21 Ibid., p. 405.
22 Ibid., p. 348.
23 CDL, in *CP*, p. 135, follows another MS, which reads:
        Purest, it is a diamond dawn of Spring,
        And yet the Veil of Venus and youth's skin
        Mauve-marbled; purpling young Love's mouth for sacred sin.
24 Ibid., p. 105.
25 Ibid., p. 104.
26 Ibid., p. 143.
27 Ibid., p. 112.
28 The MS drafts of this poem being obviously unpolished, I have silently emended the punctuation.
29 See below, p. 306.
30 See below, p. 306.
31 *CL*, p. 408.
32 Ibid., p. 410.
33 *JFO*, III, pp. 152–3.
34 Ibid., pp. 154–6.
35 Ibid., p. 158. HO says they met once more, but see *CL*, p. 418.
36 *CL*, p. 413.

Chapter 7.   *The Somme*

The principal sources for this chapter are *CL*, pp. 421–71; A. J. P. Taylor, *The First World War*, pp. 132–40; and Captain Cyril Falls, *Military Operations/France and Belgium*, 1917, London, 1940.
1   MS in the possession of Mr. George Derbyshire.
2   *Westminster Gazette*, 24 October, 1916.
3   *CL*, p. 421.
4   Ibid., p. 521. WO's recollection that he spent the night of 31 December 1916 at Étaples must surely be wrong.
5   Ibid., p. 422.

6 *Death of a Hero*, 1929, p. 305. It can hardly be a coincidence that Aldington has his hero, George Winterbourne, killed on the same day as WO, 4 November 1918.

7 *CL*, pp. 424–5.

8 Ibid., p. 425–6.

9 Lieut. W. B. St. Leger, M.C., diary in the Imperial War Museum archives.

10 *CL*, pp. 427–8.

11 Ibid., pp. 428–9.

12 Ibid., p. 430.

13 Ibid., pp. 431–2.

14 Ibid., p. 431.

15 Ibid., p. 436.

16 Ibid., p. 434.

17 HO's MS.

18 Bodleian MS.

19 *CL*, p. 437.

20 Ibid., p. 438.

21 Captain Cyril Falls, *op. cit.*, p. 87.

22 Ibid., pp. 112–4.

23 Ibid., pp. 91–2.

24 *CL*, p. 439.

25 Ibid., p. 441.

26 Ibid., p. 442.

27 Ibid., p. 443.

28 Ibid.

29 Ibid., p. 444.

30 Captain Cyril Falls, *op. cit.*, p. 115.

31 Ibid., p. 93.

32 See below, p. 309.

33 *CL*, p. 445.

34 Ibid., p. 446.

35 See *CP*, pp. 106–7.

36 *CL*, p. 447.

37 Ibid., pp. 448–9.

38 For my description of this action I am deeply indebted to the detailed account given me by Mr. George Derbyshire.

39 *CL*, pp. 449–50.

40 'Diary of Edward Thomas', edited by Professor George Thomas, *The Anglo-Welsh Review*, vol. 20, no. 45, p. 31.

41 *CL*, p. 458.

42 Ibid., pp. 453–4.

43 Ibid., p. 452.

44 Ibid., p. 453.

45 Ibid., p. 456.

46 Ibid., p. 447.

47 See p. 47 above.

48 Quoted in *CL*, p. 456 n.

49 Ibid., p. 459.

50 Ibid., pp. 461–2.

51 Ibid., p. 467.
52 Ibid., p. 471.

Chapter 8.   Craiglockhart
The principal sources for this chapter are *CL*, pp. 471–504, and *The Hydra*.
1   *CL*, p. 471.
2   Ibid., p. 473.
3   SS, *Sherston's Progress*, 1936, p. 23.
4   Ibid., pp. 86–8.
5   For a detailed account of the history of Craiglockhart, see [Mother Valerio], 'The Craiglockhart Estate', *The Buckle*, Craiglockhart College, 1968, pp. 8–18.
6   *CL*, p. 475.
7   Ibid., pp. 472–3.
8   Ibid., p. 476.
9   Ibid., p. 478.
10 Ibid., pp. 480–1.
11 See below, p. 321.
12 *CL*, p. 482.
13 WO, 'Field Club', *The Hydra*, 9, pp. 8–9. This brief article opens with his account of his own lecture, 'Do Plants Think?'
14 *CL*, pp. 483–4.
15 SS, *Siegfried's Journey, 1916–1920*, 1945, p. 58.
16 SS, 'Ancestors', *The Old Huntsman*, 1917, p. 61.
17 *CL*, p. 349.
18 Robert Graves, *Goodbye to All That*, revised edition, 1957, Penguin Books 1960, p. 214. SS gives his account of these events in *Memoirs of an Infantry Officer*, 1930, pp. 273–334.
19 *CL*, p. 485.
20 Ibid., p. 488.
21 *Siegfried's Journey*, p. 60.
22 The date on LG's draft of this poem, which is entitled 'Sonnet to Beauty'.
23 *CP*, p. 101.
24 This theory, and much of what follows, first appeared in my article 'W. B. Yeats and Wilfred Owen', *The Critical Quarterly*, autumn 1969, pp. 199–214.
25 *CP*, p. 95.
26 Ibid., p. 126.
27 *CL*, pp. 484, 488, 490, 534, and 560.
28 Manuscript notes for Chapter VI of *Siegfried's Journey*.
29 *CL*, pp. 492–3.

30 The Tynecastle School Log contains an entry dated 24 September 1917:

> During this week arrangements have been made whereby several of the officers from Craiglockhart Hospital are taking classes in certain subjects for some of the pupils. This has been done with the consent of the Board. As far as arranged at present 2 classes in Map Reading, 2 in Physical Exercises, 2 in Signalling, 1 in First Aid and 1 (twice a week) in English Literature are being taught by the officers, each of whom is an expert in his own subject. The classes meet for $\frac{3}{4}$ hour each afternoon and not more than one period is

devoted to each class.
31   *CP*, p. 86. The Sassoon quotation is the closing couplet of the closing poem in *The Old Huntsman*, 'A Letter Home [To Robert Graves]'.
32   The four principal drafts of this poem appear in facsimile in *CP*, pp. 185–8.
33   SS, 'Wilfred Owen – A Personal Appreciation', *A Tribute to Wilfred Owen*, edited by T. J. Walsh, Birkenhead, [1964], p. 35.
34   *Siegfried's Journey*, pp. 59–60.
35   *CL*, p. 496.
36   *EB*, pp. 134–5.
37   *The Hydra*, New Series, No. 1, November 1917, p. 21.
38   *CL*, p. 498.
39   *CP*, p. 67.
40   *CL*, p. 499.
41   *CP*, p. 55.
42   See W. G. Bebbington, 'Jessie Pope and Wilfred Owen', *Ariel*, vol. 3, no. 4, pp. 82–93.
43   'I used to have the *Daily Mail* (Continental) given me.' *CL*, p. 311.
44   *CL*, p. 595.
45   *CP*, pp. 103 and 99.
46   For Arthur Newboult's recollections, see *CL*, p. 594.
47   Letter from Miss Mary Newboult.
48   *CL*, p. 411, and *CP*, p. 104.
49   *CP*, p. 41.
50   What follows derives from the typescript recollections of Miss Dauthieu.
51   *CL*, p. 503.
52   See below, p. 308.

Chapter 9.   Scarborough and Ripon

The principle source for this chapter is *CL*, pp. 504–71.
1   *CL*, pp. 505–6. 'Smile the penny' and 'grame' are taken from Aylmer Strong, *A Human Voice*, 1917.
2   Ibid., p. 511.
3   Ibid., p. 508.
4   *CP*, p. 57.
5   *CL*, pp. 508–9.
6   See below, p. 313.
7   *CL*, p. 510.
8   Ibid., p. 512.
9   Ibid., p. 514.
10   *CP*, pp. 50–1.
11   *Poems, 1899–1906*, p. 22.
12   *CP*, p. 109.
13   Ibid., pp. 48–9. In a letter of 25 January 1974 to the editor of the *TLS*, Professor Dennis Welland quotes a note written to him by SS in which he accepted as 'a certainty' the date of February 1917 for the genesis of 'Exposure'. Recalling their discussions of 'Anthem for Doomed Youth' at Craiglockhart in September 1917, SS comments: 'It was the first occasion on which I was able to hail him as my equal, since he had hitherto withheld the

MSS of his most powerful poems (Exposure, for one) possibly because he feared they would pain me.' His fullest note on the subject, however, runs as follows:

> My belief is that 'Exposure' was much revised at Craiglockhart. I see in it that W. had been influenced by Barbusse's Le Feu, – the English translation of which I made known to him in Aug. 1917 – ('What are we doing here' and 'But nothing happens' are echoes from Barbusse's poilus). can't believe that W. could have written the poem in its perfected state, while on active service. But I have never drawn attention to this, because 'Exposure', being dated previous to W. knowing me, provides proof that he was working on his own creative line before that (my influence on him having been exaggerated).

I cannot believe that WO, had he written 'Exposure' in 1917, would have withheld it from SS for fear of paining him.

14 For an interesting discussion of this theme, see Jon Silkin, *Out of Battle*, 1972, pp. 48–9.
15 *CP*, pp. 183–4.
16 See below, p. 321.
17 See below, p. 308.
18 *CL*, pp. 518 and 595–6.
19 *CP*, pp. 39–40.
20 *Fairies and Fusiliers*, p. 7. See below, p. 313.
21 *CL*, p. 515.
22 Ibid., pp. 515, 530, 532, and 564.
23 *EB*, p. 125.
24 *CL*, p. 513.
25 *CP*, pp. 91–2.
26 Siegfried Sassoon, 'Suicide in the Trenches', *Collected Poems*, p. 78.
27 Ibid., pp. 69–70.
28 Barbusse, p. 288.
29 *CP*, p. 35.
30 *CL*, p. 527.
31 Robert Graves, *Goodbye to All That*, pp. 223–4.
32 *CL*, p. 499 n.
33 Ibid., p. 534.
34 *CP*, p. 59.
35 See Timothy d'Arch Smith, *Love in Earnest/Some Notes on the Lives and Writings of English 'Uranian' Poets from 1889–1930*, 1970, p. 114.
36 *CL*, p. 538.
37 Ibid., p. 543.
38 *JFO*, III, pp. 162–3.
39 Ibid., p. 170.
40 *CP*, pp. 37–8.
41 Ibid., pp. 64–6.
42 Ibid., pp. 46–7.
43 Sir Osbert Sitwell, *Noble Essences*, pp. 103–4.
44 *CL*, p. 552.
45 Ibid., p. 553.
46 Ibid., p. 561.

47 *CP*, p. 31.
48 Ibid., pp. 79 and 58.
49 Ibid., p. 102.
50 *CL*, p. 567.
51 Ibid., p. 568.
52 *CP*, pp. 80–1.
53 *The Nation & the Athenaeum*, March 1921, pp. 909–10.
54 *CP*, p. 175.
55 D. S. R. Welland, *Wilfred Owen/The Man and his Poetry* (unpublished dissertation in Nottingham University Library), 1951, p. 60.
56 *CL*, p. 571.
57 Ibid., p. 535.

Chapter 10.   France 1918

The principal sources for this chapter are *CL*, pp. 571–91; A. J. P. Taylor, *The First World War*, pp. 232–4; Brigadier-General Sir James E. Edmonds and Lieutenant-Colonel R. Maxwell-Hyslop, *History of the Great War/Military Operations/France and Belgium 1918*, 1947, pp. 463–76; and Sir A. Montgomery, *The Story of the Fourth Army in the Battles of the Hundred Days*, 1926, pp. 170–262.

 1 *CL*, p. 572.
 2 For the account of this meeting I am indebted to a letter from Mr. McClymont.
 3 *CL*, p. 574.
 4 Conal O'Riordan, 'Poets are Cheerful!', *John O'London's Weekly*, 6 June 1941, pp. 225–6.
 5 *CL*, p. 578.
 6 *CP*, pp. 77–8.
 7 Ibid., pp. 61–2.
 8 Ibid., pp. 52–3.
 9 *CL*, p. 579.
10 Findlay Muirhead, ed., *The Blue Guide to Belgium and the Western Front*, London, 1920, pp. 146–7.
11 *CL*, p. 580.
12 *CP*, p. 177.
13 *CL*, p. 581.
14 *CP*, p. 110.
15 *CL*, p. 584.
16 Ibid., p. 588.
17 Ibid., p. 589.
18 Ibid., p. 591.
19 For accounts of the passage of the Sambre Canal, see Brigadier-General Sir James E. Edmonds and Lieutenant-Colonel R. Maxwell-Hyslop, *op. cit.*, pp. 463–76; and Sir A. Montgomery, *op. cit.*, pp. 239–62.
20 *CP*, p. 178.

Afterwords

 1 *JFO*, III, pp. 198–9.

2 This revolver was found, in a cardboard box full of WO's letters, by two boy scouts commissioned to clean out the Owens' potting-shed, some time after Susan Owen's death. It was cocked and loaded.

3 Joseph Cohen's defence of Mrs. Owen's action, 'Wilfred Owen's Tombstone Inscription Reconsidered', pamphlet, 1956[?], is more gallant than convincing.

4 *CP*, p. 89.

APPENDIX A

THE OWEN AND SHAW FAMILIES

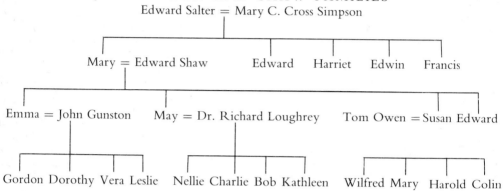

Edward Salter = Mary C. Cross Simpson

Mary = Edward Shaw   Edward   Harriet   Edwin   Francis

Emma = John Gunston   May = Dr. Richard Loughrey   Tom Owen = Susan Edward

Gordon Dorothy Vera Leslie   Nellie Charlie Bob Kathleen   Wilfred Mary Harold Colin

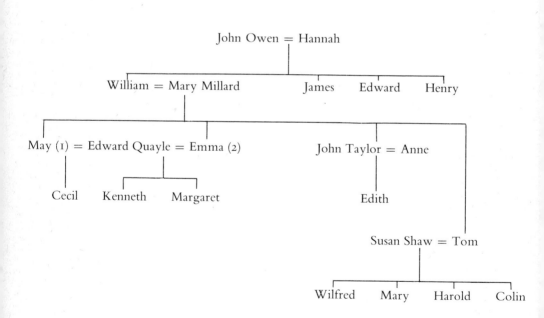

John Owen = Hannah

William = Mary Millard   James   Edward   Henry

May (1) = Edward Quayle = Emma (2)   John Taylor = Anne

Cecil   Kenneth   Margaret   Edith

Susan Shaw = Tom

Wilfred   Mary   Harold   Colin

APPENDIX B
POEMS AND FRAGMENTS NOT IN COLLECTED POEMS

Titles are printed in italic, first lines of untitled poems and fragments in roman type. The location of these mss is shown as follows: BM (British Museum), CL (*Collected Letters*, Library of the University of Texas at Austin), *and* HO (private possession of the Owen Estate).

A Contemplation   BM
A Palinode   HO
A Tear Song   HO
A Vision in Whitechapel   HO
About the winter forest loomed   HO
All Children   HO
At Dawn, I love to stray upon the meeting-line   BM
Ballad of Lady Yolande   BM & HO
Ballad of the Morose Afternoon   HO
Beat on, beat on, beat on, O heart of mine   BM
Before reading a Biography of Keats for the first time   HO
But when, O Friend, thy card this morning   HO
By thy disenchanted eyes   BM
Cortez   HO
Deep under turfy grass and heavy clay   BM & HO
Doth thy spirit, youthful poet, brood   HO
Eve of St. Mark   HO
For there's a Bishop's Teign (pr. Tin)   CL, p. 185
Full springs of Thought around me rise   CL, p. 593
Golden Hair   BM & HO
He meditates in silence all the day   CL, pp. 109–10
Hearts and Tarts   HO
Hide yet my Flower, hide close: the noon   BM
How do the heavens rule my gloomy moods   HO
I am to thee a Sunflower to the Sun   BM
I Began to Run   HO
I know that I have paid for every drop of pleasure   HO
I will adorn my garden with statues   HO
Impressionist   HO
Impromptu   HO
It was a navy boy, so prim, so trim   BM
It was the noiseless hour: [the] tremulous wood   BM
Lines Written on my Nineteenth Birthday   HO
Listen the multitude is wailing for its sins   HO
Little Claus and Big Claus   HO
Mourn for the nights to come   HO

My dearest Colin [*verse letter*]   CL, p. 67
Nights with the Wind. A Rhapsody   BM
Nocturne   BM
Now let me feel the feeling of thy hand   CL, pp. 243–4
O darkness and murmur of deaths   HO
O, Jesus, now thine own self speaking   HO
O piteous mistake: O wrong wrong word   BM
O true to the old equities & sureties   HO
On a Dream   HO
On Seeing a Lock of Keats's Hair   HO
Page Eglantine   BM
Perseus   BM & HO
Perversity   HO
Poring upon the/fairy-strange enchantments   BM
Reunion   BM
Roundel/In Shrewsbury Town e'en Hercules wox tired   CL, pp. 250–1
Science Contradicted   HO
Science has looked, and sees no Life but this   HO
Song/What time I saw her in the budding day   BM
Sonnet/Daily I muse on her; I muse and fret   HO
Sonnet/The city lights along the waterside   HO
Sonnet/When I perceive by watching other men's   HO
Sonnet/When late I viewed the gardens of rich men   BM & CL, p. 193
Sonnet/Whither is passed the softly-vanished day   HO
Sonnet/*Written at Teignmouth, on a Pilgrimage to Keats's House*   HO
Spring not, spring not in my wild eyes, O Tears   BM
Stunned by their life's explosion into love   HO
Sunrise   BM
Supposed Confessions of a Secondrate Sensitive Mind in Dejection   HO
That Heart & Soul and Spirit are only names   HO
The Ballad of Purchase-Money   HO
The Ballad of Many Thorns   HO
The Cultivated Rose/*From the Greek*   BM
The Dread of Falling into Nought   HO
The End [*not the published poem of that title*]   BM
The gay fleet hours now tired & paused and palled   HO
The Little Mermaid   HO
The Peril of Love   HO
The Poet in Pain   HO
The Rime of the Youthful Mariner   BM
The Rivals   HO
The Rumour rose by Syria & the Nile   HO
The sun, far fallen in the afternoon   HO
The Swift/*An Ode*   HO
The time was aeon; and the place all earth   BM
The Two Reflections   HO
The West! I dare not pass into the West   HO
There is a set of men today who deal   HO
They brought suggestions   HO

Thy chilly whiteness like a summer morning mist   BM & HO
Tis but love's shadow that so haunts my thought   HO
To Poesy   HO
Tom Tit   HO
Tonight, unknown maybe to her, fair sufferer   HO
Unto what pinnacles of desperate heights   HO
Uriconium/an Ode   BM
What is a poet but a hateful child   BM & HO
When on the kindling wood the coals are piled   BM
Who is the god of Canongate   BM
Why should the anguish of leaving those we love   HO
With those that are become   BM
Written in a Wood, September 1910   HO
Written On a June Night (1911)   BM

APPENDIX C

WILFRED OWEN'S LIBRARY
(now housed in the English Faculty Library at Oxford)

This, thanks to Susan Owen's belief in her son, was preserved intact at his death, and subsequently carefully kept by Harold Owen. Since it was in every sense a working library and much can be learnt from WO's annotation, dating, marginal lines, and underlining, it seems appropriate to offer an annotated checklist.

[Edmond François Valentin About], *L'Homme à l'Oreille cassée*, London, n.d.

———. *Word- and Phrasebook for L'Homme à l'Oreille cassée*, the General Editors of the [Siepmann's Elementary French] Series, London, 1911.

Bernard Adams, *Nothing of Importance*, London, 1917. Inscribed on the front end-paper 'To Wilfred Owen:/from/Siegfried Sassoon/Oct. 31. 1917.' The fly-leaf recto carries a key, in Sassoon's hand, to the characters mentioned in the book: 'Scott=Sassoon' etc. The fly-leaf verso carries a list of names of officers in the 1st RWF killed or wounded. This and the annotations throughout the book are also in Sassoon's hand. See above, p. 233.

Marion Adams, *Contes Fabuleux de la Grèce Antique*, adaptation française par Mlle Latappy, Paris, n.d. Underlining.

[Joseph Addison], *Coverley Papers from The Spectator*, with an Introduction and Notes by K. Deighton, London, 1907. Underlining.

Hans Andersen, *Little Klaus and Big Klaus*, London and Glasgow, 1906. See *CL*, p. 74.

Anthologie des Écrivains français morts pour la Patrie, par Carlos Larrarde, Préface par Maurice Barrès, vols I–IV, Paris, n.d. Vol. I is inscribed on the fly-leaf 'A W.E.S. Owen/en/témoignage de notre constante communion d'idées/et de notre/fraternelle amitié/V. P. berthaud/21.12.17.' See *CL*, p. 240 n.

Anthologie des Poètes lyriques français, Introduction par Charles Sarolea, Paris . . . New York, n.d.

An Anthology of English Verse, edited by A. J. Wyatt and S. E. Goggin, London, 1908. Marginal lines.

Antología de los mejores Poetas Castellanos, Introducción y Comentarios de Rafael Mesa y Lopéz, London and Paris, n.d.

The Apocryphal New Testament, London, n.d.

Matthew Arnold: His Poetry and Message, The Penny Poets, XXVI, London, n.d.

Jane Austen, *Pride and Prejudice*, London and New York, 1906.

Alfred Austin, *Songs of England*, London, 1898. Inscribed on the fly-leaf 'WEO/Guildford/August/1916'. Marginal lines. See above, p. 248.

W. E. Aytoun, *Edinburgh after Flodden*, London, Glasgow and Dublin, 1903.

Honoré de Balzac, *Contes Philosophiques*, Introduction par Paul Bourget, London and Paris, n.d. Some pages uncut.

———, *La Vendetta*, London, 1911.

Henri Barbusse, *Le Feu*, Paris, 1916. Inscribed on the front cover 'WEO'. See *CL*, p. 520 n.

Sir Edmund Beckett, *On the Origin of the Laws of Nature*, London and New York, 1879. Underlining on p. 83.

H. Belloc, *Esto Perpetua/Algerian Studies and Impressions*, London, 1911. Inscribed on the fly-leaf 'W. E. S. OWEN./Scarborough/Decem. 1917.'

———, *Gems from*, London, n.d. Lacking cover and title-page, some marginal markings.

F. N. Bennett, *Problems of Village Life*, London and New York, n.d. Inscribed on the fly-leaf 'W. E. S. OWEN –/EDINBVRGH./IVLY./1917.'

Arthur Christopher Benson, *Tennyson*, London, 1912. Inscribed on the fly-leaf 'W. E. S. OWEN/Edinburgh/August: 1917.' Correction made on p. 56. See *CL*, p. 532.

———, *Where No Fear Was*, London, 1914. See *CL*, p. 551.

J. D. Beresford, *H. G. Wells*, London, 1915.

T. H. Bertenshaw, *Longman's Illustrated First Conversational French Reader*, London, New York and Bombay, 1904. Certain illustrations have been coloured with crayons.

Blackie's Elementary English Grammar based on the Analysis of Sentences, London, Glasgow and Dublin, n.d. Inscribed on the fly-leaf 'Wilfred Owen. Form I/51 Milton Road/Birkenhead'. Beneath this is rubber-stamped 'WILFRED OWEN/51 MILTON RO O'. Underlining and many lesson numbers ringed in pencil.

R. D. Blackman, editor, *Composition and Style*, thirteenth edition, Edinburgh, 1908.

R. D. Blackmore, *Gems from Lorna Doone*, London, n.d.

Henry Bordeaux, *Les Roquevillard*, Paris . . . New York, n.d. Annotation and underlining.

George Borrow, *Wild Wales*, London, n.d.

Brachet & Dussouchet, *Grammaire Française Abrégée*, Paris, 1913. Inscribed on the front cover 'WEO'.

Victor Branford, *St Columba*, Edinburgh and London, 1913.

Charlotte Brontë, *Shirley*, London, 1903. Marginal markings. See above, p. 27.

Rupert Brooke, *1914 & Other Poems*, thirteenth impression, London, 1916. Inserted is a newspaper photograph of Brooke's grave. See above, p. 140.

Stopford A. Brooke, *English Literature from A.D. 670 to A.D. 1832*, London and New York, 1905. Inscribed on the fly-leaf 'W. E. Owen/Mar. 1912.' Annotation, marginal lines, and underlining.

———, *Studies in Poetry*, London, 1910. See *CL*, p. 520 n.

Elizabeth Barrett Browning, *The Complete Poems of*, vol. 2, London and New York, n.d. Inscribed on the fly-leaf 'WEO/Bouchoir/Somme/March: 1917.' Marginal lines. See *CL*, pp. 445, 479; and above, pp. 173–4.

———, *Gems from*, London and Glasgow, n.d. Inscribed on the fly-leaf 'To: Mrs Owen/From: Doris Wharmby/With love, wishing her/a very Merry Christmas /and a Happy New Year./Xmas 1911'. See *CL*, p. 263.

———, *Sonnets from the Portuguese*, illustrated by Herbert Cole, London and New York, n.d. Two title numbers circled.

Robert Browning, *Men and Women*, London, n.d.

———, *The Poems and Plays of Robert Browning, 1844–1864*, London and New York, 1908.

———. *Poems by*, The Penny Poets, LII, London, n.d.

L. M. Bull, *Easy Free Composition in French*, London, 1909.

[Robert] Burns, *The Poems of, A Selection*, with an Introduction by Neil Munro, London . . . Melbourne, 1904.

John Bunyan, *The Pilgrim's Progress from this World to that which is to come*, London, 1890. Inscribed 'Sue./With love and best wishes from/Tom/17.3.04'. See p. 30 above.

Lord Byron, *Childe Harold's Pilgrimage*, Part II, The Penny Poets, XII, n.d.

René Canat, *La Littérature Française par les Textes*, Paris, n.d. Inscribed on the fly-leaf and half-title 'R Lem'. See *CL*, p. 614.

Thomas Carlyle, *The French Revolution*, New York, 1881. Inscribed on the fly-leaf 'M Lodter[?]/Concord/Mass/U.S.A./1881'.

H. F. Cary, trans., *The Vision or Hell, Purgatory, and Paradise of Dante Alighieri*, London and New York, n.d. Marginal markings.

Les Cent Meilleurs Poèmes (Lyriques) de la Langue Française, choisis par Auguste Dorchain, Paris . . . London and Glasgow, 1913. Annotation, marginal lines, and underlining.

Chamber's Etymological Dictionary of the English Language, edited by Andrew Findlater, London and Edinburgh, 1907.

Chamber's Twentieth Century Dictionary of the English Language, edited by Thomas Davidson, London and Edinburgh, 1910. Inscribed on the title-page 'WEO'. Marginal markings.

Geoffrey Chaucer, *The Complete Works of*, edited by Walter W. Skeat, Oxford, 1906. Pages uncut.

———, *Stories from, Being the Canterbury Tales in Simple Language for Children*, Books for the Bairns, No. 83, London, n.d. Annotation and underlining.

Mary G. Cherry, *Hill and Heather, or England's Heart*, London, 1915. Front cover inscribed 'WEO'.

G. K. Chesterton, *Wine, Water and Song*, London, 1915.

Samuel Taylor Coleridge, *Biographia Literaria*, London and New York, n.d.

———, *Christabel*, London, n.d. Inscribed on the fly-leaf 'Wilfred/with best/ wishes from Leslie [Gunston]/Dec. 14. 1916.'

————, *The Golden Book of*, London and New York, 1909. Inscribed on the fly-leaf 'Christabel Rose Coleridge/Aug 10. 1910/Ernest Hartley Coleridge/Aug. 10: 1910'. See *CL*, pp. 61–2; and above, p. 52.

Charles Cowden Clarke, *Tales from Chaucer*, London and New York, 1911. See *CL*, p. 88.

W. G. Collingwood, *The Life of John Ruskin*, sixth edition, London, 1905. See *CL*, pp. 149–50, 304, 309–10.

Sidney Colvin, *Keats*, London, 1909. Inscribed on fly-leaf 'Wilfred E. S. Owen./ Torquay./Spring, 1911.' Annotation, marginal lines, and underlining. See *CL*, pp. 69, 160, 506; and above, pp. 56–7.

Albert S. Cork, *A First Book in Old English*, Grammar, Reader, Notes, and Vocabulary, Third Edition, London, 1903.

John W. Cousin, *A Short Biographical Dictionary of English Literature*, London and New York, 1910.

William Cowper, *The Poetical Works of*, Complete Edition with Memoir, Explanatory Notes, &c., London and New York, n.d. See *CL*, p. 133.

Sidney Dark, *William Makepeace Thackeray*, London . . . Melbourne, 1912.

F. J. Harvey Darton, *Arnold Bennett*, London, n.d.

Charles Darwin, *On The Origin of Species*, London . . . Melbourne, 1909.

Alphonse Daudet, *Lettres de Mon Moulin*, London, 1909. Underlining.

————, *Tartarin sur les Alpes*, adapted and edited by George Petilleau, London, 1910.

Walter de la Mare, *Motley and Other Poems*, London, 1918. Inscribed on the dust-jacket 'W E S Owen/Mahim/Monkmoor/Shrewsbury'.

————, *Poems*, London, 1906.

Xavier de Maistre, *Voyage Autour de ma Chambre*, London, 1911.

Thomas de Quincey, *The Confessions of an English Opium-Eater*, London and New York, 1910. One pencilled correction on p. 203.

Marceline Desbordes-Valmore, *Les Chefs-D'Oeuvres Lyriques de*, choix et notice de Auguste Dorchain, Paris . . . London and Glasgow, 1913. Inserted in this copy a list, in Owen's hand, of the Latin and English names of 7 plants.

Charles Dickens, *Barnaby Rudge*, London and New York, 1906. Inscribed on the fly-leaf 'Owen/Mahim/Monkmoor/Shrewsbury'.

————, *A Christmas Carol*, London, Glasgow and Dublin, n.d. Underlining. See *CL*, p. 131.

————, *A Christmas Carol*, London and Glasgow, n.d. See *CL*, p. 131.

————, *David Copperfield*, with an Introduction by G. K. Chesterton, London, and New York, n.d. Pencilled sum on back fly-leaf. See *CL*, p. 229.

Notes on Dickens' David Copperfield, by N. Stockwell, eighth edition, London, n.d.

————, *Dealings with the Firm of DOMBEY & Son Wholesale, Retail & for Exportation*, London and New York, 1910. Marginal lines. See *CL*, p. 72.

————, *Little Dorrit*, London and New York, n.d. Marginal lines and under-lining. See *CL*, p. 116.

————, *The Old Curiosity Shop*, London, n.d. One sheet containing a List of Characters inserted.

————, *Oliver Twist*, London, n.d.

————, *La Maison Hantée*, Paris, n.d.

————, *The Posthumous Papers of the Pickwick Club*, 2 vols, London, 1847.

Notes on Dickens' Tale of Two Cities by Geo[rge] M. Handley, fourth edition, London, n.d. On a home-made dust-jacket WO has written the title and below it rubber-stamped 'W. E. OWEN'. On the title-page verso and two succeeding pages he has copied out, under the heading 'Influence morale de Charles Dickens', 250 words by Ferdinand Brunetière. Annotation, marginal lines, and underlining.

A Dictionary of the English Language . . . abridged from Webster's International Dictionary, London, 1895. Inscribed on the fly-leaf 'Mary Owen,/with best love from her brother/Wilfred./Christmas, 1912.'

[Denis] Diderot, *Le Neveu de Rameau*, Les Meilleurs Livres, Paris, n.d.

Edward Dowden, *Shakespere*, London, 1907. Inscribed on the front end-paper 'W. E. Owen/June/1913'. Annotation, marginal lines, and underlining.

John Drinkwater, *Tides*, London, 1917.

[Maria] Edgeworth, *Popular Tales by*, third edition, vols II and III, London, 1807.

William Edwards, *Notes on British History*, Part II, London, 1909. Annotation, marginal lines, and underlining.

George Eliot, *Romola*, London, n.d. Rubber-stamped on the fly-leaf 'W. E. OWEN'. Underlining. See *CL*, p. 254.

————, *Silas Marner*, Edinburgh and London, n.d. Inscribed on title-page 'J G Dale'.

The English Review, vol XVIII, no. 1, edited by Austin Harrison, London, August 1914.

F. E. Feller, *A New English and French Pocket Dictionary*, vol. 1, English–French, Paris, n.d.

————, *Nouveau Dictionnaire de Poche Français et Anglais*, vol. 11, Français-Anglais, Paris, n.d. Signed on title-page 'R Lem'. See *CL*, p. 614. Some marginal drawings.

Gustave Flaubert, *La Tentation de Saint-Antoine*, Introduction par Émile Faguet, Paris and London, n.d. Inscribed on the half-title 'Wilfred Oven/le 5 septembre 1914./*Bagnères-de-Bigorre*/en souvenir de/*Laurent Tailhade*/La Gailleste. 7 sept 1914.' Tailhade also emended the title-page to read: 'le stupide ÉMILE FAGUET/*de l'Académie Française*/qui déshonore ce chef/d'œuvre'. Annotation and underlining.

The Floral Birthday Book: Flowers and their Emblems. With Appropriate Selections from the Poets, London and New York, n.d. Inscribed on the fly-leaf 'To Susy/ [Owen]/with love/17th March 1882./M.S.' M[aria] S[alkeld] was E. G. Shaw's Godmother. Many names have been entered on the blank pages facing the text.

George E. Fox, *A Guide to the Roman City of Uriconium, at Wroxeter, Shropshire,* Shrewsbury, 1911. Inscribed on the front cover 'W.O.' See *CL*, pp. 54–5, 77, 112, 153, 191, 193; and above, p. 88.

———, *Reading Public Museum and Art Gallery. Short Guide to the Silchester Collection,* third edition, Reading, 1908. See *CL*, p. 57.

C. A. Fyffe, *History of Greece,* second edition, London, 1876.

John Galt, *The Life of Lord Byron,* London, n.d.

Wilfrid Wilson Gibson, *Battle,* London, 1916. Inscribed on the fly-leaf 'W.E.S. OWEN/London: Nov: 1917'. See *CL*, p. 520 n.

Golden Sayings from F. B. Meyer, London, n.d.

Oliver Goldsmith, *Selections from,* London, n.d. There are two copies of this Arnold Prose Book.

———, *She Stoops to Conquer and the Good-Natured Man,* London . . . Melbourne, n.d.

———, *The Vicar of Wakefield,* with an Introduction by Henry Irving, London . . . Melbourne, 1906.

———, *The Vicar of Wakefield,* London, n.d.

Paul Goodman, *A History of the Jews,* London, n.d.

Eva Gore-Booth, *The Perilous Light,* London, 1915. Marginal lines.

Robert Graves, *Fairies and Fusiliers,* London, 1917.

[Thomas] Gray and [William] Collins, *The Poetical Works of,* edited by Austin Lane Poole, London . . . Bombay, 1917. Underlining.

[Thomas] Gray, [Oliver] Goldsmith, and [William] Collins, *Selected Poems of,* The Penny Poets, XL, London, n.d. Annotation, marginal lines and underlining.

The Greenwood Tree/A Book of Nature Myths and Verses, London, n.d. Annotation and marginal markings.

E. Leslie Gunston, *The Nymph and Other Poems,* London, 1917. Inscribed on the fly-leaf 'Wilfred/with best wishes/from Leslie/Nov. 1917.' See *CL*, pp. 486, 508–12, 520, 526, 588; also above, pp. 239–40.

Thomas Hardy, *Under the Greenwood Tree,* London, 1907. Annotation on p. 157. See *CL*, pp. 547–8.

William Hazlitt, *Lectures on the English Poets,* London and New York, n.d. Inscribed on the fly-leaf 'W. E. S. OWEN/Scarborough: Dec: 1917'. Underlining. See *CL*, p. 527.

Felicia Hemans, *The Poetical Works of,* London, 1886.

The Holy Bible, containing the Old and New Testaments, Oxford, n.d. Annotation, marginal lines, and underlining, all by Susan Owen.

A. E. Housman, *A Shropshire Lad,* London, 1915. Inscribed on the fly-leaf 'WEO/Witley: August 1916:'. Markings on the Contents List. Marginal lines and underlining elsewhere.

Victor Hugo, *Les Misérables,* London and New York, 1912.

————, *Notre-Dame*, London, n.d.

The Hundred Best Blank Verse Passages in the English Language, selected by Adam L. Gowans, London and Glasgow, 1905.

Leigh Hunt, *Essays and Sketches*, London, New York and Toronto, n.d.

Richard H. Hutton, *Sir Walter Scott*, London, 1909. Marginal lines and underlining.

The Hydra/Journal of the Craiglockhart War Hospital [edited by Wilfred Owen and others], nos 1 (2 copies), 2, 3, 4, 5, 6 (2 copies), 7 (2 copies), 8 (2 copies), 9 (2 copies), 10 (2 copies), 11 (2 copies), 12 (2 copies), New Series nos 1, 2 (2 copies), 3, 7, 8, and 9. Many issues of the first series 1–12 are inscribed on the front cover 'WEO', 'With the Editor's compliments', etc., and a few have annotations in the text. See above, Chapter 8.

Thomas Ingoldsby [Richard Harris Barham], *The Ingoldsby Legends or Mirth and Marvels*, First Series, London, 1889. Many pages uncut.

Washington Irving, *Life of Goldsmith*, London, 1907. Underlining. See *CL*, p. 78.

O. A. Joergens, *The Woman and the Sage and other Poems*, London, 1916. Inscribed on the half-title 'Olwen A. Joergens'. See *CL*, pp. 250, 434, 494.

H. H. Johnson, *A Short Introduction to the Study of French Literature*, London, 1910. Inscribed on the fly-leaf 'WEO'.

R. Brimley Johnson, *Leigh Hunt*, London, 1896.

Samuel Johnson, *Selections from*, London, n.d. Inscribed on the front cover 'W. Owen'. Marginal lines and underlining.

John Keats, *The Complete Works of*, Glasgow, 5 vols, 1 December 1900 – 1 April 1901. Underlining and marginal lines in vols 1, 2, and 4.

————, *Isabella or the Pot of Basil*, London, n.d. Marginal lines.

————, *Poems of*, edited by G. Thorn Drury, with an Introduction by Robert Bridges, 2 vols, London and New York, 1896. Some pages uncut.

————, *Sonnets*, London, n.d.

————, *Sonnets from*, London, n.d.

Frederick Keeble, *Practical Plant Physiology*, London, 1911. See *CL*, p. 456 n.

Janet Harvey Kelman, *Flowers Shown to the Children*, described by C. E. Smith, London and Edinburgh, n.d. Inscribed on the front end-paper 'Mary Owen/ with loving wishes/from/Mother/Christmas 1909'.

Charles Kingsley, *The Heroes*, London and New York, n.d. Some of the black and white plates have been coloured in crayon.

————, *Westward Ho!*, London and New York, 1907.

R. Kron, *Le Petit Parisien*, Freiburg (Baden), 1913. Annotation and underlining.

Charles Lamb, *Essays of Elia*, edited with Introduction and Notes by N. L. Hallward and S. C. Hill, London, 1906.

———— and Mary Lamb, *Tales from Shakespeare*, London and New York, 1907. Some line-drawings have been coloured in crayon. Inserted, a sheet of paper headed 'Two Gent: of Verona' and listing some of the characters of that play.

————, *Some Tales from Shakespeare*, second edition, The Penny Poets, LXIII,

London, n.d. Inscribed on the front cover 'Owen'.

Carlos Larronde, *Le Livre d'Heures,* Paris, 1913. Inscribed on the fly-leaf 'A M.

Wilfred Owen/avec ma cordiale sympathie/et l'espoir que ces vers/lui en feront aimer d'autres/ – plus beaux – /des Poètes que j'aime/Carlos Larronde/ Bordeaux 24 Sept. 1914'. Titles marked on the Contents list. Annotation and underlining.

G. H. Lewes, *The Life and Works of Goethe with Sketches of his Age and Contemporaries,* London and New York, n.d.

Henry Wordsworth Longfellow, *Evangeline, and Other Poems,* The Penny Poets, VII, London, n.d.

———, *The Song of Hiawatha,* London, n.d. Inscribed on the fly-leaf 'In memory of the/reading of Hiawatha/Autumn 1917. Edinburgh./M. K. Fullerton/ Alnwick/Autumn 1918.' Inscribed on the half-title 'Harold./Christmas 1923.' See *CL,* p. 496 n.

———, *Moments with,* London, n.d. Inscribed on the fly-leaf 'To Mrs Owen./ With love and best/wishes from/Doris Wharmby./Xmas 1912.' See *CL,* p. 263.

Lyric Masterpieces by Living Authors (1908), selected by Adam L. Gowans, London and Glasgow, 1914.

Bulwer [Lytton], Sir E. L., *The Last Days of Pompeii,* 2 vols, London, Edinburgh and Dublin, 1840. See above, p. 89.

Lord Macaulay, *The History of England/From the Accession of James the Second,* vols IV, V, and VI, London, 1874. Underlining in vol. IV. See *CL,* p. 62.

William Macgillivray, *A Systematic Arrangement of British Plants by W. Withering, M.D.,* fifth edition, London, 1841. Inscribed on the front end-paper 'Mary Salter/Aug 28/51.' Annotation and underlining by WO.

Laurie Magnus, *Introduction to Poetry,* London, 1902. Annotation, marginal lines, and underlining.

G. H. Mair, *English Literature: Modern,* London, n.d.

Albert Mallet, *L'Antiquité/Orient-Grèce-Rome,* 1re partie/Orient, Paris, 1902.

Christopher Marlowe, *Edward the Second,* edited with a Preface, Notes and Glossary by A. W. Verity, London, 1908. Underlining.

———, *The Tragical History of Doctor Faustus,* with Introduction and Notes by William Modlen, London, 1912. Marginal lines and underlining.

John Masefield, *The Daffodil Fields,* London, 1913. Inscribed on the dust-jacket 'WEO./First Edition!' and on the fly-leaf 'W:E:S:OWEN:/Scarborough: Dec:1917.' See *CL,* p. 494 n.

———, *Lollingdon Downs and Other Poems, with Sonnets,* London, 1917. Inscribed on the fly-leaf 'W:E:S: OWEN./Scarborough/Dec. 1917'. See *CL,* p. 520.

Flora Masson, *The Brontës,* London, Edinburgh and New York, n.d. Underlining.

Samuel Maunder, *The Scientific and Literary Treasury,* New Edition, London, 1876.

George Meredith, *One of our Conquerors,* London, 1904. Annotation, marginal lines, and underlining. Notes on front end-paper.

———, *Poems,* London, 1910. Inscribed on the half-title 'WEO/LONDON:

AUGUST: 1916). See *CL*, p. 136, but, from the dating, this would appear to be a different copy.

John Milton, *The Poetical Works of*, with Introduction, Memoir, Notes, Bibliography, etc., London and New York, n.d. Inscribed on the half-title 'W. E. Owen.' Annotation, marginal lines, and underlining.

Mary Russell Mitford, *Our Village*, London . . . Melbourne, 1909.

The Modern French Reader/Prose/Junior Course, edited by Ch. Cassal and Théodore Karcher, London, 1906. Annotation and underlining.

Molière, *L'Avare*, edited by O. H. Fynes-Clinton, London, 1908. Inscribed 'W.E. Owen'. Annotation and underlining.

Harold Monro, *Before Dawn*, London, 1911. Inscribed on the fly-leaf 'W.E. Owen'. Title-page stamped 'PRESENTATION COPY'.

———, *Children of Love*, London, 1914. Front cover inscribed 'WEO'.

F. Frankfort Moore, *The Jessamy Bride*, London, n.d.

More Songs by the Fighting Men, edited by Galloway Kyle, London, 1917. Inscribed on the fly-leaf:
    'A little book and a little song.
    The first all right and the last all wrong:
    Which is but meet, let it be known,
    Since mine the song and the book's for Owen!
    Murray McClymont – 2 Lieut/7 : 9 : 18./Base./B.E.F.'
Underlining. See *CL*, p. 573, and p. 270 above.

W. H. Morris, *Elementa Latina or Latin Lessons for Beginners*, London . . . Calcutta, 1909. Inscribed on the fly-leaf 'Mary & Colin Owen/Feb. 7th 1912.' Marginal ticks and crosses throughout.

Vincent T. Murche, *Elementary Botany for Beginners*, London, n.d.

F. W. H. Myers, *Wordsworth*, London, 1909.

Mythologie Gréco-Latine, 2 vols, Les Meilleurs Livres, Paris, n.d.

Robert Nichols *Ardours and Endurances*, London, 1917. Inscribed on the front end-paper 'WEO'. See *CL*, pp. 511, 517–8, 520.

Novum Testamentum, ex Interpretatione Theodori Bezæ, Berolini, 1909. See *CL*, p. 94 n.

Palgrave's Golden Treasury/Poetry and the Drama, with an Introduction by Edward Hutton, London, 1906. Some poem titles underlined in the list of Contents.

Notes on Palgrave's Golden Treasury of Songs and Lyrics, by J. H. Boardman, seventh edition, London, n.d. Annotation and underlining.

Notes to Palgrave's Golden Treasury of Songs and Lyrics, Books I–IV, London, 1904.

De V. Payen-Payne, *French Idioms and Proverbs*, third edition, greatly enlarged, London, 1900. Rubber-stamped on the half-title 'W.E. OWEN'. Annotation and marginal markings.

Percy's Reliques of Ancient English Poetry, 2 vols, London and New York, n.d. Each volume inscribed on the front end-paper 'WEO/EDINBURGH. IVNE. 1917'. See *CL*, p. 476.

Charles Perrault, *Contes de ma Mère L'Oie*, Les Meilleurs Livres, Paris, n.d.

Plutarch's Life of Julius Caesar, edited for schools by H. W. M. Parr, London, 1910.

Poems of Today: an Anthology, London, 1916. Inscribed on the fly-leaf 'M. Milton/Bedford Regt.' See above, p. 216.

The Poetry Review, vol. II, no. 1, edited by Stephen Phillips, London, January 1913.

Alexander Pope, *Essay on Man and Other Poems*, The Penny Poets, XXIII, London, n.d.

The Popular Guide through Shrewsbury, Shrewsbury, 1906.

Ernest Renan, *Souvenirs d'Enfance et de Jeunesse*, Paris, n.d. Inscribed on the title-page 'à Wilfred Owen/Bagnères-de-Bigorre/le 7 Septembre 14./amical souvenir des beaux après-midis de La Gailleste –/son vieil ami/Laurent Tailhade'.

Jean Richepin, *La Mer*, nouvelle édition, Paris, 1912. WO has written a French poem of 6 stanzas on the back fly-leaf.

Forster Robson, *British Trees, and How to Name Them at a Glance, Without Botany*, sixth edition, London, n.d.

William Michael Rossetti, *Life and Writings of John Keats*, London and Felling-on-Tyne, n.d. Annotation, marginal lines, and underlining. See *CL*, pp. 160–1.

——, *Life of John Keats*, London, 1887. This earlier edition of the above is inscribed on the fly-leaf 'W. E. Owen'. See *CL*, pp. 160–1.

William Rossiter, *A First Book of Botany*, fourth edition, revised and corrected, London, 1874.

The Royal Scottish Museum, Edinburgh. Guide to the Collection of Egyptian Antiquities, Edinburgh, 1913. Inscribed on the front cover 'WEO/Aug. 1. 1917'.

Kathleen E. Royds, *Elizabeth Barrett Browning & Her Poetry*, London, 1912. Inscribed on front end-paper 'Wilfred Owen with affectionate Christmas wishes from his friend Clyde Black/Xmas 1912'. See *CL*, p. 166.

John Ruskin, *Sesame and Lilies*, edited by Albert E. Roberts, London, 1910. Underlining. See *CL*, pp. 556 and 563.

——, *Sesame & Lilies/The Two Paths/& The King of the Golden River*, London and New York, 1909. Annotation.

Lady Margaret Sackville, *The Pageant of War*, London, n.d. Inscribed on the front cover 'WEO', and on the half-title 'From Margaret Sackville/1914'. Titles marked on the list of Contents.

La Sainte Bible, Version D'Ostervald, Paris, 1903. Inscribed 'Wilfred Owen/from/ Mother/Christmas 1906/I Thess 5–16–17–18'.

Egbert T. Sandford, *Brookdown and other Poems*, London, 1915. Inscribed on the front cover 'WEO'. Some pages uncut. Annotation and underlining.

Siegfried Sassoon, *Counter Attack and Other Poems*, London, 1918.

[——], Saul Kain, *The Daffodil Murderer*, London, 1913. Inscribed on the fly-leaf 'To Wilfred Owen./from Siegfried Sassoon.' See *CL*, pp. 494, 525, and above, p. 213. Marginal lines and underlining.

————, *The Old Huntsman and other Poems*, London, 1917. Inscribed on the dust-jacket 'WEO' and on the fly-leaf 'To W.E.S. Owen./from Siegfried Sassoon./Craiglockhart. August. 1917.' See above, pp. 208–9.

[Arthur] Schopenhauer, *Essays of*, with an Introduction [by R.D.], London . . . Melbourne, n.d.

D. H. Scott, *An Introduction to Structural Botany*, parts I and II, London, 1909 and 1912. Part I inscribed on the half-title 'W.E. Owen'. Underlining. Three 'Difficulty Papers' dated September 1911 tucked into Part II.

————, *The Evolution of Plants*, London, n.d. Marginal lines and underlining.

Sir Walter Scott, *The Antiquary*, London and New York, n.d.

————, *The Bride of Lammermoor*, London, n.d. Underlining on p. 209.

————, *The Fortunes of Nigel*, London, Paris and Melbourne, n.d. Stamped on the fly-leaf 'W.H. Smith & Son. 186. Strand/Library'. On the half-title recto and verso WO has written out a 'List of Characters'. Inserted, a sheet of paper bearing the words 'The eye of the Wift. Temple Thurston/The Isles of Illusion.'

————, *The Heart of Midlothian*, London . . . Melbourne, 1909.

————, *The Lady of the Lake*, London, New York and Bombay, 1905. Marginal marks in the Introduction. See *CL*, p. 100.

————, *The Lady of the Lake*, London, n.d. Inscribed on the fly-leaf 'Mary Owen,/with affectionate wishes/from Wilfred/May 30. 1913'. Underlining.

————, *The Lady of the Lake*, The Penny Poets, XX, London, n.d. There are three copies of this book. Annotation, marginal lines, and underlining in two of them.

————, *The Lay of the Last Minstrel*, London, 1806.

————, *The Lay of the Last Minstrel and Other Poems*, The Penny Poets, XXXI, London, n.d. Marginal lines and underlining.

————, *The Lay of the Last Minstrel*, with a short Biography by Andrew Lang and Introduction and Notes by Fred. W. Tickner, London, New York and Bombay, 1905.

————, *Marmion*, London and Edinburgh, 1903. The fly-leaf bears a pencil sketch of a landscape entitled 'Among the Cheviots/July 1912.' See *CL*, p. 150, and pp. 76, 138, and 191 above.

————, *The Talisman*, with Introduction and Notes, London, 1906.

William Shakespeare, *As You Like It*, with Notes etc. by W. Dycke, London . . . Calcutta, 1907. Annotation, marginal lines, and underlining.

————'s *As You Like It. A Complete Paraphrase* by Isobel Young, London, n.d.

————, *Hamlet*, edited with Notes by Henry N. Hudson, London, n.d. Underlining.

————, *Index* to The Era Shakespeare [series], edited with Notes by Henry N. Hudson, London, n.d.

————, *Jules César*, Les Meilleurs Livres, Paris, n.d.

————, *Julius Caesar*, with an Introduction and Notes by K. Deighton, London, 1904. Stamped 'BOROUGH OF SHREWSBURY HIGHER EDUCATION. PUPIL TEACHERS' CENTRE.' Annotation, marginal lines, underlining, one sheet of pencilled notes on the characters of Cassius and Mark Antony inserted.

————, *Julius Caesar*, London, n.d. Annotation, marginal lines, and underlining.

————, *King Henry IV*, Part I, with Introduction and Notes by J. V. Saunders, London, Glasgow and Bombay, n.d.

————, *King Henry the Fifth*, edited with Introductions and Notes by C. H. Herford, London and New York, 1906. Annotation, marginal lines, and underlining. See *CL*, pp. 73, 82–3, 193.

————, *King Henry V*, London, Glasgow and Bombay, n.d. Two crosses on p. 1 against the line 'That did affright the air at Agincourt?' See *CL*, pp. 73, 82–3, 193.

————, *King Lear*, edited with Notes by Henry N. Hudson, London, n.d. Dustjacket inscribed 'W.E.O.' Underlining.

————, *King Richard II*, Act III, Scene 2, Green's Scholastic Series of Poetry, No. 54, Manchester, n.d.

————, *King Richard III*, edited with Notes by Henry N. Hudson, London, n.d. Marginal lines and underlining. Inserted, a printed 'Warning to Correspondent Students' on the verso of which WO has drawn a family tree of the House of York.

————, *Le Roi Lear*, traduction de Benjamin Delaroche, Paris, n.d.

————, *The Life and Death of King John*, edited by C. W. Crook, London, n.d.

————, *Love's Labour's Lost*, edited with Notes by Henry N. Hudson, London, n.d. Marginal lines and underlining.

————, *Macbeth*, London, 1904.

————, *Le Marchand de Venise*, Paris, n.d.

————, *Measure for Measure*, edited with Notes by Henry N. Hudson, London, n.d. Inscribed on the title-page 'W.E.S. OWEN. Edinburgh: Aug: 1917.'

————, *The Merry Wives of Windsor*, edited with Notes by Henry N. Hudson, London, n.d.

————, *A Midsummer-Night's Dream/with Nymphidia or, The Court of Fairy, &c*, with an Introduction by Henry Morley, London, 1907. Draft of blank-verse poem quoted on pp. 40–1 written on the front end-paper. Annotation, marginal lines, and underlining.

————, *Much Ado about Nothing*, London . . . Melbourne, 1908. Marginal lines and underlining.

————, *Pericles*, edited with Notes by Henry N. Hudson, London, n.d.

————, *Romeo and Juliet*, edited with Notes by Henry N. Hudson, London, n.d. Annotation, marginal lines, and underlining.

————, *Select Scenes and Passages from the English Historical Plays*, edited by C. H. Spence, London, 1906. Annotation and underlining.

————, *Sonnets and Poems*, with Notes by Henry N. Hudson, London, n.d.

Inscribed 'WEO/EDINBVRGH/IVLY/1917'.

———, *The Taming of the Shrew*, Introduction by Henry Morley, London . . . Melbourne, 1909.

———, *The Taming of the Shrew*, edited with Notes by Henry N. Hudson, London, n.d. Inscribed on the fly-leaf 'W.E.S. Owen: Edinburgh: 1917.'

———, *The Tempest*, with an Introduction by Charles and Mary Lamb, The Penny Poets, LXVII, London, n.d. The title-page verso, listing the 'Persons Represented', is headed by the date 'Oct. 11. 1912.' and bear the signatures of the following: Wilfred. E. S. Owen/Flora Poole/ Emma Gunston/Herbert S Belling/E. Leslie Gunston/John Gunston/Vera Gunston. Their respective initials are set against each of the 'Persons Represented'. Marginal markings against speeches by Sebastian, Francisco, Stephano, and Iris.

———, *The Tempest*, edited by A. R. Weekes, London, n.d. Underlining.

———, *Timon of Athens*, edited with Notes by Henry N. Hudson, London, n.d.

———, *Titus Andronicus*, edited with Notes by Henry N. Hudson, London, n.d. Inscribed on the title-page 'W.E.S. OWEN/Edinburgh: Aug: 1917.'

———, *Troilus and Cressida*, edited with Notes by Henry N. Hudson, London, n.d. Inserted into this book is *The Cathedrals of Old England/Winchester* (Burrow's Cathedral Guides, no. 3, price one penny).

———, *Twelfth Night*, with an Introduction by George Brandes, London, 1904. Fabian's speeches marked throughout.

———, *Venus & Adonis and Lucrece*, edited with Notes by Henry N. Hudson, London, n.d.

———, *The Winter's Tale*, edited by J. H. Lobban, Cambridge, 1910. Dated on front end-paper 11.11.10.

[Percy Bysshe] Shelley, *Adonais*, edited by A. R. Weekes, London, n.d. Marginal lines and underlining.

———, *The Complete Poetical Works of*, edited by Thomas Hutchinson, London . . . Melbourne, 1912. Label attached to the fly-leaf inscribed 'With Best Love and wishes/for a very happy/Birthday from, Mary./Harold and Colin./March. 18th. 1914.' See *CL*, p. 237.

———, *Selections from Shelley*, chosen by William Landells, London, n.d.

Robert H. Sherard, *Oscar Wilde*, London, 1909.

Otto Siepmann, *Siepmann's Primary French Course*, part 1, new edition, London, 1910. Inscribed on the fly-leaf 'Mary Owen/May 7th 1912.' Annotations.

F. M. Sim, *Robert Browning The Poet and the Man*, London, 1912.

[Edith Sitwell, editor,] *Wheels: A Second Cycle*, Oxford, 1917.

Sacheverell Sitwell, *The People's Palace*, Oxford, 1918. Inscribed 'W.E.S.O./ from/C.K.S[cott]. M[oncrieff]./in Vid . Assumps.ᵒⁿⁱ/B. V. M./MDCCCCVIII. /Mahim/Monkmoor Rd./Shrewsbury.'

MacGregor Skene, *Wild Flowers*, London, Edinburgh, and New York, n.d.

W. F. Smith, *Notes on Thackeray's Esmond*, sixth edition, London, n.d.

Robert Southey, *Poems of*, edited by Maurice H. Fitzgerald, London, 1909.

Certain titles ticked on the Contents list.

Edmund Spenser, *The Faerie Queene*, Book II, edited by Kate M. Warren, London, 1897.

——, *The Story of St. George and the Dragon or The Redcross Knight*, The Penny Poets, XVIII, London, n.d. Annotation and underlining.

Laurence Sterne, *A Sentimental Journey*, with an Introduction by L. F. Austin, London . . . Melbourne, 1903.

R. L. Stevenson, *Essays in the Art of Writing*, London, 1912. See *CL*, p. 575.

——, *The Master of Ballantrae*, London . . . Melbourne, 1915. Inscribed on the front end-paper 'W: E: S: OWEN – /Edinburgh: Oct: 1917.'

——, *St. Ives*, London, n.d. Inscribed on the fly-leaf 'WEO' and stamped on the title-page 'Edinburgh School Board/Tynecastle Supplementary School/5 Sep 1917'. See *CL*, p. 500.

——, *Treasure Island*, London . . . Melbourne, 1903. See *CL*, p. 132.

——, *Weir of Hermiston*, London, n.d.

Aylmer Strong, *A Human Voice*, London, 1917. Inscribed on the front fly-leaf 'Owen. from SS./Edinburgh./Oct. 26th. 1917./"When Captain Cook first sniff'd the wattle,/"And Love columbus'd Aristotle." [a quotation from p. 63]. See above, p. 233.

[Jonathan] Swift, *Gulliver chez les Géants par*, adaptation française par Mlle Latappy, Collection Stead, no. 6, Paris, n.d.

——, *The Poetical Works of*, vol. I, Edinburgh, 1778.

——, *The Works of . . .*, vol. I., *containing A Tale of a Tub*, London, 1752.

Algernon Charles Swinburne, *Poems and Ballads* (First Series), London, 1917. Inscribed on front end-paper 'W.E.S. OWEN/Scarborough. Aug. 1918'. A coloured picture-postcard of 'Scarborough – St. Mary's Church' is stuck on to the front flap of the dust-jacket. On the reverse of this flap is written in SO's hand, 'This came back with his things from France'. See *CL*, p. 589, and above pp. 282 and 288.

——, *A Song of Italy*, London, 1867.

John Addington Symonds, *Shelley*, London, 1909. Annotation, marginal lines, and underlining. See *CL*, p. 106, and pp. 69–70 above.

Laurent Tailhade, *Poemes Elégiaques*, troisième édition, Paris, 1907. Inscribed on the fly-leaf 'à Wilfred E. S. Owen/en souvenir de nos belles causeries/et des beaux soirs à La Gailleste/Paris, le 4 mai 1915/Laurent Tailhade'.

Alfred Lord Tennyson, *Elaine*, London, n.d. Inscribed on the half-title 'To Wilfred/with best/Christmas/wishes/1913./from Leslie [Gunston].'

——, *The Holy Grail and other Poems*, London, 1870. Inscribed 'W.E.S. Owen –/ Edinburgh. Ivly. 1917'. Annotation. See p. 248 above.

——, *In Memoriam*, London and Glasgow, n.d. Inscribed on the fly-leaf 'To Mary/With love from Doris [Wharmby]./May 30th 1912'. See *CL*, p. 263.

——, *The Lover's Tale*, London, 1879. Inscribed on the fly-leaf 'W.E.S. OWEN/Edinburgh. Ivly. 1917'.

———, *The Poems of, 1830–1863*, London and New York, 1910.

———, *The Poetical Works of*, London, 1911. Pages uncut.

———, *Selections From*, The Laureate Poetry Books VIII, London, n.d. Rubber-stamped on the front cover 'W. E. OWEN'.

———, *Tiresias and Other Poems*, London, 1885. Inscribed on the fly-leaf 'WEO/ Gvildford: August: 1916:'. Marginal lines and underlining.

William Makepeace Thackeray, *Vanity Fair*, London and Glasgow, n.d.

Edward Thomas, *Keats*, London, Edinburgh and New York, n.d. Inscribed on fly-leaf 'WEO/June 1916/Witley Camp'. See p. 130 above.

Gilbert Thomas, *The Voice of Peace*, London, 1914. Inscribed on the fly-leaf 'W.E.S. Owen/With all good wishes/ from/Gilbert Thomas./August 19, 1916.' Inserted, a newspaper photograph of a portrait of the author. See *CL*, p. 409 n.

James Thompson, *The Seasons, and Castle of Indolence*, London, 1826.

Leo Tolstoy, *Short Stories*, with an Introduction by Frederick J. Crowest, London and Felling-on-Tyne, n.d.

J. M. W. Turner, *Liber Studiorum*, London and Glasgow, 1911.

The Twentieth Century New Testament/A Translation into Modern English, London, n.d. Inscribed on the fly-leaf 'Mother./with Love from/Wilfred./Christmas, 1912.'

R. E. Vernède, *War Poems and Other Verses*, with an Introductory Note by Edmund Gosse, London, 1917. Dust-jacket inscribed 'W.E.S. Owen'.

Alfred de Vigny, *Chatterton*, Paris, n.d.

Percival Vivian, *A Dictionary of Literary Terms*, London and New York, n.d.

Adolphus William Ward, *Dickens*, London, 1909.

William Watson, *Excursions in Criticism*, London and New York, 1893. Inscribed on the fly-leaf 'WEO/Guildford: Ivne: 1916.'

H. G. Wells, *The Discovery of the Future*, London, 1913. Some pages uncut.

Peggy Whitehouse, *Songs from the Sussex Downs*, London, 1915. Front cover inscribed 'WEO'.

Wild Flowers at Home, third series, London and Glasgow, 1908.

Oscar Wilde, *Poems by*, thirteenth edition, London, 1916.

A. S. Wilkins, *Classical Antiquities. II. Roman Antiquities*, London, 1877.

Richard Wilson, *A First Course in English Literature*, London, n.d. Rubber-stamped on the fly-leaf 'W.E. OWEN'.

A. J. Wyatt, *An Elementary Old English Grammar*, Cambridge, 1911. Annotation, marginal lines, and underlining.

———, *An Elementary Old English Reader*, Cambridge, 1908.

——— and W. H. Low, *The Intermediate Text-Book of English Literature*, London, 1907. Annotation, marginal lines, and underlining. Inserted, a half sheet of paper with 3 lines of poetry drafted on recto and literary notes on verso.

*The following titles appear in a
checklist drawn up by Harold Owen in
1920, but are not to be found in the
library today. Some, if not all,
may have been given away as presents.*

[R. A. Bremer], *Orthometry/The Art of Versification and the Technicalities of Poetry*,
    Edinburgh, 1912.
Arnold Bennett, *Literary Taste*.
A Child's History of England.
Esperanto for the Million, The Penny Poets, London, n.d.
Georgian Poetry 1916–1917, edited by Edward Marsh, London, 1917.
Grammaire Française.
Histoire Illustrée de la Littérature Française.
Matriculation English Course.
The Poets of Great Britain, 1776.
Prayerbooks.
[Abbé Prévost], *Manon Lescaut*.
[Charles Reade], *The Cloister and the Hearth*.
The Writers' and Artists' Year Book.

SELECT BIBLIOGRAPHY

Editions of Owen's Poetry and Letters
Poems by Wilfred Owen, with an Introduction by Siegfried Sassoon, London, 1920.

The Poems of Wilfred Owen, edited with a Memoir and Notes by Edmund Blunden, London, 1931.

The Collected Poems of Wilfred Owen, edited with an Introduction and Notes by C. Day Lewis and with a Memoir by Edmund Blunden, London, 1963.

Wilfred Owen/War Poems and Others, edited with an Introduction and Notes by Dominic Hibberd, London, 1973.
Wilfred Owen/Collected Letters, edited by Harold Owen and John Bell, London, 1967.

Books containing recollections of Owen
Robert Graves, *Goodbye to All That*, London, 1929.
Harold Owen, *Journey from Obscurity*, 3 vols, London, 1963, 1964, 1965.
Siegfried Sassoon, *Siegfried's Journey*, London, 1945.
Osbert Sitwell, *Noble Essences*, London 1950.
T. J. Walsh, ed., *A Tribute to Wilfred Owen*, Birkenhead, 1964.

Books about the First World War
Richard Aldington, *Death of a Hero*, London, 1929.
Henri Barbusse, *Under Fire*, London, 1917.
Edmund Blunden, *Undertones of War*, London, 1928.
History of the Great War/Military Operations, 39 vols, London, 1925-48.
Sir A. Montgomery, *The Story of the Fourth Army*, London, 1926.
E. M. Remarque, *All Quiet on the Western Front*, London, 1929.
Frank Richards, *Old Soldiers Never Die*, London, 1933.
Siegfried Sassoon, *The Complete Memoirs of George Sherston*, London, 1937.
A. J. P. Taylor, *The First World War/An Illustrated History*, London, 1963.

Anthologies of poems about the First World War

Brian Gardner, ed., *Up the Line to Death: The War Poets, 1914–1918*, London, 1964.
I. M. Parsons, ed., *Men who March Away: Poems of the First World War*, London, 1965.

Books containing critical discussion of Owen's Poetry
Bernard Bergonzi, *Heroes' Twilight: A Study of the Literature of the Great War*, London, 1965.
John H. Johnson, *English Poetry of the First World War: A Study in the Evolution of Lyric and Narrative Form*, Princeton and London, 1964.
Jon Silkin, *Out of Battle: The Poetry of the Great War*, London, 1972.
D. S. R. Welland, *Wilfred Owen: A Critical Study*, London, 1960.
Gertrude M. White, *Wilfred Owen*, New York, 1969.
William White, *Wilfred Owen (1893–1918): A Bibliography*, Illinois, 1965.
[*This lists most of the articles written on Owen's poetry up to 1965.*]

INDEX

Page references in bold type denote a manuscript facsimile
in the text.

A Christmas Carol, see Dickens, Charles
A.E., 124
'A verse-letter from somewhere in Oxfordshire', 67–9
'A Palinode', 55
'A Terre', 261, 265 n
Abbeville, 159, 162, 168
Abbotsford, Sir Walter Scott's house, 76
Adams, Bernard, *Nothing of Importance*, Sassoon gives WO his copy, 233
Adey, William More, 263 and n
Aldershot, 137
Aldington, Richard, *Death of a Hero*, 153
'All sounds have been as music', 56, 217
Allen, Alice Mary and Hilda Agnes, 80
Alpenrose, the Gunston family house at Kidmore End, 49, 55, 59, 73, 85, 126
Alpina, the Gunston family house in Wimbledon, 34, 46, 80
Andersen, Hans, 19, 74, 78–9
'Anthem for Doomed Youth', 216, **217–21**, 222, 227, 248 n
'Apologia pro Poema Meo', **250–1**, 256
Artists' Rifles, 121, 122, 123–4, 126
'Asleep', **238**
Astræa, launching of, 1; HO on board, 288
Astronomical Geological and Botanical Society, 44, 49, 199 and n
Aumont, Dr. Maurice, 97, 98
Austin, Alfred, *Songs of England*, 248–9

Bagnères-de-Bigorre, 100, 102, 106
Bainbrigge, Philip, 258, 265 n, 281
Bairnsfather, Bruce, 153 and n
'Ballad of a Morose Afternoon', 72–3
'Ballad of the Lady Yolande', 194, **195**
Barbusse, H., *Under Fire*, 242; his work as

influence on WO's poems, 242–6, 256
Barrett, Wilson, *Lucky Durham*, 201 and n, 202, 203, 204
Beaumont-Hamel, 152, 156, 202
Beaurevoir-Fonsomme Line, 277
'Beauty', 180 n
'Before reading a Biography of Keats for the first time', 56
Bellenglise, 277
Belloc, Hilaire, *Hills and the Sea*, 121; *Esto Perpetua*, 242 n
Benalder, 5, 46
Bennett, Arnold, 236, 242 n, 265 n
Bennett, Harry, 19, 21
Berlitz Schools, at Bordeaux, 93, 94, 97; at Angers, 97; 100; at Edinburgh, 199, 222
Berthaud, Pierre, 98
Bible Society Gleanings verse competition, 67
Binyon, Laurence, 124, 125
Birkenhead, ch. 2 *passim*; —Institute, 18, 21, 28, 29, 222
Blaikie, Walter Biggar, 222
Blunden, Edmund, 246
Bonsall, Mr., 119, 123
Borage Lane, Ripon, 259, 261
Bordeaux, 93; ch. 5 *passim, esp.* 94–100, 111–12, 121
Bouchoir, 164, 173
Brest, 46
Bridges, Robert, 124
British and Foreign Bible Society, 39–40
Brock, Captain, 192–3, 195, 198, 202, 252, 265 n
Brodribb, C. W., 124
Brontë, Charlotte, *Shirley*, 27

Brooke, Rupert, 104, 105, 119, 140 and n, 171 and n, 206
Brooke, Stopford, *Studies in Poetry*, 242 n
Browning, Elizabeth Barrett, *The Poems of*, 173–4
Broxton, 27–8, 124, 281
Bulman, Bill, 76, 194 n
Bulman, Blanche, 76
Bulman, John, 76, 117
Bulman, Nellie (née Roderick), as governess at Plas Wilmot, 2; 76, 193, 194, 198
Bulwer, E. L., *The Last Days of Pompeii*, 89
Bunyan, John, *Pilgrim's Progress*, 30, 158
Burlington Magazine, 263

Canon Street, Shrewsbury, 13
Castelnau, picnic at, 98–9
Celtic origins of Owen family, 3–4; WO's pride in, 57
Chantilly Conference of Allied Commanders, 150
Chapman's *Homer*, 57
Childs, Dr., 73–4
Clarence Gardens Hotel, Scarborough, 239, 253, 264
Clark, Dudley, 124, 125
Clemenceau, Osbert Sitwell's epigram on, 265; his speech to Senate, 273
Cleveland Place, Shrewsbury, 37
Coleridge, Christabel Rose, 52
Coleridge, Ernest Hartley, 52
Coleridge, Samuel Taylor, 52
Colvin, Sidney, *Keats*, 56–7, 88, 89, 236 and n
Connacher, W. S., 18, 29
'Conscious', 256
Cousin May, 30–2
Cowper, William, 28, 74 n
Craiglockhart War Hospital, 106, 140, 188, ch. 8 *passim*, 252
'Cramped in that funnelled hole', 246, 256, 257
Crichton Green, Captain H. R., 155 and n
Cross Simpson, Mary C. (WO's great-grandmother), 1
Cummings, Mr., 126
Cunynghame, Lieutenant-Colonel Sir Percy, 152

Dauthieu, Albertina Marie, 231
Davies, W. H., 206
de la Mare, Walter, 124, 125
de la Touche, Anne, 112, 113, 114, 115, 116, 117, 119, 161 n
de la Touche boys, Johnny, Bobbie, Charles, David, 112, 113, 114, 115, 116, 118, 119, 123, 125, 126, 139, 161 and n, 236; Johnny to receive a copy of WO's book, 265 n
de Puységur, Mlle, 114
de Vigny, Alfred, 121
'Deep under turfy grass and heavy clay', 80–1, 256
Dempster, Major, 187 and n, 188
Dickens, Charles, 21, 127, 230
'Disabled', **224–6**; Graves's reaction to, 229; 265 and n
Downside, 112, 117, 126, 161 n
Dubo, Mme, 97
'Dulce et Decorum Est', 105, 156, 226–8
Dunsden, WO's first visit to, 55; first visits to vicarage, 60, 62; description of vicarage, 63–4; ch. 4 *passim, esp.* 66–7, 69–70, 73, 74, 80, 82–3, 85; 97, 105 n, 109, 137, 199

Edinburgh, 75, ch. 8 *passim, esp.* 189, 201, 222; 240, 252
Edwards, Mr., 58
Elm Grove, Birkenhead, 14
English Review, 263
Étaples, 151, 253, 269
Etretat, No 1 General Hospital, 187
'Exposure', 246–8

Farrell, Miss, 19, 28
Fayet, 181 n, 199
Field Club (Natural History Club at Craiglockhart), 197–8, 199, 202–3, 210, 214–15, 222
Flaubert, Gustave, *La Tentation de Saint Antoine*, 111
Fleetwood, *see* Musketry camp
Fleury, Mr. and Mrs., 23, 24
Flodden Field, 76
Forrest, Walter, 76, 194 n
Fox, George, *Guide to the Roman City of Uriconium*, 88

France, WO's first visit to, 46; doctor recommends visit to, 93; ch. 5 *passim*, ch. 7 *passim*, ch. 10 *passim*
France, Anatole, 111
'From my Diary, July 1914', 106, 122, 211
'Futility', 266

Gailly, Casualty Clearing Station, 171, 172, 184, 260
Gaukroger, 2nd Lieutenant, 182 and n
German, Edward, *Merrie England*, 231 n
Gibson, Wilfrid, *Battle*, 242 n
Gilbert and Sullivan, 15
'Golden Hair', 161–2
Goodwin, Miss ('Goody'), 40
Gosse, Edmund, 206
Graves, Robert, 207–8, 223, 226, 227, 229, 235 and n, 242 n, 250, 'Two Fusiliers', 252; WO attends his wedding, 257–8; 264, 265 n
Great Indian Peninsular Railway, 5, 7
Great Western Railway, 4, 45
'Greater Love', 230–1
Grenfell, Julian, 119, 124
Grimm, Brothers, 19
Gunston, Dorothy (WO's cousin), 34
Gunston, Emma (née Shaw, WO's aunt), 2–3, 11, 34
Gunston family, 34, 39, 46, 49
Gunston, Gordon (WO's cousin), 34
Gunston, John, 3, 34, 49, 55
Gunston, Leslie (WO's cousin), 34, 44, 49, 73, 121, 122, 124, 125, 161 and n, 162, 194, 198, 211 n, 237; *The Nymph and Other Poems*, 239; WO's reactions to, 239–40; 265 n, 282
Gunston, Vera (WO's cousin), 34, 44
Gurney, Ivor, 180

Haig, General Sir Douglas, 150, 181
half-rhyme, 70, 141, 211 n; *and see* para-rhyme
Halloy, 152, 153
Hancourt, 279, 280
'Happiness', 161 n, **162**, 163
Hardie, Private Sam, 148, 151, 177, 178
Hardy, Thomas, 124
Hare Hall Camp, WO posted to, 129; HO visits, 130–34; Officers' School at, 136

Harrow, 267–8
'Has your soul sipped?', 106, 141–2
Hastings, 267
Haughmond Abbey and Hill, 48, 282
Hawthorn Villa, Shrewsbury, 23, 37
Heinemann, William, 263
Henderson, Miss, 194
Hewitt, Miss, 92
Heydon, 2nd Lieutenant A., 155 and n
Hindenburg Line, 166–8, 172, 279
Hood, Basil, *Merrie England*, 231 n
Hope, Anthony, *The Prisoner of Zenda*, 124
'Hospital Barge at Cérisy', 184, 248, **249**, 256
Housman, A. E., *A Shropshire Lad*, 138
Hulcoop, Mr., 93
Hunt, Holman, 66
Hydra, The, 193, 198, 201, 204, 214–15, 256

'I saw his round mouth's crimson deepen as it fell', 280
Iles, Dorothy, 48
'Insensibility', 261
'Inspection', 266
Ireland, 1898 holiday in, 13; 1902 holiday in, 23–6
'It was a navy boy, so prim, so trim', 142–3

Joergens, Olwen, 126, 161 and n, 162, 211 n
Jones family of Glan Clwyd, 32–3

Keats, John, 27, 40, 46; his influence on WO's 'To Poesy', 53; WO reads W. M. Rossetti's *Life and Writings of*, and Colvin's biography of, 56–7; and visits his Teignmouth house, 57; WO goes to see his MSS. and his house, 62; 69; his influence, 78–9; 85; WO visits his Teignmouth house again, 86–8; 88, 107, 113, 123, 124; Edward Thomas's book on, 130; 175–6, 221, 235, 236 and n, 248, 264, 281
Kelso, 75–6, 194
Kemp, *see* Saxelby-Kemp, Alfred
Kendrick School, Reading, 73
Keswick, 76–7
Kidmore End, 49, 55, 59, 62, 126

Kings College School, Wimbledon, 34, 73

Kipling, Rudyard, 119, 124

Kirk, 2nd Lieutenant James, 285, 288

La Sainte Bible, 36

Lamb, Charles, 66

Langholz, M., 97

'Le Christianisme', **183**

Le Roux, Xavier, 124

Léger, Mme, 100, 101–2, 104, 107, 111

Léger, M., 100, 101

Léger, Nénette, 100, 102, 106–7

Lem, Raoul, 98, 99, 100, 111

'Lines Written on my Nineteenth Birthday', 71

'Little Claus and Big Claus', 74

Locke, W. J., *The Usurper*, 194

London Matriculation Examination, 60, 61, 62

'Long Ages Past', 111

Loughrey, Dr. Richard, 3

Loughrey, May (née Mary Shaw, WO's aunt), 2–3

Lucky Durham, see Barrett, Wilson

Ludendorff, General, 166, 167, 269

Luxmoore, Lieutenant-Colonel, 152, 183

Macaulay, Thomas Babington, 40

McClymont, 2nd Lieutenant Murray, 269–70, 273

McHutcheon, Miss, 23

McNaught, Maurice, 48

Maddox, the drapers, Shrewsbury, 4

Mahim, named by Tom Owen, 50 and n; 69, 82, 86, 96; Raoul Lem visits, 100 and n; 119, 146

Maitland, F. E., 124, 125

Mametz Wood, 266

Manchester Regiment,

    5th Battalion: WO 'gazetted' as 2nd Lieutenant in, 136; 137; to be posted abroad, 146–7; arrive in France, 148; Reserve Battalion in Scarborough, 239;

    2nd Battalion: WO joins, 151; in Halloy, 152; move to Beauval, Bertrancourt, 153–4; in Front Line, 156–9; in trenches near Fresnoy,

168–9; in action near Savy Wood, 177–8, 180–2; 'rest' period at Quivières, 182–3; August 1918 engagements, 272; WO rejoins near Amiens, 272; move up to Front Line, 277–8; move back to Lehaucourt, 279; into action on Sambre and Oise Canal, 283–6

Marlborough College, 205

Marmion, see Scott, Sir Walter

Masefield, John, 242 n

Marsh, Edward, 206

Marshall, Major J. N., 276–7, 285–6, 288

Mary Millard (HO's model ship), 47

Massingham, Henry, 206, 237 and n

'Maundy Thursday', 118 n, **120**, 121, 210

'Mental Cases', 263 and n, 265

Meredith, George, 75

Mérignac, 112, 113, 114, 115, 121, 123, 124

Merrie England, see Hood, Basil, *and* German, Edward

Milford Camp, near Witley, *see* Witley

Millard, Mary, *see* Owen, Mary

Milnathort, 231

Milton, John, 28, 75

Milton Road, Birkenhead, 14, 21, 29, 35

'Miners', **254–5**, 257

Monkmoor Road, Shrewsbury, 50. *See also* Mahim

Monro, Harold, 127, 128, 129; discusses WO's sonnets with him, 135–6; 261

Montague, Milly, 67

Moore, Mrs, 35

Morgan, Rev. John, 82

Morley, Miss Edith, 75, 126, 136

Morrell, Lady Ottoline, 206, 232

Morris, William, 66

'Music', 140, 230

Musketry camp (at Fleetwood, near Aldershot), 137, 153, 170

'My Shy Hand', **212–13**

Nantwich, home of Owen family, 4

Natural History Club (at Craiglockhart), *see* Field Club

Newbolt, Henry, 124, 125

Newboult, Arthur, 229–30

Newboult, Mary, 230

Nichols, Robert, 124, 242 n, 265 n

Nicholson, Frank, 222
'Nights with the Wind. A Rhapsody',
 79–80
'1914', 105, 210
'Nocturne', 105, 106
'Now, let me feel the feeling of thy hand',
 122, 123
Noyes, Alfred, 124

'On a June Night (1911)', 90–1
'On my Songs', 210
'On Seeing a Lock of Keats's Hair', 78
Onion, Mrs., 9
O'Riordan, Conal, 269, 271
Ors cemetery, 288
Oswestry, ch. 1 *passim*, 146, 156
Oswestry and Border Counties Advertizer,
 announcement of WO's birth in, 1
Owen, Anne (WO's aunt), 4; *and see*
 Taylor, Anne
Owen, Colin (WO's brother), born, 19;
 special friendship with Harold, 42;
 working on farm, 174; poem to, 174–5;
 as cadet in Royal Flying Corps, 267
Owen, Emily, *see* Quayle, Emily
Owen family, leave Plas Wilmot for
 Birkenhead, 12–13; and 1898 holiday in
 Ireland, 13; rift in, 14–15; and 1902
 holiday in Ireland, 23–6; and Broxton
 holiday, 27–8; sense of solidarity in,
 30; and holiday in Scarborough, 32;
 move to Shrewsbury, 36–7; move in
 to Mahim, 50; and holiday in Scotland,
 75–6;
 incidents relating to: Hindustanis to
  supper, 17; swimming bath expeditions, 18; encounter with tramp, 20;
  Tom nearly drowned, 23–4; shark
  fishing, 24; psychic experience, 25–6;
  'Wilfred's Church', 39; discovery of
  Uffington, 42–4; visit to fair, 60–1;
  burning the tar barrel, 91–2
Owen, Hannah (WO's great-grandmother), 4
Owen, Harold (WO's brother), born, 13;
 visits docks with Tom 16; stays weekend
 with Miss Farrell, 28; taken away from
 school, 29; sent to free board school in
 Shrewsbury, 38; special friendship with

Colin, 42; discovers interest in painting,
 46–7; told to find a job, 82; goes to
 sea, 86; returns from first voyage, 91;
 visits WO at Hare Hall Camp, 130–4;
 goes to cinema in London with WO,
 134–5; second visit to WO in Camp,
 144–6; in air crash, 163; last talk with
 WO, 260–1; psychic experience on
 board the *Astræa*, 287
Owen, John (WO's great-grandfather), 4
Owen, Mary (WO's sister), born, 10;
 bullets remind WO of her canary,
 156; WO copies passages of Elizabeth
 Barrett Browning for, 173–4; twenty-
 first birthday, 186
Owen, Mary (née Millard, WO's grandmother), 4, WO visits, 23; Owen
 family stays with, 37
Owen, May, *see* Quayle, May
Owen, Susan (née Shaw, WO's mother),
 born, 2; falls in love with Tom Owen,
 5; calls him back from India, 7; marries,
 8; children born: Wilfred, 8–9; Mary,
 10; Harold, 13; Colin, 19; takes WO
 to Broxton, 27–8; visits Alpenrose to be
 near WO, 85; visits Nellie Bulman to be
 near WO in Craiglockhart, 198; stays
 in Hastings to see WO and Colin on
 leave, 267;
 and anxiety to keep up standards, 14, 48;
 and early ambitions for WO, 9, 16, 22,
  96;
 and obsession with health, 18, 19, 48,
  78, 95, 96, 170, 282;
 and religion, 10, 22, 39–40
Owen, Tom (WO's father), born in
 Nantwich, 4; at Dame School, 4;
 joins G.W.R., posted to Oswestry, 4;
 falls in love with Susan Shaw, 5; goes to
 India as Ordinary Seaman, joins Great
 Indian Peninsular Railway, 5–7; called
 back to England, 7; marries, 8; builds
 S.S. *Susan*, 10; stationmaster at Woodside station, 13; promoted, 36; takes
 WO on holiday to Brest, 46; visits WO
 in Bordeaux, 95–6;
 and music: 15, 30;
 and physical exercise: swimming, 18,
  23–4; early morning expeditions,

41–2; skating, 45; shooting, 60;
and the sea: prized Discharge Certificate,
5–6; builds model ships, 10, 47; and
sailors next door, 14–15; visits docks,
16; invites Indian sailors to supper, 17;
'sailors' fo'c'sle food' ritual, 30;
WO's changed attitude to, 236
Owen, Wilfred,
and archaeology: Uriconium, 48–9,
88; Silchester remains, 49;
and botany: his 'Vegeatble Garden',
23; formation of AGBS, 44–5; at
Dunsden, 73–4; 159; Craiglockhart
Field Club, 197–8; 'Can Plants
Think?', 199; 275–6;
and health: early preoccupation with,
47–8; eyes, 78; 95, 96–7, 118–19; no
longer concerned by, 170;
and interest in language when young:
learns Hindustani phrases, 18; word-
game with Paton, 21; learns Welsh
phrases, 33; 'faring very sumptuously',
33–4; attachment to books, 36; works
at night, 37–8, 41;
and literary and historical pilgrimages:
Coleridges, 52; Keats's house in
Teignmouth, 57, 86–8; British
Museum, 61–2, 78; Keats's House
in Hampstead, 62; Shelley's cottage
near Dunsden, 69; Scott's house at
Abbotsford, 76; Flodden Field, 76–7;
battlefield of Castillon, 124; Tamworth, 137–8;
and religion: 39, 60, 75, 83, 85, 175,
185, 203, 258, 265;
and stages in army career: enlists, 127;
first drill, 128–9; Hare Hall Camp
training, 129; Balgores House Officers'
School, 136; 'gazetted' as 2nd
Lieutenant, 5th Manchesters, stationed
at Witley, 136; musketry courses at
Aldershot, Fleetwood, 137; to France,
139; joins 2nd Manchesters, 152;
leads platoon to Front Line, 156–9;
to Abbeville on transport course,
159–61; joins B Company, sent up
near Front Line, 168–70; concussed,
sent to Gailly, 171–2; rejoins 2nd
Manchesters near St. Quentin, 178;

fighting, 178–80, 181–2; 'rest' period
at Quivières, 183; back to Gailly with
shell shock, 184; invalided back to
England, 187–8; to Craiglockhart,
188; rejoins Regiment in Scarborough, 239; transferred to Ripon,
258; back to Scarborough, 264;
returns to France, 269; joins 2nd
Manchesters near Amiens, 272; moves
up to Front Line, 277; wins Military
Cross, 279; 'rest' period at Hancourt,
279–80; back into Line on Sambre
and Oise Canal, 283
Owen, William (WO's grandfather),
apprenticed as shoemaker to his father,
4; marries, 4; moves to Shrewsbury, 4;
WO visits, 23; Owen family stays with,
37

pararhyme, 105, 106, 141, 211 and n
Paton, Alec, 21; on holiday with WO in
Wales, 32–4; 48
'Perversity', 210
Peyronnet, M., 116, 119, 121
Pilgrim's Progress, see Bunyan, John
Plas Wilmot, the building of, 1–2;
economies introduced in the running of,
8; auctioned 11–12; standards to be
maintained, 14; linen and silver stolen,
35
Poems of Today, 1916, 216
Poetry Bookshop, the 127–8, 129, 134,
236, 265 n
Poitou, Mlle Henriette, 99
Pope, Alexander, 45
Pope, Jessie, 226–7
Potts, 2nd Lieutenant F., 271, 278
Preface, WO's draft for planned collection
of poems, 266
Priestley, Lieutenant, 264
Pringle Bank, the Bulman family home in
Kelso, 75–6
'Purple', 139, 161 n

Quayle, Edward, 93, 98, 117, 146
Quayle, Emily (née Owen, WO's aunt), 4
Quayle, May (née Owen, WO's aunt), 4
Quivières, 182–3

Ragge, John, 48
Raleigh, Sir Walter, 66
Rampton, Vivian, 67, 83
Rawlinson, General Sir Henry, 148, 149, 150
Rayner, Miss M. M. C., 74, 265 n
Reading, 63, 66, 73, 85, 137;
—Museum, 49
Regent Palace Hotel, Piccadilly, 126, 236, 280
Renan, Ernest, *Souvenirs d'Enfance et de Jeunesse*, 111
Rhewl, Denbighshire, 32
Richepin, Jean, 124
Rimbaud, Arthur, 238
Ripon, WO transferred to, 258; 259–60, 261
Rivers, Dr. W. H. R., 190 and n, 232
Robson, Rev. Herbert, 59, 60
Roderick, Nellie, *see* Bulman, Nellie
Ross, Robert, 234, 235, 236, 257, 262–3, 281
Rossetti, W. M., *Life and Writings of John Keats*, 57, 78
Royal Flying Corps, WO applies for transfer to, 143–4; 168; Colin Owen cadet in, 267
Royal Victoria Hospital, 187
Royal Welch Fusiliers, 1st, 233
rue Beaubadat, Bordeaux, 121
rue Blanc Dutrouilh, Bordeaux, 111
rue Desfourniels, Bordeaux, 111
Rupprecht, Crown Prince, 166, 172
Ruskin, John, 66, 75
Russell, Bertrand, 206

S.S. *Susan* (WO's model ship), 10, 47
St. Quentin, 178, 181, 260;
—Canal, 277, 279
Salmond, 2nd Lieutenant J. B., 201
Salter, Edward (WO's great-grandfather), comes to Oswestry and marries, 1; builds Plas Wilmot, 1–2; dies at thirty-two, 2
Salter, Mary, *see* Shaw, Mary
Sambre and Oise Canal, 283–6
Sassoon, Siegfried, 201, 204–13; *The Old Huntsman*, 204, 208–9; 'The Deathbed', 209–10; 'They', 210; 'Vision' 212; *The*

Daffodil Murderer, 213; 'Dreamers', 215; 'The Rear-Guard', 215, 256; his influence on WO, 216, 217–18, 221–2, 223, 226; 231, 232–4, 235, 242, 243, 264, 265 n, 266, 267, 272, 274; *Counter-Attack*, 279
Savy Wood, 178, 181, 182 n
Saxelby-Kemp, Alfred, 63, 64, 74
Scarborough, holiday with Cousin May in, 32; ch. 9 *passim*, *esp.* 238–9, 252
Scotland, Owen family holiday in, 75–6
Scott Moncrieff, Captain Charles, 263 and n, 265, 266, 267
Scott, Sir Walter, *Marmion*, 21, 76, 138 and n, 191, 194
Secker, Martin, 210
Service, R. W., 242 n
Shakespeare, William, 21, 31, 40, 62; *A Midsummer Night's Dream*, WO's copy with poem on fly-leaf, 40–1, 53
Shaw, Edward (WO's uncle), 2; as sportsman, 3; meets Tom Owen 4–5; leading a wild life, finally disappears, 7
Shaw, Edward (WO's grandfather), comes to Oswestry and sets up as ironmonger, 2; marries Mary Salter, 2; plays leading role in local affairs, 2; saddened by death of wife, disappearance of son, 7; retires, 8; dies, 10–11
Shaw, Emma, *see* Gunston, Emma
Shaw, Mary (née Salter, WO's grandmother), left in possession of Plas Wilmot, 2; marries Edward Shaw and has four children, 2; dies, 7
Shaw, Mary or May, *see* Loughrey, May
Shaw, Susan, *see* Owen, Susan
Shelley, Percy Bysshe, 66, 69, 73; *Complete Works* as 21st birthday present, 98; 256, 265 and n, 267
Sherard, Robert, *The Real Oscar Wilde*, 242 n
Shirley, *see* Brontë, Charlotte
Shrewsbury, WO's grandfather moves to, 4; 13; Owen family moves to, 37; ch. 3 *passim*; 82, 119, 126, 136, 235; WO's last visit to, 260–1;
—Museum, 48, 89;
—School of Art, 46;
—Technical School, 40, 46, 58

Siegfried-Stellung, 166–8
Silchester excavations, 49
Simpson, Joseph, 125
Sitwell, Edith, 265 and n
Sitwell, Osbert, 262–3, 265, 267
'Six o'Clock in Princes Street', 214
Smallpage, Eric, 29; on holiday in Wales with WO, 34
Smallpage, James, 29, 34
'Smile, smile, smile', 273–4, 276
Somme offensive, 148–50, 206
'Song of Songs', 210, 211, 214
'Sonnet Autumnal', 210
'Sonnet: to a Child', 229–30
'Sonnet with an Identity Disc', **175**, 176
'Sonnet written at Teignmouth', **58**
Sorrel, Lieutenant S., 168 and n, 169
'Spells and Incantation', 280–1
'Spring Offensive', 44, 274–6
Stevens, F. W., 7
Stevenson, Robert Louis, 222, 242 n
Stonyhurst College, 161 n
'Storm', 139
'Strange Meeting', 215, 256, 265 n
'Sunrise', 184
Swinburne, Algernon Charles, 35, 230, 282, 288
Symonds, John Addington, *Shelley*, 69–70, 211 n

Tagore, Rabindranath, 124, 125, 129, 159 n, 267
Tailhade, Laurent, 108–9; his *Lettre aux Conscrits* and *Pour la Paix*, 109; 111, 112, 265 n
Tamworth, 137–8
Tarr, Ralph Stockman, 52
Tarr, Russell, 52
Taylor, Anne (WO's aunt), 52, 56, 86
Taylor, Edith (WO's cousin), 52
Taylor, John, 52, 56, 86
Taylor, Miss, 30
Taylor, 2nd Lieutenant, 178
Teignmouth, 57–8, 86
Temperance Society, 39
Tennyson, Alfred Lord, *Tiresias*, 138; *The Lover's Tale*, 202; biography of, 202; 204, 248–9
'The Ballad of Peace and War', *see* 'The

Ballad of Purchase-Money/s'
'The Ballad of Purchase-Money/s', 104–5, 111
'The Calls', 266
'The Chances', 265 n
'The Dead-Beat', 265 n
'The Dread of Falling into Naught', 80
'The End', 85, 161 n, 288
The Faerie Queene, 40
'The Fates', 194
'The Imbecile', 105
'The Kind Ghosts', 256, 266
'The Last Laugh', 258
'The Little Mermaid', 78–9, 80
The Nation, 206, 237, 259
'The Next War', 216
'The One Remains', 210
'The Peril of Love', 72, 210
'The Prelude' *see* Wordsworth, William
The Prisoner of Zenda, see Hope, Anthony
'The Rivals', 54–5
'The Send-off', 261–2
'The Sentry', 157, 265 n, 274
'The Show', 158 n, 182 n, 242, **243–4**, 245, 256, 265 n
'The Sleeping Beauty', 106–7
'The Swift', 73
'The time was aeon; and the place all earth', 71–2
The Times, on day of WO's birth, 1; *War Poems from*, 124; reports Clemenceau's speech to the Senate, 273
'The Wrestlers', 194, **195–6**, ('Antæus') 210, 252
theatre, WO's interest in dressing up, acting, 22, 39; SO's disapproval of, 31, 107; WO acting and writing for at Craiglockhart, 200, 201 and n, 204
Thirteenth Casualty Clearing Station, *see* Gailly
Thomas, Edward, 130, 179–80
Times of India, 7
Timpany, Mr., 59
Transport Duties Course, WO on, 159–63
'To—', **138**, 139, 210
'To a Comrade in Flanders', 140
'To Eros', **84**
'To Poesy', 53–4
Tofield, Mr., 94

Torquay, WO's visits to, 52, 56, 86, 88

Tynecastle Secondary School, 215, 222, 253

Uffington, 42–4, 92, 184
Uncle Remus, 35, 118
University College, Reading, 66, 73–4, 75, 92, 199
University Correspondence College, 66
'Unto what pinnacles of desperate heights', **81**
Uriconium, 49, 88, 281
'Uriconium/An Ode', 88–90, 257

Vachell, Horace, *The Hill*, 268
Vernède R. E., *War Poems and Other Verses*, 242 n

Waenfawr, Caernarvonshire, 34
Wales, Owen family origins in, 3–4; WO stays in with Paton family, 32–4; WO stays in with Smallpage family, 34; Keats's mother's name from, 57
War, outbreak of, 102; WO's initial reactions to, 104–5; changing attitude to, 109–10, 112, 121; his desire to fight in, 123–4; progress of, ch. 7 *passim, esp.* 148–50, 164–8, 172; 258, 260; ch. 10 *passim, esp.* 269, 272
War Poems from the Times, 124
Watson, William, 124, 125
Weaver, Mr., 46–7

Well Walk, Hampstead (Keats's house), 62
Wells, H. G., 210, 236, 242 n, 265 n
Westminster, Duke of, 18; Junior Scholarship, 34
Wheels, 265 and n, 270
'Who is the god of Canongate?', **240–1**
Wigan, Rev. Herbert, 59; first meetings with WO, 60, 62; description of, 63; 64; WO's first impressions of, 66; WO's relationship with, 75, 82, 83, 85; 137
'Wild with All Regrets', 248, 256, 261
Willmer Road, Birkenhead, 13
Wimbledon, 34, 46, 61
Winchester, 237
'Winter Song', 229
'Within those days', 40
Witley Camp, 136, 137, 155
Wood, Frederick and Arthur, 185
Wood, Harry Plant, 19
Woodhouse, Violet Gordon, 267
Woodside Station, 13
Wordsworth, William, 'The Prelude', 45, 261
Wright, Miss, 40
Wroxeter, 49
Wyle Cop School, Shrewsbury, 58–9

Yeats, W. B., 213–14, 244–5, 265 n
Young Abstainer's Union, 22

Zangwill, Israel, 188 and n

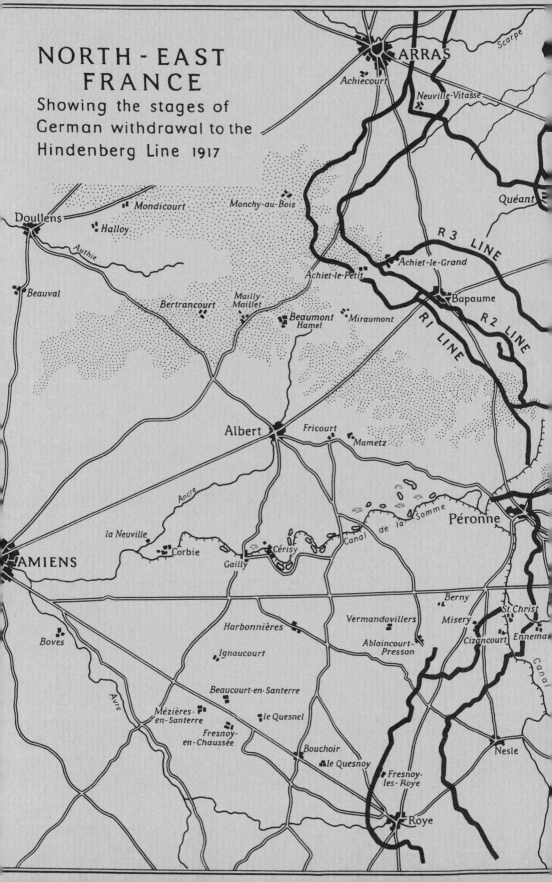

NORTH - EAST FRANCE

Showing the stages of
German withdrawal to the
Hindenberg Line 1917

Scarpe

ARRAS

Achiecourt

Neuville-Vitasse

Quéant

Mondicourt

Monchy-au-Bois

R 3 LINE

Doullens

Halloy

Achiet-le-Grand

Authie

Achiet-le-Petit

R1 LINE

Bapaume

R 2 LINE

Beauval

Bertrancourt

Mailly-
Maillet

Beaumont
Hamel

Miraumont

Albert

Fricourt

Mametz

Ancre

de la *Somme*

Péronne

la Neuville

Corbie

Cérisy

Canal

AMIENS

Gailly

Berny

St.Christ

Vermandovillers

Misery

Ennema

Boves

Harbonnières

Ablaincourt-
Presson

Cizancourt

Ignaucourt

Avre

Beaucourt-en-Santerre

Canal

Mézières-
en-Santerre

le Quesnel

Fresnoy-
en-Chaussée

Bouchoir

Nesle

le Quesnoy

Fresnoy-
les-Roye

Roye

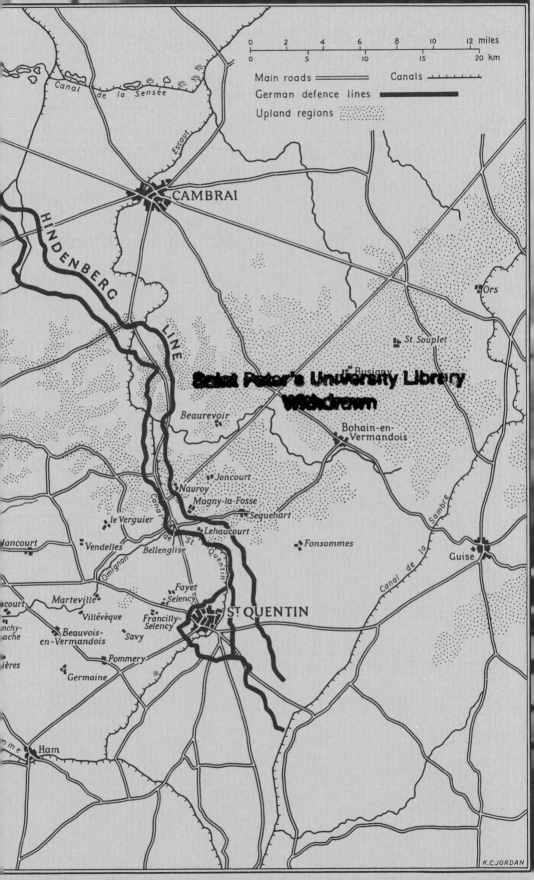

CAMBRAI

HINDENBERG LINE

Canal de la Sensée

Escaut

Ors

St. Souplet

Busigny

Beaurevoir

Bohain-en-Vermandois

Joncourt

Nauroy

Magny-la-Fosse

Sequehart

le Verguier

Lehaucourt

Canal de St. Quentin

Fonsommes

Vendelles

Bellenglise

Omignon

Guise

Canal de la Sambre

Fayet

Selency

Marteville

Villévèque

Francilly-Selency

ST QUENTIN

Beauvois-en-Vermandois

Savy

Pommery

Germaine

Ham

Main roads   Canals

German defence lines

Upland regions

0 2 4 6 8 10 12 miles

0 5 10 15 20 km

K.C.JORDAN